General Editors
Steven Connor and Thomas Healy

The Reinvention of the World

English Writing 1650–1750

Douglas Chambers

Professor of English,
University of Toronto, Canada

A member of the Hodder Headline Group
LONDON • NEW YORK • SYDNEY • AUCKLAND

First published in Great Britain in 1996 by
Arnold, a member of the Hodder Headline Group
338 Euston Road, London NW1 3BH
175 Fifth Avenue, New York, NY 10010

Distributed exclusively in the USA by
St Martin's Press Inc.,
175 Fifth Avenue,
New York, NY 10010

British Library Cataloguing in Publication Data
A catalogue entry for this book is available from the British Library

Library of Congress Cataloging-in-Publication Data
Chambers, Douglas.
    The reinvention of the world : English writing, 1650–1750 /
Douglas Chambers.
        p.   cm.
    Includes bibliographical references (p.   ) and index.
    ISBN 0–340–66242–5 (hardbound).—ISBN 0–340–58478–5
(pbk.)
        1. English literature—18th century—History and criticism.
    2. Space and time in literature.   3. English literature—Early
modern, 1500–1700—History and criticism.   4. Literature and
history—Great Britain—History—18th century.   5. Literature
    and history—Great Britain—History—17th century.   6.
Knowledge, Theory of, in literature.   7. Geography in literature.
                                    I. Title.
PR448.S69C48   1996   96–36365
820.9′004—dc20

ISBN 0 340 58478 5(Pb)
ISBN 0 340 66242 5(Hb)

Typeset by Phoenix Photosetting, Chatham, Kent
Printed and bound in Great Britain by J. W. Arrowsmith, Bristol

Contents

For Craig

General Editors' Preface

The title of this series intimates the reciprocal relations of writing and history that its contributors seek to encourage: literature acting as history and history acting in literature. Writing in History aims to write history back into the practices of literary study, at a time when the demands made by literary and cultural theory on the time and attention of student and teacher alike may effectively have written history out of the picture. But the history that this series aims to write back in is neither a simple alternative nor antidote to 'theory'; rather, it is the reasoned consequence of the heightened levels of theoretical awareness and debate within literary studies.

The series title points to an enlarged conception of the historical embeddedness of all forms of writing, whether literary or non-literary, a conception of writing not merely as the register of history, but as itself a form of historical event, action and effect. According to this view of the relations between writing and history, there is no particular value in the distinction between the worldly purposes of legal, religious, medical, scientific, or political writing and the literary writing which W. H. Auden gloomily concluded 'makes nothing happen'. The writing in 'Writing in History', is more verb than noun, more process than product. To read historically is to catch writing in the act: to watch it happening.

The phrase 'writing in history' is meant to remind the authors and readers of these books that the understanding of history is always itself determined by historical conditions; determined both in the negative sense that we are limited by who we are, and what our condition enables us to see, and also in the positive sense that our limited perspective is what makes possible the renewal and discovery of different relations to the past. In the writing of history, we are always partly writing the stories of our relations to the past.

The last years have seen an explosion of guides to theory which enable students to question most aspects of literary study. Surprisingly, though, there has been no concerted attempt to inform them of the changes in history and literary history: e.g. the rethinking of ideas of period, the greater prominence given to social and cultural history, and the emergence of new areas of focus such as gender history. This series given students of literature access to recent ideas about history and involves them in measuring their implications for critical practice. Writing in History refuses to allow history to be imagined either as existing only in writing, or as a retrieval of the past as background to literary expression. Using exemplary work to explore key interactions between writing and history, the series makes accessible their complexities and the critical excitement they generate in reconsidering literary and historical experience. Each book exemplifies the varieties of theoretical methodologies and histories available, and challenges the conventions of traditional literary history.

One of the most acute difficulties for students confronting new issues of writing in history has been the unfamiliarity and inaccessibility of many of the texts studied and discussed. Writing in History helps overcome some of this difficulty by providing an appendix to each volume, in which difficult to obtain material (such as trial transcripts, sermons, popular literature, political pamphlets, medical writing, journalism, or chronicles and historical writing) is reproduced in full or in longish extract. This appendix offers a complementary reader, where the book's arguments can be tested and where texts difficult for students to locate may be compared with those more frequently studied.

Steven Connor and Thomas Healy
London

♈

Preface

This book traces the rise of the mechanical model of the world to a position of dominance in the late seventeenth and early eighteenth centuries. It also examines the resistance to that domination in popular culture and in other, rival models of knowledge. Specifically, it is largely about space, both metaphorical and literal, and about domination and subordination. The book also argues that what came to be called 'Augustanism' was by no means monolithic: that some of the strongest resistance to the exclusively mechanical model of knowledge came from major writers of the period.

The texts for this study are not simply what is usually thought of as 'literary'; though many of them are by major figures, I have tried to suggest how such writers as Milton and Pope are both denser in their argumentation and poetic and closer to contemporary cultural issues than is sometimes suggested. This has involved a complex interweave of what traditionally have been thought of as 'literary' and 'non-literary' texts: a distinction that has served to privilege one sort of voice over another.

There are many authors to whom I am indebted here: Raymond Williams, E. P. Thompson, and John Barrell among them. But I am also indebted to my late friend Geoffrey Summerfield, and especially to his *Fantasy and Reason*, for first suggesting to me how childhood and writing for children can be a legitimate cultural text. And I am indebted to another former colleague, John Dixon Hunt, for introducing me to the 'texts' of gardens and landscapes.

Work of this kind can be done from printed sources, but I am grateful also to those who have helped me with manuscript material: John Wing, of Christ Church, Oxford for his unfailing help with the Evelyn papers before their transfer to the British Library, and Frances Harris of the British Library for suggesting that I look at the Trumbull manuscripts.

Many others have given help and useful criticism: John Baird, Guy de la Bedoyère, Brian Corman, François Lachance, Andrew Gray, Sheila Gray, Tom Healy, Jeanette Neeson, Craig Patterson, Stephen Pender, Sandra

Raphael, Bruce Redford, Jonathan Sawday, and Robert Williams. For the material on childhood I am indebted to the enthusiastic staff of the Osborne Collection of Early Children's Books in Toronto. This book, like most of my writing, would have been impossible without the British Library and its helpful staff and without the unfailing good nature of the staff of the library of Trinity College, Toronto, especially Elsie del Bianco.

|1|

Introduction: Methodically Digested

In the year 1658, as the founders of the Royal Society were discussing the reform of education and the foundation of modern science, James Ussher, future Archbishop of Armagh and Primate of Ireland, published his *Annals of the World*. Described as 'collected from all History, as well Sacred, as Prophane, and Methodically digested,'[1] it is most famous for 'establishing' that the world was created in 4004 BC.

Speculation about the date of the creation had been going on for centuries,[2] and was the subject of such great encylopaedias as Zanchius's *De Operibus Dei* (1591). Indeed, such speculation is the sort of subject debated by the fallen angels in Book II of *Paradise Lost*. Ussher's 'Methodically digested' work, however, settled the controversy in an opening sentence that must be among the most breathtaking of any book ever published:

> In the beginning God created Heaven and Earth, *Gen*. I. *v*. 1. Which beginning of time, according to our Chronologie, fell upon the entrance of the night preceding the twenty third day of *Octob*. in the year of the Julian Calendar, 710.

In retrospect, such assurance seems worthy of the academicians of Lagado in *Gulliver's Travels* or of the scientist described by Pope in *An Essay on Man*:

> Go wond'rous creature! mount where Science guides,
> Go, measure earth, weigh air, and state the tides; . . .
> Go teach Eternal Wisdom how to rule –
> Then drop into thyself, and be a fool.
>
> (II. 19–20, 29–30)[3]

The refusal of Pope and Swift to accept the universalizing claims of the new science reflects a more general scepticism in the early eighteenth century about certitude in knowledge as a whole, the sort of certitude implied in Newton's Preface to his *Principia* (1686):

> by the propositions mathematically demonstrated in the former books, in the third I derive from the celestial phenomena the forces of gravity with which bodies tend toward the sun and the several planets. Then from these forces, by other propositions which are also mathematical, I deduce the motions of the planets, the comets, the moon and the sea. I wish we could derive the rest of the phenomena of Nature by the same kind of reasoning from mechanical principles, for I am induced by many reasons to suspect that they may all depend upon certain forces by which the particles of bodies, by some causes hitherto unknown, are either mutually impelled toward one another and cohere in regular figures, or are repelled and recede from one another.[4]

In the light of this sort of mechanical explanation, it seems less surprising that Newton was closer to Ussher's sort of schematizing than is often recognized. Like Ussher, moreover, he spent a great deal of his later life calculating the generations that had passed since the Creation, just as John Wilkins, the effective founder of the Royal Society, had spent some of his time calculating the dimensions of Noah's ark.[5] But Newton never came to any conclusion as to whether the wave or particle theory of optics was true. In fact, Newton's other writings indicate that he was much less certain about the mechanical operation of the world than his Preface suggests. 'Alchemy,' A. Rupert Hall observes, 'seems to have given him a greater sense of the ultimate mystery than his unfolding of the celestial system.'[6]

No more certain was 'the founder of modern chemistry', Robert Boyle, who continued to interest himself in alchemy and believed that the chemical elements were inhabited by angels. Indeed, although Boyle removed the theory of the four elements from chemistry, he himself never drew up a final list of what the chemical elements were. That Boyle's first biographers subsequently censored his papers to remove material 'not suited to the genius of the present age',[7] however, suggests how quickly the new science was moving to eradicate what Milton meant when he claimed that truth 'may have more shapes than one'.

But no period is a cultural monolith, not even the early eighteenth century. The 'Augustans' did not speak with one voice. The later seventeenth century, too, is at least as culturally various. The restoration of Charles II neither silenced the many voices of dissent that had flourished during the interregnum nor did it usher in a triumphalist revival of Stuart mythology, though arguments about the nature of the British state continued to revolve around Stuart claims until the extinction of the Jacobite cause in 1745. Supporters of the Parliamentary cause, like General Monck (who became Lord Albermarle) and Edward Mountagu (who became Earl of Sandwich), temporized with the new regime and got titles for their pains. But John Evelyn, who had remained an Anglican Royalist throughout the

Commonwealth and Protectorate, was no more favourably disposed to the dissolute culture of Charles II's court than the itinerant Baptist writer, John Bunyan, who pilloried its hypocritical corruption in *Pilgrim's Progress* (1678).

Milton, who had been Latin Secretary for the Commonwealth, lived on to publish his greatest work, *Paradise Lost* (1667), under a revived monarchy. And his protégé, Marvell, who had learned to be equivocal about the republican power he endorsed, lived on as a satirist in an age of satire; his *Poems* (1681) was published posthumously in the same year as Dryden's *Absalom and Achitophel*. The study of English literature is bedevilled by periodization and the clichés that accompany it. Often this is at the expense of looking at the response that works received in the culture in which they were published. *Paradise Lost* and Marvell's *Poems* were as much works of the Restoration as the tag-ends of early-seventeenth-century poetic traditions. As a work that plays with structure and illusion, *Paradise Lost* is part of the argument between Palladian and Baroque style that was central to late seventeenth-century taste: John Evelyn's translation of Freart de Chambray's *A Parallel of the Ancient and Modern Architecture* (printed three times before 1715), or Wren's rebuilding of St Paul's after the Great Fire. And Marvell's early mockery of pastoral, 'A Dialogue Between Thyrsis and Dorinda' (*c*.1645), is part of the debate about pastoral in which Pope and Gay engaged with Ambrose Phillips in the first decade of the eighteenth century.

Among the premises of this book are that truth is dialectical and that culture is multivalent. English literature, in the period between 1650 and 1750, was both more heterogenous and contradictory than many critics and historians have allowed. The current argument between historians of the left and right about the nature of history in this period is intimately connected with arguments about the canon of English literature and the nature of genres.[8] And one of the things that makes any study of this period interesting is that, as in the 1640s, it is (in Milton's words) engaged in 'disputing, reasoning, reading, inventing, discoursing, ev'n to a rarity, and admiration, things not before discourst or written of'.[9]

Anyone who has listened to a radio survey of recordings of a work such as Handel's *Messiah* is aware that there are many possible 'readings' of it available. In the first place, *Messiah*, like many of the poems of the seventeenth century, exists in more than one score. Is a modern performance to follow the original Dublin score of 1742 or that of the later London performance of 1754? Is the orchestra to be scored for baroque instruments when modern audiences no longer hear the pitch of those instruments as original audiences did? And what is the exact nature of the voices and the singing style to be deployed? These are questions, like similar ones about 'original' performances of Shakespeare and reconstructions of his theatre, that can never satisfactorily be answered except in the recognition that no performance can ever claim to be authentic. The great harpsichordist,

Wanda Landowska, is said to have observed to a fellow pianist, 'You play Bach in your way and I will play him in his.' This sort of comic absurdity none the less still haunts the criticism of many figures of the period 1650–1750: the desire for a finite or definitive reading.

We look at the history of science, and indeed at the history of history itself, retrospectively, searching in it for confirmation of our own beliefs. Neither the history of science nor of culture generally is straightforward. A widespread interest in codes, signs, allegories, and portents in the late seventeenth and early eighteenth centuries suggests that 'rational method' did not sweep all before it in the late seventeenth century. T. M. Greene has described the culture of the late sixteenth century as including:

> a polysemous allegorical tradition, dream vision, pastoral eclogue and elegy, emblems and emblem books, devices (*imprese*), 'Hieroglyphs', a vast and confusing body of mythographic materials, elements of liturgical and sacramental symbolism, interpretations of the 'Book of Nature' including hermetic correspondences, astrological, mathematical and scientific speculations.[10]

A century later many (though by no means all) of these 'rival knowledges' had been eclipsed, but not the habit of mind that could dwell as happily in one model as another. The resistance of Pope and Swift to the claims of 'scientific certitude' were in fact more rational than many, but their position exemplified a widespread disquiet about the claims of a narrow rationalism.

John Byrom, the poet and author of the popular hymn 'Christians Awake', was the reputed lover of Queen Caroline and a friend of Sir Hans Sloane, the great botanist and effective founder of the British Museum. Fascinated by secret knowledge and secret codes, Byrom had among his drawings one that he believed depicted the 'perfectly rounded sphere which reveals the eternal pattern of the universe'.[11] This cabbalistic belief in the nature of the universe he shared with Newton and Boyle, and indeed with many of those 'encyclopaedists' like the diarist John Evelyn, who resisted the drive towards specialization. For them the universe remained full of mysteries. Byrom's resistance to Bishop Butler's rationalist *Analogy of Religion* (1736) was not a resistance to religion but to a definition of religion based solely on ratiocination. Goodwin Wharton, an aristocrat and Whig member of the House of Commons for life, who was made a Lord of the Admiralty in 1697 by William III, was not mad; but he believed in the power of fairies in a way that makes some sense of Locke's hostility to such stories. Throughout his life Wharton clung to the conviction that a buried treasure guarded by the fairies would be the making of his fortune.[12]

My argument in this book is that the rationalist consolidation taking place during this period – whether ideological or material – was not accomplished without considerable resistance to its exclusion by what I have called 'rival knowledge'. This latter sort of knowledge has been the subject of much modern attention, in neurology as much as in literature. The recent work of Oliver Sacks among the autistic has demonstrated that perception does not necessarily lead to conception. And Sacks's *Seeing Voices*, on the world of the deaf, has confirmed what his studies of the blind have also shown: that to restore the sensation of hearing or seeing is not to render either of those sensations intelligible to someone who has never learned how to make sense of their information. Prelingual deafness, Sacks claims, prevents the ability to propositionize, and yet of the deaf he says, 'I get an overwhelming feeling not only of another mode of communication but of another mode of sensibility, another mode of being.'[13]

An Imaginary Life, the novel about Ovid's exile on the Black Sea by the Australian writer, David Malouf, similarly presents the reader with an articulate and educated adult relearning, from a wolf-boy he has been set to teach, the feral knowledge that he 'knew' as a boy but from which his 'civilisation' has sundered him. This is the knowledge of Ted Hughes's poem 'The Thought Fox' and Thom Gunn's 'Yoko'. And is it not this knowledge that Conor Cruise O'Brien alludes to when he says: 'The Enlightenment we need is one that is aware of the dark, especially the dark in ourselves'?[14] But it is precisely this knowledge that Locke wanted kept from children.

Not until the nineteenth century was there as articulate a celebration of that kind of knowledge as Thoreau gives in *A Week on the Concord and Merrimack Rivers* (1849), in a passage in which he describes the American Indian:

> He has glances of starry recognition to which our saloons are strangers. The steady illumination of his genius, dim only because distant, is like the faint but satisfying light of the stars compared with the dazzling but ineffectual and short-lived blaze of candles.[15]

And yet Margaret Cavendish, Duchess of Newcastle, had some intimation of this in the mid-seventeenth century too. In her romance novella, *The Blazing World* (1666), the central figure, a European woman marooned in the Arctic, is made Empress by 'Bear-men' who introduce her gradually to all the other inhabitants of the country. Far from seeking to impose her names and classifications on them (as European settlement was already doing), she listens to their descriptions of themselves and wishes to write them down.

What, if anything, Cavendish can have known about Amerindian ethnography is difficult to determine. Her attachment to the household of Queen Henrietta Maria in the early 1640s, and her subsequent residence in Paris, however, would have exposed her to French taste in the period. And among the eagerly awaited cultural events each year in the French court was the publication of the *Jesuit Relations*: accounts of the French missions in North America, among which certainly were surveys of the culture and beliefs of the first-nation peoples.

Even earlier in her writing career, in determining the relation between the imagination and the passions, Cavendish elaborated an epistemology that was not simply empirical. She insisted that what she called 'the rational animate matter' was unencumbered by the senses:

> for the Senses only present the Objects, the Rational the Passions; which shews, the Rational Animate matter is as much in the Heart, as in the Head, and may be of the same Degree of Strength, although they Work Different wayes, as being Different figures, yet there is such Sympathy with each other, whether by Recourse or otherwise, as Passions will Raise Imaginations, Corrupt Judgement, Disorder Reason, and Blind-fold Understanding; And Imaginations will raise Passions, as Fear, Love, Hate, Doubt, Hope, and the like.[16]

'Nothing is in the mind that was not first in the senses,' Comenius wrote on the title-page of his influential picture-book for children, *Orbis Sensualium Pictus*, first published in the same year as Ussher's *Annals*. But Comenius himself included in his engraving of serpents many (such as dragons and basilisks) that he knew to be fanciful. And many a nursemaid continued to convey to her charges the oral tradition of supernatural ballad, folk-tale, and fairytale that John Locke sought to exclude from the child's upbringing in his *Some Thoughts Concerning Education* (1693). Much of this world of fantasy was the very stuff not only of Bishop Percy's famous anthology, *Reliques of Ancient English Poetry* (1765), but of the Gothic novel of the latter part of the eighteenth century. Moreover, one might argue that for all Fielding's mock-emplacement of the novel within traditional genres such as epic, the novel itself as a form was subversive of the very attempt to fix genres and establish polite literature.

Newton's mechanical explanation of the world's operation, however, satisfied an increasing tendency in the later seventeenth century to place method (whether empirical or Cartesian) before inquiry: a modernist position which Swift pilloried in *The Battle of the Books* (1704). One of the most quoted references to Newton from the Augustan period is Pope's famous epitaph on him:

> Nature, and Nature's Laws lay hid in Night.
> God said, *Let Newton be!*, and All was *Light*.
>
> (1–2)

Given Pope's scepticism about the perfectibility of human knowledge, these lines seem strangely ironic, not least in the context of his observation on Newton in *An Essay on Man* (1732–4). The word '*Light*', however, suggests that Pope's praise is restricted to that most popular of Newton's discoveries, the refraction of light in his *Optics* (1704). Pope wrote those lines in about 1730 for an intended memorial to Newton, but the position they appear to endorse was elaborated by Addison nearly twenty years earlier in his celebrated 'Newtonian' ode, 'The Spacious Firmament on High':

What though, in solemn silence, all
Move round the dark terrestrial ball?
What though nor real voice nor sound
Amid their radiant orbs be found?
In reason's ear they all rejoice,
And utter forth a glorious voice,
For ever singing, as they shine,
'The hand that made us is divine.'[17]

Although Addison is here describing a geocentric universe, his model of that universe is a modern machine, indeed something very like the machine that his partner, Sir Richard Steele, had described a year earlier in *The Englishman*. Designed by George Graham and made by John Rowley, it demonstrated the circulation of the planets around the sun, and was named an 'Orrery' after the fourth Earl of Cork and Orrery who, as one of the 'moderns', was central to the 'ancients and moderns' controversy which Swift deployed in *The Battle of the Books*.

The idea of such a machine was indebted to a mechanical model of the world which was also reflected in William Harvey's notion of the heart in *On The Motion of the Heart and Blood in Animals* (first published in 1628). Harvey wrote of the heart as

a piece of machinery in which, though one wheel gives motion to another, yet all the wheels seem to move simultaneously; or in that mechanical contrivance which is adapted to firearms, where the trigger being touched, down comes the flint, strikes against the steel, elicits a spark, which falling among the powder, it is ignited, upon which the flame extends, enters the barrel, causes the explosion, propels the ball, and the mark is attained.[18]

Newton's contemporaries are even closer to Harvey's language in their formulations. 'All nature is one great *Engine*, made by, and held in His [God's] Hands,' says Nehemiah Grew (1682); and Locke refers to 'our Planetary World' as 'this stupendious Machine'. Even Robert Boyle wrote that 'the [mechanical] philosophy teaches, that the phenomena of the world are physically produced by the mechanical properties of the parts of matter.'[19]

What both Ussher's *Annals* and Newton's *Principia* reflected was an increasing desire to account for the world methodically in one coherent system: a clearing away of the rubbish of medieval speculation along the lines recommended by Bacon in *The Advancement of Learning* (1605). Indeed, it was to Bacon that the Royal Society looked back for justification of their elevation of inductive experience over deductive speculation or the writings of antiquity.

But Bacon was himself an heir to reforms intended to make discourse 'scientific'. In *The Advancement* he wished to rid science of what he called the idols of the tribe, the cave and the marketplace: that is, to render it culturally and personally neutral. Mary Louise Pratt, noting the attempts of twentieth-century ethnography to be 'scientific', describes a similar desire. Ethnographers, she explains, want 'a neutral, tropeless discourse that would render other realities "exactly as they are", not filtered through our own values and interpretative schema.' It is a process that she identifies as a wild-goose chase,[20] perhaps ultimately attributable to the publication in 1735 of Linnaeus's *Systema Naturae* (*System of Nature*) or to the French expedition of that year designed to discover the exact shape of the earth.[21]

What Dijksterhuis has called 'The Mechanisation of the World Picture' goes back at least to the Greeks, however, and may be intimately connected with what Robert Logan has called 'The Alphabet Effect',[22] or the ability of western cultures to outstrip the East by being able to systematize knowledge with a small number of characters or letters. This desire for a 'real' or universal character (that is, a standard set of signs for all languages) was a special concern of Bacon's followers who set up the Royal Society. John Wilkins, in his *Essay Towards a Real Character* (1668), drew heavily upon the earlier works both of the Scotsman George Dalgarno (1661) and the Londoner Francis Lodowyck (1646, 1652); and yet all of them (as Lodowyck recognises) are indebted to the 'hieroglyphical representation of words'[23] in older cultures, a subject also pursued by the seventeenth-century Jesuit antiquarian Athanasius Kircher.

Bacon had also been preceded in his desire for such a neutral discourse by the so-called reforms in logic and rhetoric of Petrus Ramus (Pierre de la Ramée) in the mid-sixteenth century, reforms which had a profound impact on late sixteenth-century England. Animated by a belief in the necessity of separating thought from expression, Ramus gave to logic all the processes of thought and left rhetoric with what is now commonly meant by the word 'rhetoric': that is, simply the means of expression.

But classical rhetoric had had many subjects for argument (or 'topics of invention') that were not included in the new topics given to logic: such arguments as 'the usefulness or honour of a thing' or 'the character of the person speaking'. These were the '*loci communes*' or 'commonplaces' that shared with emblem literature a sense of truth as polysemous. A whole range of arguments and evidence was thus excluded from thought and deemed to be extraneous to it. One of the results was that Eurocentric scientific thought could be presented as free of cultural and personal values. Thomas Lodowyck could imagine, in other words, that because all western European countries recognized that the sign '5' meant 'five' in whatever language, this would be true for the rest of the world.

Swift, who had no love for the Royal Society and its works, attacks this kind of reduction in his description of the 'Oratorial Machines' in *A Tale of a Tub* (1704). There the hack scholar refers to:

a Number I was resolved to establish, whatever Argument it might cost me; in imitation of that prudent Method observed by many other

Philosophers and great Clerks, whose chief Art in Division has been, to grow fond of some proper mystical Number, which their Imaginations have rendered Sacred, to a Degree, that they force common Reason to find room for it in every part of Nature, reducing, including, and adjusting every *Genus* and *Species* within that Compass, by coupling some against their Wills, and banishing others at any Rate.

He has been most preoccupied with 'the profound Number THREE,' he says, and 'reduced the *Senses* and the *Elements* under its Banner,' having 'brought over several Designs from its two great Rivals, SEVEN and NINE.'[24]

Ramus's stress on method was equally influential in this rearrangement of knowledge. No one who has seen the binary schemes of Ramistic texts can doubt their legacy to the branching system of directories and files in information science or the schemes of taxonomic knowledge. Whether embraced or rejected, Ramus's *Dialectica* (1555) made method central to the agenda not just of logic but of any learned discipline; for although his title invoked *dialectica*, his work was in fact about *scientia*. Not so much about inquiry as about instruction, Ramus's 'method' was a scheme more for conveying information than for making inquiries.[25]

Bacon's 'transparent' discourse and method are two of his important legacies to the generation of the Royal Society. His 'valueless' language is exactly the sort of transparent and universal discourse recommended by Thomas Sprat in his 'Proposal for erecting an English Academy' (1667), 'A fixt and *Impartial Court* of *Eloquence*, according to whose Censure all Books or Authors should either stand or fail.'[26] This is a theme put into practice in Mandeville's *An Enquiry into the Causes of the Frequent Executions at Tyburn* (1725), where the author argues that 'the Pleasure there is in imitating Nature in what Shape soever is so bewitching, that it over-rules the Dictates of Art'.[27] Things as they are, in other words, do not need to be 'to Advantage drest' but may be described 'transparently', in their stark reality. This assurance about transparent language is allied with an assurance about classification and standards in a remark by the poet Thomas Tickell (one of Pope's 'dunces') in 1713:

> Men, who by long study and experience have reduced their ideas to certain classes, and consider the general nature of things abstracted from particulars, express their thoughts after a more concise, lively, surprising manner.[28]

Both assurances are allied in Sir John Hill's work on plants, significantly titled *Eden* (1757). As the first translator of Linnaeus into English, Hill writes about method and about his own language as if it too had become a universal character available to all:

> The GREEK, though no Gardener's Tongue, is not an unknown Language; nor are the Depths of Nature unfathomable. The want of a

Work on Gardening, in which this Method should be explained, was
the principal Occasion of the present Undertaking; and we propose in
it to make this SWEDE speak ENGLISH, and to deliver his Method in such
a Manner, that all may comprehend it.[29]

But what is the source of these universal and impartial standards, these
'classes' and 'general nature' about which Dr Johnson also seemed so sure?
As S. M. Walters has pointed out:

the whole idea of genus and species [in botany] is a natural product of
European thought of the seventeenth and eighteenth centuries, based
on Aristotelian logic ... What reason have we to think that the demar-
cation of the largest Angiosperm families would look even approxi-
mately like the one we use (with very little dispute) at the present day,
if Angiosperm taxonomy had been born in, say, New Zealand, instead
of Europe?

Why was the rose (the family *Rosaceae*) chosen as the central genus by such
seventeenth-century botanists as Tournefort and Bauhin, asks Walters?

The answer is clear. This was happening in seventeenth-century
Europe, where for centuries previously art and literature had been full
of certain symbolic flowers. How could any other choice have been
made? The 'indefinable' families, then, are associative [i.e. culturally
constructed]; the type genus is an important European plant; and the
shape of the family is a product of this thought-process.[30]

Looking back over the history of physics, Einstein observed that the chief
fault with the mechanical system upon which Linnaeus grounded his
taxonomy was

the fundamental assumption that it is possible to explain all events in
nature from the mechanical point of view ... Science is not just a
collection of laws, a catalogue of unrelated facts. It is a creation of the
human mind, with its freely invented ideas and concepts.[31]

What Einstein has to say about the contingency of physics was recognized
by Boyle and Newton: that is, that all systems are only hypotheses of order.
But a whole host of lesser thinkers, many of them associated with the Royal
Society, saw in the mechanical model of the world a means both of reform
and possession, a reinvention of the world that would allow them to
quantify and possess it in a way only dreamt of by Bacon in his *New
Atlantis*. 'On the authority of Isaac Newton,' says Donald Worster, 'English
biologists ... were encouraged to take up the mechanical philosophy, and
its companion, a utilitarian bias toward nature, followed closely behind.'[32]

At the beginning of the seventeenth century, the word 'invention' still
retained its ancient sense 'to come upon': from the Latin verb, *invenio*. In
one of his sermons on the anniversary of the Gunpowder Plot, Bishop

Lancelot Andrewes associates the modern sense of invention, the 'inventions' of the plotters, with the devil. By the end of the century, how- ever, the word had commonly come to mean what we now mean by it, and to have largely scientific overtones. This was due in no small measure to the legacy of Bacon and the rise of the Royal Society.

It was a shift not simply linguistic, but cognitive too. Implicit in it was the belief that men might remake or reinvent the world; that (as at the end of *Paradise Lost*) the Fall might be irreversible, but it was not irremediable. In fact, Milton gives short shrift to this modern sense of the word 'invention' in his epic. The word 'inventions' in this sense is associated with the comic farcicality of the fallen angels' invention of cannon (VI. 631). But what the fallen angels are up to in the War in Heaven – a remaking of the cosmos in their own image – is very much parodic of the increasing association of 'invention' with the great new work of dominating the world.

In his 'Notes Toward a Supreme Fiction,' the twentieth-century American poet Wallace Stevens contemplates the consequence of this development:

> But to impose is not
> To discover. To discover an order as of
> A season, to discover summer and know it,
>
> To discover winter and know it well, to find,
> Not to impose, not to have reasoned at all,
> Out of nothing to have come on major weather,
>
> It is possible, possible, possible. It must
> Be possible.
>
> (Sect. VII)

Even Linnaeus came ultimately to doubt the system upon which he had constructed modern botany: a system that carried within it the belief in a world that might be (in Wordsworth's phrase) 'parcelled out with geometric rules'. It may well be that the taxonomy to which Linnaeus has given his name sought to avoid the rigid mechanism of Descartes, but the imperialism of its model was indebted ultimately to Bacon and, beyond that, to a mechanical reading of the Creation of the world, in which the word 'dominion' was read as meaning 'power' or 'control', but without the responsibility that the Hebrew word and its culture implied.[33]

The title-page of Bacon's *Instauratio Magna* (1620) shows a ship sailing beyond the Pillars of Hercules, pillars which he understood allegorically to mean the limits of knowledge as defined by Aristotle. Bacon's text is from the book of *Daniel* ('Many shall run to and fro and knowledge shall be increased'); it overtly links the augmentation of knowledge to geographical discovery, a meaning concealed in the design's origin as an emblem of the dominion of Charles V of Spain.[34] Charles II was in no doubt that the 'real' or universal character proposed by George Dalgarno in 1661 would be of use not simply for the communication of knowledge or the promotion of religion, but for 'encreasing Traffique and Commerce'.[35] The metaphors of travel and commerce lurk not far beneath the surface of ostensible science, and with them the very sort of possession and empire that Pope seems to celebrate at the end of *Windsor Forest*.

In fact, scepticism about man's capacity to reinvent the universe on a mechanical model was, and remained, widespread. Milton is alert to the discursive slippage between knowledge and dubious power in *Paradise Lost*, where Satan waits like a pirate scout for argosies to plunder, or as a city-rapist to trap the innocent milkmaid Eve (ii. 630–42; ix. 445–57). A modern reinventer on an epic scale, Satan reads Earth as a development site:

> O Earth, how like to Heav'n, if not preferrd
> More justly, Seat worthier of Gods, as built
> With second thoughts, reforming what was old!
> For what God after better worse would build?
>   (IX. 99–102)[36]

Satan, moreover, uses the discourse of a 'projector': one who employs the advances of science to speculative and lucrative ends. His country-house vocabulary of building and property comes out of the satiric comedy of Ben Jonson's *The Devil is an Ass* (1631), where land speculation is at least as rapacious as the speculation in the South Sea Bubble of nearly a century later. Satan's first sight of Eden leads him to think of suburban development:

> Hell shall unfould
> To entertain you two, her widest Gates,
> And send forth all her Kings; there will be room,
> Not like these narrow limits, to receive
> Your numerous offspring.
>   (IV. 381–5)

Milton, moreover, was only too conscious of the gap between language and its ostensible referent. The invocation to Book VII of *Paradise Lost* asks the assistance of Urania, the goddess of heavenly wisdom; but it is 'the meaning not the name' of Urania that the poet seeks. Underneath Raphael's disquiet about describing the creation of the world, even in Adam's unfallen language, is the distance between the events described and the words available to describe them:

> to recount Almighty works
> What words or tongue of Seraph can suffice,
> Or heart of man suffice to comprehend?
>   (VII. 112–14)

Here, in the centre of the greatest epic in the language, a doubt even about its possibility is a central subject. But Milton was writing the poem in the midst of the very debate about language and things to which I have referred. By no means confined to the Royal Society and its antecedents, this debate was central to the agenda of humanism from at least Erasmus onwards. Erasmus's *De Copia Verborum ac Rerum* (1512) was a blow against the mere concern with eloquence in much late medieval thought, but it none the less recognized the interdependence of words and things in the construction of knowledge.

This debate arises again in *The Schoolmaster* (1570), by Queen Elizabeth I's tutor, Roger Ascham. Ascham's observation that 'ye know not what hurt ye do to learning that care not for words but for matter'[37] is contradicted by Bacon in an extraordinarily 'rhetorical' sentence. 'The affectionate studie of eloquence and copie [copiousness],' Bacon said, led to a situation in which

> men began to hunt more after words than matter; and more after the choiceness of the phrase, and the round and clean composition of the sentence, and the sweet falling of the clauses, and the varying and illustration of their works with tropes and figures, than after the weight of matter, worth of subject, soundness of argument, life of invention, or depth of judgment.[38]

And yet Bacon's contemporary, Ben Jonson, believed that '*Language* best shewes a man: speake that I may see thee.'[39] Jonson also believed that facts for their own sake were of little importance to true wisdom. 'What is't to me,' he wrote in one of his poems,[40] 'whether the French Designe | Be, or be not, to get the *Val-telline?*' At the end of the century Charles II's court preacher, Robert South, could write: 'What am I benefitted whether the sun moves about the earth, or whether the sun is at the centre of the world, and the earth is indeed a planet and wheels about that?'[41] In his conversation with Raphael in Book VIII of *Paradise Lost*, Milton's Adam is similarly sceptical about what constitutes right use:

> not to know at large of things remote
> From use, obscure and suttle, but to know
> That which before us lies in daily life,
> Is the prime Wisdom.
>
> (191–4)

It is one of Milton's ironies that 'obscure' and 'suttle' are two of Satan's adjectives.

The argument about use is also central to the temptation. Eve has to believe what the Lady in *Comus* does not, that use is immediate, empirical, and quantifiable, and that ignorance (even of the 'obscure and suttle') is its enemy. Satan's is the same kind of Lucretian argument as that used by Cecropia against Pamela in Sidney's *Arcadia* (iii. 5): that nature, not God or Providence, provides the fruitfulness of the earth; that the prohibition of any kind of knowledge is a tyranny; and that use consists of immediate enjoyment.[42]

Paradise Lost was being written as the first publication of Lucretius in English was published: John Evelyn's edition of Book I in 1656. In his preface to the *De Rerum Natura*, Evelyn, like his continental predecessor Gassendi, tried to reconcile the work to Christianity; but it was no easy argument to make. Lucretius had been associated with a nature that overthrows moral and social restraint. This is Edmund's nature in *King Lear*:

> Thou, Nature, art my goddess; to thy law
> My services are bound. Wherefore should I
> Stand in the plague of custom, and permit
> The curiosity of nations to deprive me,
> For that I am some twelve or fourteen moonshines
> Lag of a brother? Why bastard? Wherefore base?
>   (I. ii. 1–6)[43]

Satan's tree is the 'Mother of Science' which allows him, he says, 'to discerne things in their Causes'. But 'science', or '*scientia*', as Milton understood the word, is not wisdom or even knowledge: not 'sapience', in other words, whose meaning Milton invokes at the beginning of Book VII. 'Experience is the common schoolhouse of fools and ill men; men of wit and honesty be otherwise instructed,' says Ascham, paraphrasing Erasmus.[44] The knowledge Satan offers Eve is merely empirical: one in which tasting, touching, and smelling outweigh other kinds of knowing. What Satan offers Eve is the very sort of hidden knowledge that Adam has already rejected, and which is rejected, too by the tradition of Christian humanism.

The curriculum of Milton's *Of Education* is one 'which fits a man to perform justly, skilfully and magnanimously all the offices both private and public of peace and war'.[45] Milton echoes Spenser in invoking the discourse of civic humanism. It is not my business or intention to trace all the permutations of this debate about the kinds of knowledge; suffice to say that the debate was not settled even by 1750, and that an admirer of Erasmus such as Swift was by no means persuaded of the claims for a 'real' or universal character. In the third book of Gulliver the academicians of Lagado are engaged in exercises little different from those of Wilkins, Lodowyck, and Dalgarno. Indeed, the preface to Dalgarno's *Ars Signorum* (1661) is written in a strange neo-language that looks remarkably like the speech of the Lilliputians.

It used to be commonplace to think of rationalizing empiricism as sweeping all before it from the Restoration of 1660 onwards in a great age of enlightenment. But the retrospective history of thought frequently omits the inconvenient and the unfashionable. Robert Boyle's first biographer, as I said, destroyed papers that did not suit 'the present age'. Medieval scholasticism was neither simply preoccupied with word-spinning nor with merely deductive generalizing. Nor were its logic and rhetoric simply swept away by Ramistic and Baconian 'reforms' that displaced old-fashioned 'scholastic' or syllogistic deduction with induction.

The great systems of knowledge and language contained in John Wilkins's *Real Character* (1668), for example, owe as much to the encyclopaedias of the previous century as they do to scientific induction. Indeed, even Bacon himself has been described as 'one of a group of Renaissance encyclopedists': a man whose limitations and strengths owe more to his cultural milieu than has often been recognized.[46]

In fact, one of the more interesting seventeenth-century scholars of the process of induction, the 'scholastic' logician John Poinsot, wrote what semioticians now regard as a significant re-evaluation of that process. Bacon's *Novum Organum* (1620) had argued most strenuously against syllogistic deduction and for induction; but Poinsot's book on logic, called *Liber Tertius Summularum* (1631), pointed out that induction was not simply deduction in reverse, but a more complex process. In it the mind was not simply engaged in dealing with the sensations of things but reconciling them to already established truths. Poinsot was as prepared as any later member of the Royal Society to recognize that knowledge arises from sensations, but he did not accept that it was 'transparent'. Knowledge in that sense could never be free of what Bacon called 'the idols of the theatre' or what we would now call 'cultural construction'.[47]

Even Sir Thomas Browne, who wrote his *Vulgar Errors* (1646) in response to Bacon's appeal for a book to rid science of superstition, believed that 'the wisest heads prove at last almost all Scepticks, and stand like *Janus* in the field of knowledge'.[48] And Milton, himself an educational reformer and a friend of Galileo, created in *Paradise Lost* an epic that uses both heliocentric and geocentric models of the world. Both were equally useful as myths of a world that man could never completely know: a world that Blake would describe as 'hid by thy senses five'.

This position finds an echo in the twentieth century in the writings of the American poet, Charles Olson. In *Human Universe* (1965), Olson writes:

> There are laws, that is to say, the human universe is as discoverable as that other. And as definable.
>
> The trouble has been, that a man stays so astonished he can triumph over his own incoherence, he settles for that, crows over it, and goes at a day again happy he at least makes a little sense. Or if he says anything to another, he thinks it is enough – the struggle does involve such labor and some terror – to wrap it in a little mystery: ah, the way is hard but this is what you find if you go it.
>
> The need now is a cooler one, a discrimination, and then, a shout. Der Weg stirbt [the way has disappeared], sd one. And was right, was he not? The 'indefinable' in the question is: was ist der Weg [what is the way]?[49]

The 'way' that Olson refers to as having died in the early twentieth century is what Blake called 'the ratio of the five senses' which hides the greater truths of the imagination. Olson's crowing intellect is also like the cockerel of Wallace Stevens' poem, 'Bantams in Pine Woods'. 'Damned universal cock,' the poet writes, 'as if the sun I Was blackamoor to bear your blazing tail.'[50] It is a 'crowing' which Pope and Swift found profoundly objectionable.

The post-Romantic reaction against what Blake called 'the mills of Newton and Locke' also included a revulsion against method. The period with which I am dealing in this book (about 1650 to 1750) is the period during which method (Cartesian and otherwise) was increasingly consolidated, from the appearance of Ussher's *Annals* to the final establishment of Linnaeus's taxonomic system with the publication of his *Species Plantarum* in 1753.

How did this entrenchment come about and what are its implications for the reading of literature? Who decided that statistics (that late-seventeenth-century invention) were more important than narratives, or even free of them? In his biography of the computer pioneer Alan Turing, Andrew Hodges refers to the early work of Turing's colleague, Michael Polanyi, who held the Chair of Chemistry at the University of Manchester before the Second World War. Polanyi, Hodges observes, believed

> that science was all in the mind anyway, and had no meaning apart from the 'semantic function' which the human mind alone could supply. [The philosopher] Karl Popper, who held similar views, said in 1950 that 'It is only our human brain which may lend significance to the calculator's senseless powers of producing truths.'[51]

That is an observation that Milton, himself a contemporary of the first calculators, would entirely have understood. Part of our difficulty in reading the literature of the late seventeenth and early eighteenth centuries is in recovering a pre-mechanical culture: one in which what John Barrell calls 'civic humanism' and its discourses had not been overwhelmed by the claims of political economy 'to offer a thoroughly systematic account of history and of economic and social organisation'.[52]

But equally, literary criticism has frequently marginalized itself behind a screen of impenetrable verbiage. What follows is an account of only a few areas of discourse and thought in which we can trace the battle in this period for possession not just of knowledge but also of culture. Mapping, travelling, farming, owning, and childhood are by no means the only 'territories' in which these intertextual and intercultural skirmishes can be traced. Although it is not possible to pursue all that might be said even on these few topics, the chapters are each arranged internally in a generally chronological manner in order to suggest the development of the subject within the period 1650 to 1750.

Notes

1 Title-page (London, 1658).
2 See Arnold Williams, *The Common Expositor: An Account of the Commentaries on Genesis, 1527–1633* (Chapel Hill, NC: University of North Carolina Press, 1948).
3 Except where noted, quotations from Pope are from *The Poems of Alexander Pope*, ed. John Butt (Twickenham edition, London: Methuen, 1939–67).
4 *Newton's Philosophy of Nature: Selections from his Writings*, ed. H. S. Thayer (New York: Macmillan-Hafner, 1953), pp. 10–11. It seems likely that Newton was much less a 'mechanist' than his followers, who took their cues from the mechanical explanations in his work, thought him to be.
5 By recreating the scientific context of the later seventeenth century in England, A. Rupert Hall asserted, 'we may then perceive that the intellectual link between Archbishop Ussher and Isaac Newton was no freakish, archaic absurdity'. 'English Scientific Literature in the Seventeenth Century', *Scientific Literature in Sixteenth- and Seventeenth-Century England* (Los Angeles: UCLA, William Andrews Clark Memorial Library, 1961), p.44. For Wilkins, see *An Essay Towards a Real Character and a Philosophical Language* (London, 1668), pp. 162–8.
6 *The Scientific Revolution 1500–1700* (London: Longman, 1954), pp. 258, 244.
7 I am grateful to Michael Hunter's inaugural professorial lecture at Birkbeck College for this phrase from Boyle's biographer, Thomas Birch.
8 See J. C. D. Clark, *English Society 1688–1732* (Cambridge, 1985), E. P. Thompson, *Whigs and Hunters* and *Customs in Common* (London: Allen Lane, 1975, 1993), Joanna Innes, 'Jonathan Clark, Social History and England's "Ancien Regime"' *Past and Present*, 115 (1987), and Michael McKeon, *The Origins of the English Novel 1600–1740* (London: Century Hutchinson, 1988), pp. 205–11, 226–37.
9 *Areopagtica, The Prose of John Milton*, ed. J. Max Patrick (New York: New York University Press, 1968), p. 323.
10 *The Light in Troy: Imitation and Discovery in Renaissance Poetry* (New Haven: Yale University Press, 1982), p. 20.
11 Joy Hancox, *The Queen's Chameleon: The Life of John Byrom* (London: Cape, 1994) p. 231.
12 See J. Kent Clark, *Goodwin Wharton* (Oxford: Oxford University Press, 1984).
13 *Seeing Words: A Journey Into the World of the Deaf* (Berkeley: University of California Press, 1989), pp. 19, 130. Brian Friel's most recent play, *Molly Sweeney*, deals with the destructive consquences of giving sight to a blind woman. Jane Urquhart's novel *The Whirlpool* (1986) presents the genius of an autistic rearranging the world as Sacks has done in *An Anthropologist on Mars* (1995).
14 *On the Eve of the Millenium* (Toronto: Anansi, 1994), p. 30.
15 New York: Holt, Rinehart and Winston, 1963, p. 62.
16 *Philosophical and Physical Opinions* (London, 1663), pp. 265, 262. The first edition was in 1655. The British Library 1663 edition is inscribed 'Ex dono nobilissimae Heroinae, Authoris' and seems to have been corrected by her hand or at least that of a contemporary.
17 *The New Oxford Book of Eighteenth Century Verse*, ed. Roger Lonsdale (Oxford: Oxford University Press, 1984), p. 45.
18 Trans. Robert Willis, ed. E. A. Parkyn (London: Dent & Co., 1906), pp. 37–8.

19 The quotation from Locke is from *Some Thoughts Concerning Education* (1693), in *The Educational Writings of John Locke*, ed. James L. Axtell (Cambridge: Cambridge University Press, 1968), p. 306. The quotations from Grew and Boyle are cited in A. R. Hall, *The Scientific Revolution 1500–1800* (Boston: Beacon Press, 1966), pp. 191, 212.

20 'Fieldwork in Common Places', *Writing Culture: The Poetics of Ethnography*, ed. James Clifford and George Marcus (Berkeley: University of California Press, 1986), p. 27.

21 I am here conflating Pratt's article with her later work, *Imperial Eyes: Travel Writing and Transculturation* (London: Routledge, 1992), pp. 15–16.

22 *The Mechanisation of the World Picture*, trans. C. Dickinson (Oxford: Oxford University Press, 1961); *The Alphabet Effect: The Impact of the Phonetic Alphabet on the Development of Western Civilisation* (New York: Morrow, 1986).

23 *A Common Writing* (London, 1647), sig. A2. For a more extensive discussion of the history of this phenomenon see Umberto Eco, *The Search for the Perfect Language* (Oxford: Oxford University Press, 1995).

24 *Gulliver's Travels and Other Writings*, ed. Ricardo Quintana (New York: Modern Library, 1958), p. 278.

25 In *Voltaire's Bastards* (Toronto: Penguin, 1992, pp. 14, 7, 15, 50), John Ralston Saul observes that reason in western culture has become not a weapon of moral inquiry but 'a disinterested administrative method'. 'Our reality,' he notes, 'is dominated by elites who have spent much of the last two centuries, indeed of the last four, organizing society around answers and around structures designed to produce answers.' Saul sees this as a legacy of the Inquisition's demand for right answers, but none the less a legacy that has come down to us indifferently through Descartes, Locke, and Marx. Saul's account of the process of exclusion is superficial, but not in its sense of something having been excluded: what he calls 'common sense' but what I have been calling 'rival knowledge'. See also Morris Berman, *The Reenchantment of the World* (Ithaca, NY: Cornell University Press, 1981).

26 *The History of the Royal Society* (1667), *Critical Essays of the Seventeenth Century*, ed. J. E. Spingarn (Oxford: Oxford University Press, 1957), ii. 114.

27 sig. [A5v].

28 *The Guardian* 23, 7 April 1713, (London, 1756), i. 92.

29 London, 1757, p. 3.

30 'The Shaping of Angiosperm Taxonomy', *New Phytologist*, 60 (1961), pp. 75, 78. It seems to me more likely that the 'logic' is a combination of Ramistic and Cartesian, but the indebtedness of botanic systematization to Anglo-French philosophical preoccupations none the less stands. I am grateful to Professor Polly Winsor for drawing my attention to this article. Walters also defers to A. J. Cain, 'Logic and memory in Linnaeus's system of taxonomy', *Proceedings of the Linnaean Society of London*, 169 (1958), p. 144.

31 Albert Einstein and Leopold Infeld, *The Evolution of Physics* (New York: Simon and Schuster – Touchstone, 1986), pp. 120, 294.

32 *Nature's Economy* (Cambridge: Cambridge University Press, 1983), p. 40.

33 See the chapter 'The Empire of Reason' in Donald Worster, *Nature's Economy* (Cambridge: Cambridge University Press, 1985), pp. 26–55. See also the notes to *Genesis* 1: 26 in *The JPS Torah Commentary: Genesis* (Philadelphia: Jewish Philosophical Society, 1989), pp. 12–13.

34 See Margery Corbett and Ronald Lightbown, *The Comely Frontispiece: The Emblematic Title-Page in England 1550–1660* (London: Routledge and Kegan Paul, 1979), p. 186.

35 George Dalgarno, *Ars Signorum* (London, 1661), sig. [A4v].

36 The quotations from *Paradise Lost* throughout are taken from *The Poetical Works of John Milton*, ed. Helen Darbishire (London: Oxford University Press, 1958). Darbishire's text follows closely the editions printed under Milton's supervision and so preserves many of the meanings that are effaced by modernizing the spelling.

37 *The Schoolmaster*, ed. Lawrence V. Ryan (Ithaca, NY: Cornell University Press, 1967), p. 115.

38 *Of the Advancement of Learning*, 'The First Book', *The Philosophical Works of Francis Bacon*, ed. John M. Roberston (London: George Routledge & Sons, 1905), p. 54. Even Robert Boyle, however, has been accused by a modern historian of science as being 'prolix, loose and wandering': A. Rupert Hall, 'English Scientific Literature in the Seventeenth Century', p. 34.

39 *Timber: Or, Discoveries, Works*, ed. C. H. Herford, Percy and Evelyn Simpson (Oxford: Clarendon, 1947), viii, p. 625.

40 'An Epistle Answering to One that Asked to be Sealed of the Tribe of Ben', 31–2, *Works*, viii. 219.

41 Cited in A. R. Hall, 'English Scientific Literature in the Seventeenth Century', p.38.

42 See D. P. Walker, 'Ways of Dealing with Atheists: A Background to Pamela's Refutation of Cecropia', *Bibliothèque d'Humanisme et Renaissance*, 18 (1955), pp. 252–77.

43 London: Methuen, Arden Edition, 1957, p. 24.

44 *The Schoolmaster*, Part I, p. 51.

45 *The Prose of John Milton*, ed. J. Max Patrick (New York: New York University Press, 1968), p. 232.

46 See Virgil K. Whitaker, 'Francis Bacon's Intellectual Milieu', *Essential Articles for the Study of Francis Bacon*, ed. Brian Vickers (London: Sidgwick & Jackson, 1968), p. 29.

47 For this account I am much indebted to John Deely, *Introducing Semiotic: Its History and Doctrine* (Bloomington: Indiana University Press, 1982), pp. 71–73, 182.

48 *Religio Medici, The Works of Sir Thomas Browne*, ed. Geoffrey Keynes (London: Faber and Faber, 1964), i. 83.

49 *Selected Writings of Charles Olson*, ed. Robert Creeley (New York: New Directions, 1966), p. 53.

50 *The Palm at the End of the Mind* (New York: Knopf, 1971), p. 75. All subsequent quotations from Stevens are taken from this edition.

51 *Alan Turing: The Enigma* (New York: Simon and Schuster, 1983), p. 414.

52 *The Birth of Pandora and the Division of Knowledge*, (London: Macmillan, 1992), p. xiv.

|2|

The Geographical Part of Knowledge: Mapping and Naming

All study is in some sense a kind of mapping, and the study of cartography itself is revealing about the way in which any generation views itself and the world around it. Within the last decade, such books as Hugh Brody's *Maps and Dreams* (1987) and Bruce Chatwin's *The Songlines* (1987) have made us aware that there are other ways of reading the map of the world than those canonized by traditional western geography. Brody's discovery that the First Nation peoples of northern British Columbia hunt by dream maps, like Chatwin's recognition that aboriginal Australians sing their geography, points to something that we had forgotten: that mapping is a construction, not a given. Recently the ambulance-drivers of Toronto refused to use the official government map of the city streets, claiming that it did not correspond to the way they knew the streets of the city. And anyone who has grown used to the abstract diagrams that map the subways of London and New York will know how confusing it is to try to reconcile that diagram with an ordinary street map. 'A map,' Alfred Korzybski has observed, 'is *not* the territory it represents, but, if correct, it has a *similar structure* to the territory, which accounts for its usefulness.'[1]

In his book *How to Lie With Maps* Mark Monmonnier draws attention to the way in which the density of place is eroded by what a map tells:

> A good map tells a multitude of little white lies; it suppresses truth to help the user see what needs to be seen. Reality is three-dimensional, rich in detail, and far too actual to allow a complete yet uncluttered two-dimensional graphic scale model. Indeed, a map that did not generalize would be useless. But the value of a map depends on how well its generalized geometry and generalized content reflect a chosen aspect of reality.[2]

Equally the sense of where we are depends upon the social construction of place espoused by our culture. William Boelhower cites a story used by Northrop Frye in *The Canadian Imagination*,[3] in which a doctor journeying with an Innu in the Canadian Arctic is rebuked for thinking them lost: 'We are not lost. We are here.' In this light, as Boelhower has observed, 'the map is not so much a representation of space but . . . a space of representation'.[4]

More recently, Marcia Kupper has explained that our problem with understanding the meaning of such medieval world maps as the *Mappa Mundi* in Hereford Cathedral is the result of our not understanding their cultural milieu. Typically treated by their original readers 'not as autonomous objects but rather as elements subsumed within greater pictorial ensembles, architectural settings or intellectual projects', they reveal 'the layering of different epochs within the map's unified field [that] allows the correlation of geographical description with historical exposition'. Once one recognizes, in other words, that these 'maps' do not represent geographical space as modern maps do, but are a sort of encylo-pedia, they can be seen to 'reveal the terrestrial sphere as the zone where macrocosm and microcosm interlock . . . [and to] relate the existence of peoples, even the human body itself, to divine law'.[5]

Responses to mapping and location, however, are more variable than is often supposed by cultural historians. The earliest European settlers of present-day Sydney believed that they were nowhere until someone built a road to them.[6] How did that sense of where we are, our need to locate our-selves in geographical space, come about, and what relevance has it to the literature of the early modern period? How is it the product of what Carlos Fuentes calls 'geocentrism and scholasticism'; and how is that related to what the Mexican historian, Edmundo O'Gorman, means when he says 'that America was invented rather than discovered'?[7]

In Book I of Spenser's *Faerie Queene*, Redcrosse, like Dante's persona in *The Divine Comedy* and countless romance figures before the sixteenth century, is lost in a wood of error, a word which means 'to wander'. Like the drear wood of 'the misled and lonely Traveller' in *Comus*, this is uncharted territory. In Bunyan's *Pilgrim's Progress*, however, Christian knows the way. He is neither *picaro* nor romance hero; his pilgrimage is through a landscape already named and mapped, from the City of Destruction to the Celestial City. Like any modern traveller, he may lose his way or be led astray by a detour or the promise of an easier road; but the approved route is not in doubt.

Between Spenser and Bunyan two major cultural revolutions occurred in Britain: the decline of romance as a genre, and the rise of modern carto-graphy to a science. In a sense Spenser's *Faerie Queene* marks the end of the possibility of romance, dependent as romance is upon a land elsewhere, unmarked and uncharted: a land of monsters, the land of Prester John and Sir John Mandeville's *Travels*.[8] During the seventeenth century in England, romance decayed from a discourse of political power that was meant to shape 'a knight in vertous and gentle discipline' to something like what we mean by it today: the 'hearts and flowers' entertainment of much of popular culture. Within a decade of the publication of *The Faerie Queene*, romance had been parodied by Cervantes in *Don Quixote*.

Not that romance ceased to be a popular form in the seventeenth century; Sidney's *Arcadia* went through ten editions before the end of the century. But romance came to be seen not as a vehicle for the serious business of religious and political allegory, but in its modern sense: light reading, primarily for women (and increasingly children). John Evelyn says as much when he writes to his daughter Susanna to reprove her for her conduct. 'If you look for perfection,' he writes, 'and all things agreeable to the *Ideas* you reade in *Romances*, or indeede, conceive to be in nature: let me tell you, there is no such thing.'[9] By the time that Evelyn wrote that, the ersatz pastoralism of romance had been discredited by its identification with the political mythology of Stuart absolutism. The 'romance' of Charles I's wooing of the Infanta of Spain in 1623 while ostensibly disguised as a shepherd became the dominant fiction of his court. In the last of the masques, Davenant's *Salamacida Spolia* (1640), Charles I appeared as the shepherd-lover of his people only two years before the outbreak of the Civil War. By the end of the century, however, romance had became the province of otiose French fiction, the stuff that Fielding was to use comically in *Joseph Andrews* (1742).

A change in reading both reflects and impels a change in thought. The early eighteenth century saw the rise of the realistic novel in the work of Defoe. Even *Pilgrim's Progress* was a romance only in the bones of its structure; its real attractions were in the recognizable topography of England, its street fairs and its country houses. Bunyan was imprisoned in Bedford, and knew Houghton Lodge in Bedfordshire;[10] the first is recognizable in the prison of Vanity Fair, and the second in the gracious courtesy of the Palace Beautiful.[11] Bunyan's novel, moreover, has an imaginary map that also starts from the empirical 'where we are', not from the great chain of being or from the Ptolemaic spheres.

The world had been changed utterly by Charles I's execution. The monarchy that was restored in 1660 was, as Charles II recognized, not a facsimile of the world of Divine Right for which his father had sacrificed his life. Nor, on the other hand, was it any longer possible to believe in the millenarian model of the state, the rule of the saints in expectation of an imminent last coming. Both continued to have their adherents, especially amongst churchmen, but the world had begun to go elsewhere: into systems of mensuration and statistics, of which cartography was a part. No longer were maps a matter of fanciful decoration embellished with '*ultima thule*' and 'here be monsters'.

When Defoe's Captain Singleton and his crew set out to cross Africa from Mozambique to the west coast, its territory (says Singleton) was even worse than Greenland because it was inhabited by wild beasts and savages. Retrospectively the narrator can speak of their journey as 'one of the rashest and wildest, and most desperate Resolutions that ever was taken by Man';[12] but the crew's initial fears can only have been in their imaginations. Their mental map of Africa is an oxymoronic mixture of horrific danger and undreamed-of riches, savage beasts and men alongside elephants' grave-yards of ivory and streams thick with gold. What sets Singleton above them is that he understands the importance of 'the Geographical Part of Knowledge', whereas his men lack what he calls 'counsel'. From the gunner in their crew, 'an excellent Mathematician', he learns about the sciences and a method for making use of them. It was this gunner, says Singleton, who:

> laid the Foundation of a general Knowledge of Things in my Mind, gave me just Ideas of the Form of the Earth and of the Sea, the Situation of Countries, the Course of Rivers, the Doctrine of the Spheres, the Motion of the Stars; and, in a word, taught me a kind of System of Astronomy, which I afterwards improv'd.[13]

And indeed it is this gunner who persuades the crew later, by showing them a map of southern Africa, that they must head directly westward and not follow an easier route to the north.

In England maps were needed to serve the world of commerce, now expanding with the first flush of empire and the reform of trade and agriculture. John Evelyn's friend and correspondent, John Beale, himself the virtual founder of the cider industry in Herefordshire, kept up an extensive agricultural and commercial correspondence with New England and Virginia. And such novels by Defoe as *Captain Singleton*, *Colonel Jack*, and *Robinson Crusoe* reflect the dependence of maritime trade on charting and mapping in the late seventeenth century.

As Marcus Rediker has observed, 'English trade routes constituted the arteries of the imperial body between 1650 and 1750.'[14] Nor were merchants ignorant of their importance. Behind Thomas Coram, in Hogarth's 1740 portrait of him, are the sea and sailing ships; at his feet is the globe that makes such trading voyages possible. In Holbein's famous painting 'The Two Ambassadors', the two men who are its ostensible subject stand behind a table that holds globes among other mathematical instruments. For them, globes are signifiers of knowledge. Coram's globe is an instrument of his wealth; it is placed in subjection below his feet.

The globe had, in fact, begun to be placed under the control of merchants a century earlier. What sets the English apart from the Portuguese empire in the late sixteenth century, Richard Helgerson observes, is that the Portuguese myth was one of noble glory, the English of mercantilism. Maps may be the symbol of the state, but they are even more the symbol of how the state thinks of itself, its mythology. Writing of the publication of Richard Hakluyt's *Principal Navigations of the English Nation* (1599), Helgerson remarks that it 'brings merchants into the nation and brings gentry into trade'.[15] Certainly it was trade that animated the younger Richard Hakluyt's 'Discourse of Western Planting' (1585), both trading vessels throughout the known world, and the establishment of a whole new market in America for English manufactured goods.

By 1713 trading ships in Pope's *Windsor Forest* represent imperial glory

as much as (or more than) the navy, while the River Thames's exultation is
a warehouse catalogue:

> For me the Balm shall bleed, and Amber flow,
> The Coral redden, and the Ruby glow,
> The Pearly Shell its lucid Globe infold,
> And *Phoebus* warm the ripening Ore to Gold.
>   (393–6)

By the time Hogarth painted his portrait of Coram, the merchant was an old
man. In his 1720 novel, *Captain Singleton*, Defoe reflected the world in
which Coram had made his fortune at the beginning of the century: a world
in which British trading posts were already established in India, and piracy
of European ships was already a lucrative trade even off the coasts of China
and Japan.[16] When Singleton returns from a lucrative tour that extends as
far as the Philippines, he and his mate William arrive in Venice

> with such a Cargo, take our Goods, and our Money, and our Jewels
> together, as I believe was never brought into the City by Two single
> Men, since the State of *Venice* had a Being.[17]

It was the merchants of the city of London like Coram who funded John
Ogilby's great project, *A Geographical Description of the Whole World*, a
project whose first manifestation was the publication of his *Britannia* in
1675, a year before his death. His great predecessor, Hollar, had been
appointed 'Scenographer and designer of prospects' by Charles II in 1660,
and Ogilby himself had been a translator and publisher of classical texts
until the destruction of his house and stock in the Great Fire of London in
1666. Ogilby's immediate turn to cartography is a metaphor of the time: the
turn from antiquity to modernity,[18] from description to definition, from
chorography (local description) to geography. In the process he swept away
the old conventions of cartography as completely as the Great Fire of 1666
swept aside the city itself. And it was the merchants of London who were to
benefit from the establishment of the Royal Observatory at Greenwich and
the appointment of John Flamsteed to 'find out the so-much desired longitude for the perfecting of the art of navigation'.[19]

Between Spenser and Bunyan, in other words, came a major cartographical revolution, one with profound consequences for the imagination
of space, place, and distance. In the 1590s John Norden's map of England
was the first to show roads, thereby establishing them on the ground and as
part of the consciousness of place.[20] Gresham's almanac of 1603, *A
Prognostication of the foure quarters of the yeere*, included, for example, 'A
perfect direction of the best and readiest High wayes, from any notable
towne in England, and from the Cittie of London to any nottable [*sic*]
towns.' What was called 'chorography', a science akin to topography that
concerned itself with the art of describing local regions on a map, began to

give way to what we now mean by geography, a science ruled by Mercator's projections.

William Boelhower sees this tendency as early as Edward Wright's 1599 map of America. Its 'peremptory confidence in the culture of *technics*', he observes, allows us to see 'the map's double function of opening up and closing a territory', that is, revealing and claiming it. 'In this light,' he continues, 'the map's progress in plotting America is a pilgrim's progress. It traces the *peripli*[21] of a people and thus pertains to the order of story': a story, he points out, often accompanied by the dubious figure of Hermes the deceiver. In America this expansion was animated by the mythology of previous European discovery and settlement, most notoriously by the myth of Madoc, a medieval Welshman who had founded a tribe of 'white Indians'.[22]

Maps of unknown territory make explicit what is implicit in all mapping in the early modern period. Early maps of America were caught between the chorographic and the geographic, the descriptive and the definitive, 'the image and the Euclidean line', and thus 'reflect a vision of America as a place and as a passage, respectively'. 'One is contemporaneously presented with the history of America's enchantment and the advance of the culture of technics.'[23]

The difference between chorography and geography is primarily that the first describes a particular country or district. In so doing chorography overlaps with topography and shares with it a primarily pictorial sense of landscape, one in which the viewer's eye, even in maps, is at ground level. In the famous *Civitates orbis terrarum* (Cologne, 1572–1617) by Georg Hoefnagel, the artist frequently places himself within the scene being described, thereby drawing the reader/spectator into the subject through the human scale of its creator.[24] The same is true of many of the engravings of Wenceslas Hollar:[25] his views of Lord Arundel's estate at Albury in Surrey, for example, done for the absent Earl during the early 1650s. It is also the world of Thomas Coryate's *Crudities* (1611), Samuel Purchas's *Purchas his Pilgrimage* (1612), and of the work of Purchas's mentor and source, Richard Hakluyt: *Voyages* and *Principall Navigations* (1582–98). Probably the greatest chorographical work of the early seventeenth century, Drayton's *Poly-Olbion* (1612), has as its full title 'A *Chorographicall* Description of *Tracts, Rivers, Mountaines, Forests,* and other parts of this renowned *Isle* of *Great Britaine*, With intermixture of the most Remarquable *Stories, Antiquities, Wonders, Rarityes, Pleasures, and Commodities* of the same'.

Chorography animates John Stow's *Survey of London* (1598) as it does James Howell's *Londinopolis* (1657), but Howell is not so simply interested in history as Stow.[26] To him, Rome 'in point of people . . . may be called a Wilderness . . . like a tall man, shrunk into the skin of a Pygmey'. In his account of London, however, his book swarms with the linguistic life of a city aware of itself as a place with its own vocabulary. The Wardmote Inquest he describes as those who inquire after Riotors, dissolute persons, and Barrators, walking by nightertayle . . . after Potours, Panders, and Bawds, common harzardors, Champarators, maintainers of quarrels, or embracers of Inquests . . . after Witches, Strumpets, common Punks, and Scolds . . . after Women-Brokers, such as use to resort to mens Houses, to suborn young Maydens with promise to help them to better service.[27]

In the early seventeenth century, Richard Helgerson argues, this celebration of the *country* of England in its multitudinousness was at the expense of the centralizing impulse of the crown and its imperial titles and ambitions. Elizabeth I might have displaced the Virgin Mary as Virgin Queen, but Drayton displaces the royal figure with a personified map of England itself in his *Poly-Olbion*. James I was the first monarch of the empire of Great Britain; but the many 'kings' and 'queens' of local legend asserted a multiplicity of local monarchies represented by parliament.[28] Chorography was on the side of the country; it survived, even subsumed in geography, as a kind of popular resistance and a mythology of the resistance to absolutism.[29] Pope's celebration of the genius of a familiar wild landscape in *Windsor Forest* is consistent with his resistance to the mere rules of art in his *Essay on Criticism* (1711). It is also consistent with his earlier draft of *An Essay on Man* (1733) in which he wrote of 'this scene of man' as 'a mighty maze of walks without a plan'.[30] Pope's celebration of Newton in that poem is another instance. For Pope, Newton represented inductive variety; for Blake he represented deductive geometrical control.

Geography, on the other hand, deals with the *geos*, the world at large. Its perspective is aerial and abstract, a matter of mathematics and calculation.[31] It is more concerned with possessing and claiming than with describing, and as such it is a discourse appropriate to the 'solitary flight' of Milton's Satan in *Paradise Lost*, Book ii, figured as an aerial merchant trader:

> As when farr off at Sea a Fleet descri'd
> Hangs in the Clouds, by *Aequinoctial* Winds
> Close sailing from *Bengala*, or the Iles
> Of *Ternate* and *Tidore*, whence Merchants bring
> Thir spicie Drugs: they on the Trading Flood
> Through the wide *Ethiopian* to the Cape
> Ply stemming nightly toward the Pole. So seemd
> Far off the flying Fiend.
>
> (637–44)

Geography is Cartesian and deductive; even within the inductive world of Locke, the pre-existent discourse of reason which shapes that induction precludes chance. 'Reduction to the logic of the grid,' Paul Carter writes of the settlement of Australia in the late eighteenth century, 'has the strategic advantage of simplicity. As a spatial strategy, it corresponds admirably to

Locke's injunction to avoid the sinuous paths of metaphor when writing the expository prose of reason.'[32] Locke was doing no more than echoing Sprat and the approved model of Royal Society prose.[33] Even the aerial views of Kip and Knyff's *Britannia Illustrata* (1700) make claims about the nature of space, understanding, and possessing. The radial avenues of the Duke of Beaufort's estate, Badminton, for example, cannot be seen on the ground; Kip's bird's-eye engraving validates their territorial claims.[34]

To use the rhetorical terms of the period, geography is concerned with quantity and definition, chorography with quality and description. 'Chorographie,' as William Cunningham put it in 1559, 'consisteth rather in describyng the qualitie and figure, then [than] the bignes, and quantitie of any thinge.'[35] Indeed, the rise of modern geography reflects the same 'scientific' or rationalizing impulse in the early modern period that removed the topics of invention from rhetoric and confined them to logic, reducing them from more than 300 to ten.[36] Sir Thomas Browne spoke for the old chorographical world when he wrote, in *Religio Medici*, 'I am now content to understand a mystery without a rigid definition in an easie and Platonick description.'[37] Implicit in the post-Ramistic reforms of logic and rhetoric, however, was the empowerment of definition; the very scheme of this 'reform' is a definitive one.[38]

Geography is ultimately indebted to the ancient writer Ptolemy, as chorography is ultimately indebted to Strabo. Strabo's legacy is a descriptive one; Ptolemy's is mathematical. His legacy in the early modern period was first of all the sailing charts called *portolani* (or 'Waggoners' in England after the most popular Dutch versions created by Lucas Waghenaer in 1584).[39] From Ptolemy came what one critic has called 'an objectivist vision of the world no longer contaminated by imaginary fictions or literary and theological opinions'.[40]

In this process of objectification, the imaginary fictions of distant and foreign places began to acquire 'a local habitation and a name', or rather to be replaced with familiar European names. The wild frenzy of the poet's eye came to rest far from the chorographic imagination, in the world of maps and naming. Not a little of *A Midsummer Night's Dream* (from which the quotation comes) concerns the tension between Count Theseus's 'map' of real power and the will-o'- the-wisp world of romance, metamorphosis, and the imagination that serves as its critique.

In the late sixteenth and early seventeenth centuries, the word 'map', for example, still meant primarily a picture of a local place or a defined area; early map-sellers were also printsellers. The literal and the metaphorical lay as close together as the the literal and the allegorical in poetry. Although William Cunningham's *The Cosmographicall Glasse* (1599) made the claim that maps represent geography truly, many 'readers' of maps could no more comprehend what the representation of a country as a whole meant than most viewers at the beginning of the twentieth century could understand the narrative of moving pictures.

What might be called the symbolic resistance of chorography, moreover, was still strong in the culture. In James Howell's *Survey of Venice* (1651) Venice continues to be primarily a symbolic place, as it had been for nearly two centuries. His title-page and dedication link Venus and Venice, both rising from the sea, and analogous to Britain as an island state. Similarly, many of the maps of London from the Agas map in the mid-sixteenth century to Ogilby's in the late seventeenth were at least as concerned to ground London in the myth of Troy restored as to give exact geographical detail.[41] This reinscription of Britain in antiquity was part of the same mythologizing that led John Evelyn to call his great work on the history of gardens (begun in the late 1650s) *Elysium Britannicum*.

In the 1585 collection of sonnets, *Emaricdulfe*, the author finds in the house of fame 'a map of honours in a noble frame' (Sonnet 38, 3),[42] and in 1596 Francis Sabie pictures Adam reflecting on himself as the 'true figure, perfect map of future evilles'.[43] As in Anthony Copley's 'map of Doomsday, and Hell in fearfull formes',[44] we are still in the anthropomorphic world of Spenser.[45] In *Albion's England* (1602),[46] William Warner writes of men mapping themselves (i.e. understanding their motivation); and even as late as 1628 Joseph Fletcher refers to a man's mind as 'a Mappe with such varietie fraught | As in the greater World at large are taught'.[47] In 1625 John Stradling could refer to God's covenant with Israel as a chart or map with which to sail safely[48], but for George Wither a literal map was still no occasion for a poem. In response to a gentleman who left him alone to contemplate a map, Wither wrote a comic 'blazon': a joking poem that simply listed all the counties of England, as if that were all that a real map could tell.

But although the metaphoric sense of 'map' continued to be potent, a new denotative sense of the word also began to enter the language in the late sixteenth century.[49] Poetry, however, was less prompt than prose to respond to this change. For Donne (1633), a map was still primarily a metaphor, either of himself (as in 'Hymn to God my God in my Sicknesse') or of a devotional truth. In so far as he employs the discourse of geography (as in 'To his Mistris Going to Bed' or 'A Valediction Forbidding Mourning') it is as a metaphor of amatory empowerment.[50] For Herbert, whose poems were published in the same year, the topography of travel was even less chartable than for Donne; his 'Pilgrimage' is through unmapped territory.

In Herrick's *Hesperides* (1648), however, maps are external texts, already part of a scientific discourse. On one hand he can congratulate his brother Thomas for not needing the 'painted Countries' of maps to 'securely saile' in the chorographic map of his country life at home. And on the other he can praise his brother Nicholas for offering, as a traveller, 'the truth of Travails' (descriptive geography) more than 'in Varnisht maps; by'th'helpe of Compasses' (mathematical geography). In both cases, for Herrick, maps are the opposite of the self; they are texts, or even, as he calls them, 'Volumes'.[51]

Henry King's sense of map in his 1657 poems is instructive of the change that was to take place partly in response to the military campaigns of the Civil War and the mapping which they entailed.[52] King refers to the delightful rapture of the spirit that may

> descry
> As in a Map, Sions Chorography
> Laid out in so direct and smooth a line,
> Men need not go about through Palestine.[53]

In his poem 'To my Noble and Judicious Friend Mr Henry Blount upon his Voyage,' King writes of beguiling himself with maps:

> Thus by Ortelius' and Mercator's aid
> Through most of the discover'd world I strai'd.
> I could with ease double the Southerne Cape,
> And in my passage Affrick's wonders take.

But he contrasts 'the Common Place of Travailours, who teach | But Table-talk' with the true chorography of Blount's book.[54]

For King, Sion was still a local and familiar place, the province of chorography or topography; it was not to be found by maps or travelling, but by the 'streight Rode' of belief in Christ. That he could think of the possibility of a straight road at all, however, was a testament both to the commonplace notion of direct roads created by the almanacs and to John Norden's map-making successors.

One of these was Sir William Petty. Referred to by Marx as the founder of political economy, and trained as a physician and anatomist, Petty was also the first Englishman to create a map in the modern sense. In the wake of the conquest of Ireland in the Civil War, Petty was appointed by a committee of the House of Commons to do a survey so that the cashiered soldiers of that campaign could be paid in forfeited land. Called the Down Survey, because it was the first to mark the topographic details down on a map, Petty's task, he said, included 'the whole art of surveying into its severall parts, viz. Ffield worke; 2, protracting; 3, casting ; 4, reducing; 5, ornaments of the mapps; 6, writing fair bookes; 7, examination of all and every the premises.'[55]

Brian Friel's play, *Translations* (1981), set in the midst of the Ordnance Survey remapping of Ireland in the nineteenth century, makes clear the implication of 'writing fair bookes': that it involves the renaming of the country, as it also did in North America and elsewhere. The nearest village to where I live in the countryside of Ontario in Canada is called Chepstow. The original Irish settlers in the 1850s wanted to call it Emmet after one of the leaders of the 1803 Rebellion in Ireland; but the imperial government of the time said that it would be called Chepstow after the first English Earl to suppress the Irish. Similarly, one of the early instructions by the Canada Company to its agent, the novelist John Galt, twenty years earlier was to remove the native name of a river, Menesetung, and replace it with the name of the colonial governor, Maitland.

If, as William Boelhower observes, 'every toponym . . . contains the story of its own origin',[56] the removal or extirpation of local names is an act of violence against what Pope called the 'genius of the place'. And yet this is exactly what happened over and over again in the expansion of the empire, an expansion that included Ireland. In many places, moreover, it meant riding roughshod over the topography of the country with a grid that paid absolutely no attention to the topography of the place: in effect extirpating its chorography in the interest of geography.

What was beginning to happen in the late seventeenth century was not so much a 'shift in sensibility', as Eliot called it, as a shift in the model of what was deemed to be knowledge. In the process, learned culture was hived off from popular culture. Barbara Duden has chronicled a similar shift in relation to the body in her book, *The Woman Beneath the Skin*. 'The geometrization of space in the seventeenth century as expressed in new body disciplines' she sees as analogous to the Cartesian mind-set which created French houses and gardens of the period. The great avenues of Versailles and Vaux-le-Vicomte that extirpated villages in the interest of dominant survey were part of 'a reduction of the spatial experience to visual dimensionality . . . space was deprived of its reality perceivable through nose, ear, and touch, and was assigned a new geometrical disciplining function'.[57]

Like the word 'map', 'survey' continued to have older meanings, including the sense of 'to look upon or to look down upon', especially in poetry. These are the senses in which Milton, Dryden, and Pope commonly employ it throughout their work, and which it retains in Isaac Watt's famous hymn, 'When I survey the wondrous Cross' (1707), and Joseph Addison's 'When all thy mercies, O my God | My rising soul surveys' (1712). Well into the seventeenth century the word 'surveyor' meant what John Fitzherbert had defined it to mean in his classic sixteenth-century book on husbandry: 'The name of a surveyor is a frenche name and is as moche to say in Englysshe as an overseer'.[58] In 1654, the year after the Down Survey was first commissioned, Richard Whitlock used the word in this sense in his account of English society called *Zootomia*. 'Geometry, it may be, teacheth me Wisdome,' he observes, 'not to lose a Pearch[59] of my many Acres through imperfect Survey.'[60]

Whitlock thought such knowledge inferior to moral instruction; death, he observed elsewhere, presents us with 'how contracted a *Map* . . . of all those *large Possessions* of the *Rich* and *Mighty Ones* of the World'.[61] But the tide which was to be in full flood after the Restoration, when map-selling increased enormously, was already changing. Increasingly 'survey' came to acquire the panoptic and dominating associations described by Foucault in *Discipline and Punish*[62] as arising in the late seventeenth century. He cites there a plague regulation dividing a city into partitions for strict surveillance.[63] Edward Laurence's *The Duty of a Steward to His Lord* (1727) is illustrated with an estate survey of this kind in which 'Mr. Jonathan Sisson's new Invented Theodolite for Surveying and Levelling' is prominently featured. And Lawrence leaves his reader in no doubt that the former 'common methods' of surveying are inadequate to defending owners from the tricks of tenants.[64] As it became 'the process (or art) of surveying a tract of ground' (*New OED* 5a), then, the word 'survey' shifted from being an 'act of viewing, examining, or inspecting in detail'(*New OED* 1) or the 'act of looking at something as a whole'(*New OED* 3) to meaning 'oversight, supervision, superintendence' (*New OED* 2).

In the process also, a discursive sense of land possession was surrendered to a mathematical one. What had been known in local oral history as a parcel of land became a matter of protractor and stakes.[65] As early as 1650, William Leybourn (whom John Ogilby was to employ in his survey of London) published his *Planometrica: or, the whole art of Surveying*; and in 1653 he published *The Compleat Surveyor*. Republished in 1674 after Leybourn had been appointed Ogilby's assistant, it gave details of how 'to take the Ichnography or Ground-plot of Cities, Towns, Hamlets, etc.'.

Ichnography, though not a new word, was newly fashionable in the late seventeenth century. Though it had previously been used to identify the ground-plan of a building, it now came to characterize the sort of map which identified on the ground the outlines of all the buildings on it. It was, in other words, a new element of scientific discourse, one that was to prove useful in describing the layout of the landscape gardens of the following century. It is also an instructive metonym for the shift from ancients to moderns exemplified by Ogilby's own career; from being a pre-Fire publisher and translator of Homer, Aesop, and Virgil, he became a pioneering cartographer.

Certainly ichnography was what Ogilby was doing in his *Large and Accurate Map of . . . London* (1676). This work was accompanied the next year by an *Explanation* which included inventories of '*Streets* and *Lanes*, With the *Courts*, *Yards* and *Inns*, *Churches*, *Halls* and *Houses of Note*'. Here is the detailed topography of Pepys's London and what was to be Defoe's London: the London of *Roxana* and *Moll Flanders* and *The Journal of the Plague Year* and *Colonel Jack*.

Moll Flanders was supposedly 'written in the year 1683' (7 years after the appearance of Ogilby's map); but it was actually published in 1722, two years after John Strype's publication of ward maps of the city in his *A Survey of the Cities of London and Westminster*. Maps of this kind, however, are only one figuration of the city's complexity; they suggest its intricacy while failing to account for the other ways of knowing it. Like the literature of prospect poetry, they seem to give possession to the viewer, but there are other kinds of possession or knowledge at work which are equally or more significant. Like twentieth-century maps of the countryside in western culture, although Strype's maps seem to reveal what is there, they in fact do not denote the topography as the native knows it.

Moll's London, like most of modern Tokyo, is a city without street signs: a city in which districts are known intimately through a complex range of signifiers. Roland Barthes has written of Tokyo as 'practically unclassified', a city in which, although there is a map, it is useless in finding streets that are unnamed: Tokyo

> reminds us that the rational is merely one system among others . . . this city can be known only by an activity of an ethnographic kind: you must orient yourself in it not by book, by address, but by walking, by sight, by habit, by experience.[66]

Moll Flanders similarly inhabits a charted but mysterious and sinister world of streets and alleys; the known but unmapped world subverts the charted place. Moll, to paraphrase Barthes, must establish in her memory her own way of writing what this place means. Falling through sexual liaisons and bad marriages from gentility into crime, she finds herself tempted to steal a bundle of goods from an Apothecary Shop in Leadenhall Street. Her flight with it establishes a modern urban metaphor or mental space, one that most modern readers would think of as Dickensian:

> I cross'd the Street indeed, and went down the first turning I came to, and I think it was a Street that went thro' into *Fenchurch-street*, from thence I cross'd and turn'd thro' so many ways and turnings that I could never tell which way it was, nor where I went, for I felt not the Ground, I stept on, and the farther I was out of Danger, the faster I went, till tyr'd and out of Breath, I was forc'd to sit down on a little Bench at a Door, and then I began to recover, and found I was got into *Thames-street* near *Billingsgate*.[67]

London, as a text to be read in a map, begins to become a Dantesque metaphor of moral complexity and intrigue:[68] what Jonathan Keates has called 'an imaginative construct, its profile etched by fancy and desire'.[69] Moll refers to the possible danger of arriving in London unmarried and friendless and so needing to come to her future husband 'for the first Night's Entertainment'. Whether she is conscious of it or not, this is a reference, surely, to her lot as Scheherezade in the *Arabian Nights Entertainments*, a work first published in English in 1705 which became a touchstone of narrative complexity. Like Scheherezade, Moll is obliged to tell incomplete fictions, to save not her life, but her honour and fortune.

A decade later, in *Trivia* (1716), Gay makes his way through 'spacious streets' and 'winding alleys' to explore 'the silent court, and op'ning square' as well as the 'long perplexing lanes' that are the map of early eighteenth-century London. This is not an easy text to understand, and the poem describes the confusion of the expanding city to the countryman newly arrived and unable to 'read' its map:

> Here oft the Peasant, with enquiring Face,
> Bewilder'd, trudges on from Place to Place;
> He dwells on ev'ry Sign with stupid Gaze,
> Enters the narrow Alley's doubtful Maze,
> Tries ev'ry winding Court and Street in vain,
> And doubles o'er his weary Steps again.[70]

On the eve of the Restoration John Evelyn adopted the character of a Frenchman to describe the chaos of London society:

> I did frequently in the spring, accompany my *Lord* N. into a field near the Town, which they call *Hide-Parke*; the place not unpleasant, and which they use, as our *Course*; but with nothing that order, equipage and splendor, being such an assembly of wretched *jades*, and *Hackney Coaches*, as next a regiment of *Carre-men*, there is nothing approaches the resemblance.[71]

Twenty-four years later, Moll Flanders' St James's Park is accurately described by Lord Rochester, in his poem about it, as a place where the classes may be indiscriminately mixed together and vice may flourish.[72] It is for just this reason that Lady Woodville denounces it in Etherege's play *The Man of Mode* (1676). There, too, in Congreve's *The Way of the World* (1700), Marwood can spy Lady Wishfort's servant, Foible, in conference with her mistress's enemy, Mirabel, in a scene which establishes the social disorder which will permit Mirabel's servant, Waitwell (disguised as Sir Roland), to trick Lady Wishfort into accepting an offer of marriage that disgraces her.

Westminster is also a place of secret assignations and debauches, the coffee-house world of the opening scene of *The Way of the World*, or of Mr Wilson's recollections of his youth in Fielding's *Joseph Andrews*. In *Trivia* Gay describes a whore plying her trade in 'the rounds of Drury Lane' and leading a 'willing Victim to his Doom, | Through winding Alleys to her Room'.[73] *Trivia* is a catalogue of the streets and courts that are also the settings for *The Beggar's Opera* and Swift's 'An Evening Shower', for the indiscriminate cultural mix of Hogarth's 'The Times of Day' or 'Gin Lane' and 'Beer Alley', or for John Bancks's 1738 poem 'A Description of London':

> Lawyers, poets, priests, physicians;
> Noble, simple, all conditions:
> Worth beneath a threadbare cover;
> Villainy – bedaubed all over.[74]

Not everyone, obviously, was pleased with this human *olla podrida*. *Trivia* is full of the noise that maddens Hogarth's 'The Enraged Musician': a discord in which harmony is drowned rather than understood. And Pope, in one of his imitations of Horace published the year before Bancks's poem, makes poetic order (the device is called 'zeugma') out of a similar disorder:

> But grant I may relapse, for want of Grace,
> Again to rhime, can *London* be the Place?
> Who there his Muse, or Self, or Soul attends?
> In Crouds and Courts, Law, Business, Feasts and Friends?[75]

The mixed social jumble bespeaks a disordered world, just the world that Swift reflects in Section X of *A Tale of a Tub* (1704). Almost at the end of his work, Swift's hack proposes a Preface in which, along with thanks to everyone from the king to 'the *Clergy*, and *Gentry*, and *Yeomantry*', he adds, 'But in a more especial manner, to my worthy Brethren and Friends at *Will's Coffee - House*, and *Gresham - College*, and *Warwick - Lane*, and *Moor - Fields*, and *Scotland Yard*, and *Westminster Hall*, and *Guild - Hall*.'[76]

What London was not, then, was what Wren and John Evelyn hoped it might become after the Fire: a *tabula rasa* upon which an orderly baroque geometrical plan could be inscribed 'for the honour of our imperial city', as Evelyn was to put it.[77] By the 1680s, London was again the warren that it had been, a place where Defoe's Colonel Jack and his boy accomplice could escape from the forces of law and order through a maze of courts and alleys and make their way across the river to Southwark, an area famous even in Shakespeare's time as a refuge from the law.

Evelyn and Wren both drew up plans for the rebuilding of London after the Fire; Evelyn's was very much animated by his dislike of London's social disorder and its increasing pollution.[78] This new *imperium* was not to be of Papal dominion (though its model was ancient Rome) but of commerce, sanitation, and order: the sort of 'rationalistic, authoritarian project' that Defoe's H. F. recommends, in case of a future outbreak of plague, in *A Journal of the Plague Year*. But although that novel, like the plans of Wren and Evelyn, may represent London as 'accessible, comprehensible and controllable',[79] it was not.

That neither plan prevailed is an interesting footnote to the publication of *Paradise Lost* in 1667, a poem in which Satan's Pandemonium rises resplendent in the architecture of Papal and ancient Rome:

> Built like a temple, where pilasters round
> Were set, and Doric pillars overlaid
> With golden architrave.
>
> (I. 713–15)

These plans by Wren and Evelyn are also an interesting analogy to the continuing attempt to impose an order on the English language through an academy or a rule on English prosody. All of them were attempts to control a culture that was no longer restrainable by older forms and myths. In Defoe's *Moll Flanders*, Moll goes to Virginia, a kind of ur-Botany Bay where representatives of state power are former criminals. As her mother tells her: 'Many a *Newgate* Bird becomes a great Man, and we have *continued she*, several Justices of the Peace, Officers of the Train Bands, and Magistrates of the Towns they live in, that have been burnt in the Hand'.[80]

Indeed, Moll, disgraced and imprisoned as a thief, like Colonel Jack returns to Virginia at the end of the novel to re-inscribe herself as a gentle-woman on a map with few fixed places. In all this, the new world challenges the old order. If the English in America ceased merely to be the English abroad,[81] so did the English at home cease to be what they had been because of what the unmapped *terra incognita* of America represented: the possi-bility of the sort of continuous reinscription that Moll effects.[82]

The countryside, or at least the conception of it, was also changed by mapping. Defoe made his first *Tour* in the 1720s, but 40 years earlier Celia Fiennes prefaced the account of her equally prodigious tour with this rebuke:

> if all persons, both Ladies, much more Gentlemen, would spend some of their tyme in Journeys to visit their native Land, and be curious to Inform themselves and make observations ... it would ... form such an Idea of England, add much to its Glory and Esteem in our minds and cure the evil Itch of overvalueing foreign parts.[83]

Both Defoe and Fiennes were the beneficiaries of Ogilby's *Britannia* and its offshoots, the improvement of roads and the proliferation of stage-coaches.[84] Introduced in the late 1630s, coaches were not widely popular until the mid-1650s when (in 1655) there were two coaches a day between London and Southampton and (in 1657) three a week between London and Chester. Indeed, the first appearance of the word 'highwayman' in 1649 suggests an increase in this sort of traffic. The inevitable improvement in roads meant that Pepys, for example, could ride to Cambridge from London in four hours in 1661 where it took Lancelot Andrewes, as a student in the late sixteenth century, the better part of two days to cover the same distance. One historian of travel has claimed that the rapid increase in the number of stage-coaches in the following decades may be compared to the effect of the railways nearly two centuries later, though the former were obviously much slower.[85]

The building works of Book X of *Paradise Lost* are a curious footnote to road-making in this period. In building the bridge from Hell to Earth, Sin and Death follow Satan's initial 'track' and vow to 'found a path | Over this Maine from Hell to that new World'. But what they build is, in effect, a recreation of an ancient Roman viaduct – a 'stupendious Bridge', as the poem calls it – that unites 'Hell and this World, one Realm, one Continent | Of easie thoroughfare'. The 'Rode' to hell having been paved with what Satan calls 'this glorious work,' he proceeds 'down | The Causey to Hell Gate', where before he had had to steer through unknown territory. The difference between 'track' and 'road' is as significant as the difference between the plainly marked roads to earth, hell, and heaven in this passage, and the world of the 'misled and lonely Traveller' in the 'perplex't paths' of *Comus*'s 'drear Wood'. Ogilby had yet to publish any of his maps, but by the 1660s the climate for their publication was obviously well-established by a sense of the country as mappable and towns as interconnected by stages and roads.

The proliferation of stage-coaches, however, did not go unchallenged. John Cresset who, as an inn-keeper, was deprived of part of his trade by them, was obviously a biased witness against them. In his *A copy of a letter* (1672), however, when he described the conditions that Moll Flanders also experienced, he cannot have been too far off the mark. Citing the problems of heat and cold, the frequent absence of food, and the unpleasantness of the company, he says:

> Is it for a Mans pleasure, or advantagious to their healths and Business, to travel with a mixt Company that he knows not how to converse with; to be affronted by the rudeness of a surly, dogged, cursing, ill-natured Coachman; necessitated to Lodge or Bait at the worst Inns on the Road, where there is no accommodation fit for a Gentleman; and this merely because the Owners of the Inns, and the Coachmen, are agreed together to cheat the guests?[86]

Many a traveller in early eighteenth-century literature was acquainted with what Pope called 'the worst inn's worst room', and the whole plot of Farquhar's *The Beaux Stratagem* (1707) rests upon the socio-economic anonymity made possible by such hostelries, in which servants can be confused with master, and vice versa. Cresset's description is also true of a good part of *Joseph Andrews* (1742), where the coachman carrying Mrs Slipslop describes his passengers as 'a parcel of squinny-gut b-s,' and says, 'I have a good mind to overturn them.' There are, as Fielding's authorial persona observes, 'many surprising adventures' in the novel that are 'scarce credible to those who have never travelled in a stage-coach',[87] not least the adventures at inns. Like one of its sources (*Don Quixote*), *Joseph Andrews* uses the structure of romance, but its travellers are in a world of bourgeois realism. They stay not in the castles of romantic idealism but in the inns of Dutch realism; Rubens has been displaced by Rembrandt.

Cressett published more than one of these 'letters', but despite his desire to keep them secret from the stage-coach lobby, his claims did not go unchallenged. An anonymous reply, called *Stage-Coaches Vindicated*, takes up the case on the other side and gives an interesting account of how dependent large sections of society already were upon this mode of travel. Claiming that many people already 'do frequently come from all parts of the Country to *London*', it points out that the old and infirm as well as women and children can only travel this way, and that all travellers from abroad, even those from Scotland, Ireland, and Wales, are obliged to travel in this manner. Coaches, says the writer, are:

the occasions of preventing many accidents which they are subject to who travel on Horseback; as falls from Horses, catching Colds, and other Distempers in wet and unseasonable weather; especially of Casualties by rising of waters and Fords, which many Passengers are subject to: whereas the Stage-Coachmen by their constancy upon the Roads, are generally acquainted with, and therefore are often assistant to Noblemen and Gentlemens Coaches in guiding them the best ways.[88]

The anonymous author concludes with an afterthought about the many 'Trades and Sorts of people that would be much damnified by the putting down of Stages'. His catalogue is like a list of the characters of the new bourgeois realist fiction, the sprawling world of Moll, so far away from the cloistered world of romance:

Mercers, Taylors, Haberdashers, Hosiers, Exchange-people, and all that Trade in things belonging to Cloathing or Apparel; Vintners, Victualers, Alehousekeepers, Brewers, Butchers, Poulterers, Strongwater-Shops, Mum and Coffee-houses, and all that deal in any sort of Provisions or Commodities for the Belly; All persons who live by Rents of Houses, by Tabling of people, or letting Lodgings; and generally all Schools of Learning, besides those Imployments which are for mens Pleasure, Health or Ease: Also Porters, and the Hackney-Coachmen, and Watermen themselves, who joyn'd in the Petition against these Stage-Coaches.[89]

'All that Trade in things belonging to Cloathing or Apparel' were in fact only one of the many sorts of merchants liberated by the Act of Union in 1707 to trade anywhere in Great Britain.[90] Although the impact of trade on road-building was not to be felt until later in the eighteenth century, an increasing traffic of all kinds animated it; while the order of mapping produced a disorder of social station.

Only a decade before the ostensible date of Moll Flanders's composition, town and country began readily and regularly to exchange with one another, and the social confusions of town began to become a feature of the rest of the country too. It is tempting to suggest, then, that the rise of the novel owes as much to the ability of large numbers of people to travel relatively easily about the country as it does to the development of the notion of character. If romance was the product of a primarily sedentary and rural society, the novel arose from a culture in which, thanks largely to travel, relationships were no longer fixed and obvious. What would Tom Jones or Joseph Andrews be without it, or even the claustrophobia of Pamela? Similarly the poetry of prospect, whether Cotton's Wonders of the Peak or Dyer's Grongar Hill or even Richard Jago's 'Edge-Hill', depended upon the notion, already inculcated by the Grand Tour, that one might travel around one's own country with all the apparatus of coaches and stages that was already in place for Moll Flanders.

The corollary was the gradual disappearance of the great-country-house poem that had been a phenomenon of the early and mid-seventeenth century. It had been dependent upon a myth of permanence and continuity closely linked[91] to the myth of landed value, a myth the more strenuously defended as the rising mercantile middle class eroded it with international trade. From the early sixteenth century onward, however, the advent of new wealth made such a myth increasingly unsustainable. Charles I's attempts to get his nobility and gentry to live on their estates was unsuccessful precisely because power was shifting from country and land to city and money. In Jonson's 'To Penshurst' the vulgar display of the Cecils at Theobalds [92] is (like Timon's villa in Pope's 'Epistle to Burlington') the supposed exception that proves the rule. Landed money should mean proper stations; but, as Alastair Fowler notes, 'new methods of mapping and accounting make the large impersonally administered estates of absentee landlords more viable'.[93]

And yet many of the supposedly ancestral families had fortunes and power of no longer standing than the redistribution of land after the dissolution of the monasteries in the 1540s. Indeed, the Sidneys had owned Penshurst only since 1552. The family tree of the Cecils at Hatfield creates a lineage for the family that stretches back to Adam, one of the many ways in which new money of the sixteenth century grounded itself in a fictive past. Rows of ersatz ancestral portraits made to create a lineage were another. Lord David Cecil's history of his family[94] does not refer to the family tree, nor does he note that the interests of the founding patriarch, Lord Burghley, in botany and mapping were congruent with his public role as a statesman. The names of plants, like the radiating compass lines on Burghley's maps, are a controlling grid.

At the end of the seventeenth century, John Evelyn, writing to William Wotton about Wotton's projected life of the chemist Robert Boyle, mocked these absurd claims to antiquity in relation to his own family. Evelyn concludes the main body of his letter with an ironic aside not just on his own pedigree but also on the genealogies invented by Sir Willam Dugdale and the College of Heralds:

> what the Heralds write is often sufficiently mercenary Enough {and able to bring any Upstart, as far as Sir Thomas Urquhart dos his}: and I am able to bring my own Pedigree from one Evelyn, Nephew to Androgius, who brought Julius Caesar into Britain the second time. Will you not smile at this? Whilst [the families of] *Onslow, Hatton* and *Evelyn* came I suppose much at the same time hapless out of Shropshire into Surry and the adjacent Countys (from places still relating their names) sometime during the Barrons Warrs.[95]

Marvell's *Upon Appleton House* (*c*.1651), a poem celebrating classical retreat from the vices of society, was the last significant manifestation of the country-house poem. Thereafter we have, instead, poems of prospect and landscape. Indeed, it is noteworthy that Dryden's one poem of such a kind is on Lord Arlington's town garden rather than on his country estate, Euston.

The retrospective literary fiction of the country-house poem had as its corollary the absence of any urban poetry. Although the life of the city enters the city comedies of Jonson and his successors, there is little contemporary city culture in Shakespeare. Thomas Heywood's urban comedy, *The Four Prentices of London* (published 1615), adapts the world of romance to the Plautine world of the city, and is mocked for doing so by Francis Beaumont's *The Knight of the Burning Pestle* (1607?), a play in which the rude mechanicals of modern London attempt to assume traditional romantic roles. Even Jonson mocked these urban 'presumers on their own naturals' in his court masques and frequently introduced them as comic grotesques in the anti-masques.

Ogilby's *London* (1676), on the other hand, is the commercial London of George Lillo's *The London Merchant* (1731). His map may have been drawn up under the watchful eye and advice of Fellows of the Royal Society[96], but it is not a merely royal enterprise. Indeed, in a way it is an inscription of the evidence of mercantile resistance to royal power: the insistence of London merchants on property rights over royal plans after the Great Fire. Its intention, moreover, is overtly commercial: that it be 'equally Accommodated for Importing Merchandise from Abroad, and receiving necessary Supplies of Provisions at Home.'[97]

Ogilby's *London* formed part of his major work on the whole of England, *Britannia*. Published a year earlier than *London*, it was almost immediately reissued in a portable version known as *Mr Ogilby's Tables of His Measur'd Roads*. These were first issued in pocket octavo form in 1719, and gave rise to a great number of such guides. *Britannia* itself was also issued in 1675 in another format: *Itinerarium Angliae: or, A Book of the Roads*. The map-seller Philip Lea is another good example of the nature of this popular trade. His 1694 reissue of Christopher Saxton's map of 1589 had roads added to it, and he also advertised maps 'on Silke for a Sarsh Window, or to carry in the Pocket'.[98]

Ogilby also gave rise to a tradition of new and more accurate maps of London and Westminster, of which the most famous early eighteenth-century examples are those by Thomas Badeslade and John Rocque which showed in detail, as Ogilby's seldom do, the nature of the gardens included. But his chief legacy was to the maps of England. Ogilby had been authorized by Royal Warrant not only to make these maps, but to affix 'sufficient Marks for the better Direction of Travellers'.[99] In the process of this exercise, he established the British statute mile as 80 chains or 1760 yards, not the 2428 yards that it had previously been. The 1699 edition, called *The Traveller's Guide*, advertised itself as 'Being Mr. OGILBY's ACTUAL SURVEY, and Mensuration by the Wheel.' As with the map of London, Ogilby's *Roads* spawned a large literature of traveller's companions,[100] even *The Travels of Tom Thumb over England and Wales* (1746). This was published by the pioneer of children's literature, Mary Cooper, who had published the first collection of nursery rhymes, *Tommy Thumb's Pretty Song Book*, two years earlier.

What Ogilby established, in England at any rate, was a new sense of place: the old chorography attached to the new geometry of surveyed maps. Two years after the publication of John Ogilby's *Tables of his Measur'd Roads . . . to which is added, A true account of the markets and fairs* (1676), Bunyan published *Pilgrim's Progress*. I am not suggesting that Bunyan was influenced by Ogilby; but rather that the work of both manifested a new sense of direction, distance, and location. Christian's burden is sin, Ogilby's is commerce, but both travel by the same road.

Seven years later, John Evelyn records seeing at court the new coastal maps of Captain Collins:

> which that industrious man now brought to show the Duke [of York], having taken all the coastings from the mouth of the *Thames* as far as *Wales*, and exactly measuring every Creeke, Iland, Rock, Soundings, harbors, Sands, Tides and intending this next Spring, to proceede til he had finish[ed] the [whole] Iland: and that measured by Chaine, and other Instruments: a most exact and usefull undertaking.[101]

Between 1703 and 1714 Defoe travelled over much of England and into Scotland as a government agent, journeys that were to reappear in his *A Tour Through the Whole Island of Great Britain* in 1724. His Colonel Jack, fleeing from the fear of imprisonment or hanging in the 1680s, also makes for Scotland through a maze of interconnecting roads that seems as intricate as the map of London. Indeed, the intricacy of the maze of roads is as complex as the intricacy of discourse and intention. Jack and his brother know where the Great North Road is, but they no more follow it than Defoe follows a straightforward narrative. Hypotaxis is concealed beneath parataxis, as Jack explains:

> But upon the whole, this was my Rule, that when we enquir'd the way to any Particular Place, to be sure we never took that Road, but some other; which the accidental Discourse we might have, should bring in, and thus we did here, for having chiefly ask'd our way into the Northern Road, we resolv'd to go directly for *Lynn*.[102]

By the 1720s, the time of the novel's publication, George Wither's notion that a map was a risible poetic subject had been displaced. Samuel Wesley's 1693 reading of the map of Sion was a long way from that of Henry King. As Wesley looked at a topographical map of Jerusalem, his faith was led not to leap over the map itself but to look closely at one of its details: the brook of Kedron.[103] La Hire's map of France, published in the same year, shifted the west coast of France one and a half degrees east, thereby, declared Louis XIV, costing him more of his domains than a disastrous battle.[104] In this context Stephen Clay could write (in 'An Epistle from the Elector of Bavaria to the French King') of the consequences of Marlborough's victory at Blenheim in terms of their cartographical result:

> Thy spreading map each year did larger grow,
> New mountains still did rise, new rivers flow
> But now surrounded by thy ancient mound
> Dost inward shrink from thy new-conquer'd bounds.[105]

Certainly by the beginning of the eighteenth century the science of mapping had changed to the point where not only the maps of Europe and the rest of the known world could be laid out in latitude and longitude, but the world of antiquity could also be plotted on this grid and laid out in British statute miles.[106] Herman Moll's *System of Geography* (1701) complains of previous work as 'immethodicall', and Moll writes of the great advances that have been made since Peter Heylyn's *Cosmographie* (1652). What Moll means by 'methodical', however, is considerably different from what Laurence Eachard meant only a decade earlier in his *An Exact Description of Ireland: Chorographically Surveying all its Provinces & Counties*. Though Eachard claims that his work is 'done according to the latest Surveys' and that he has 'set the Longitude *and* Latitude *of all the* Towns *and* Castles' according to Moll's maps, his notion of 'methodical' is that each province of Ireland have the same number of paragraphs. His book, moreover, is indistinguishable in its interests from the sort of thing that Drayton was doing ninety years earlier.

The introduction to Moll's work by Robert Falconer, though it includes some of the terminology of geography and cosmography, signals the advent of a specialized discourse which only a few could understand. As Eileen Reeves has pointed out, these 'few' did not include women.[107] Richardson's Pamela has no map when she sets out from Booby Hall, nor could she read one if she had. Falconer has omitted an explanation of how maps are made, he says, 'because these cannot be fully understood without the knowledge of the Rules of Perspective'.[108] In his expansion of this work, *The Compleat Geographer*, Moll subsumed chorography, topography, and hydrography under geography. The local and practical are to be seen as part of the universal: for him, even cosmography is a part of geography.[109]

Into this new geographical world comes *Robinson Crusoe, of York, Mariner* (1719): a work in which marine charts and local mapping (chorography) are seen within the geography of a still-unknown great world. By the fourth edition in the same year a map of Crusoe's island was included.[110] Seven years later Swift parodied cartographical exactitude in the four maps of *Gulliver's Travels* precisely for Richard Whitlock's reasons: that this kind of knowledge had nothing to do with knowledge of the self. The factoid discourse of the Grand Academy of Lagado had been substituted for knowledge.

Notes

1 *Science and Sanity: An Introduction to Non-Aristotelian Systems and General Semantics* Lakeville, Colo.: The International Non-Aristotelian Library Publishing Co., 1950) p.58. Korzybski also compares languages to maps:' at best they must be considered *only as maps*. A word is *not* the object it represents' p. 58.

2 Chicago: University of Chicago Press, 1991, p. 25.

3 Cambridge, Mass.: Harvard University Press, 1977, p. 27.

4 'Inventing America: A Model for Cartographic Semiosis', *Word and Image*, 4 (1988), pp. 475, 479. Barry Lopez also writes of 'two landscapes – one outside the self, the other within.' *Crossing Open Ground* (London: Pan, 1989), p. 64; 'Inventing America', p. 479.

5 'Medieval World Maps: Embedded Images, Interpretive Frames', *Word & Image*, 10 (1994), pp. 263–4.

6 Paul Carter, *The Road to Botany Bay* (London: Faber, 1987), Ch. 10.

7 O'Gorman's book *The Invention of America* is cited in Fuentes's essay, 'Gabriel Garcia Marquez and the Invention of America', published in *Myself with Others* (New York: Farrar, Straus & Giroux, 1988), p. 183.

8 Mandeville's work was written in about 1357, but was not properly edited until 1725.

9 British Library, Evelyn MSS., Letterbook II, Letter 442, fo. 28. The Evelyn manuscripts were purchased by the British Library in 1995 and have yet to be recatalogued there.

10 Houghton Lodge or Houghton Park House was built by Mary Sidney, Countess of Pembroke, as a hunting lodge and is thought to be the model for Basilius's house in Sidney's *Arcadia*.

11 See the Introduction to Alastair Fowler's *The Country House Poem* (Edinburgh: Edinburgh University Press, 1994); pp. 1–11.

12 *Captain Singleton*, ed. Shiv K. Kumar (Oxford: Oxford University Press – World's Classics, 1990), p. 47.

13 Ibid. p. 56.

14 *Between the Devil and the Deep Blue Sea: Merchant Seamen, Pirates, and the Anglo-American Maritime World, 1700–1750* (Cambridge: Cambridge University Press, 1987), p. 21.

15 *Forms of Nationhood: The Elizabethan Writing of England* (Chicago: University of Chicago Press, 1994), p. 176.

16 The English had established several trading posts in India in the seventeenth century: Surat (1612), Madras (1639), Bombay (1665), and Calcutta (1690).

17 *Captain Singleton*, p. 272.

18 The 1699 edition of Ogilby's survey of the roads of England has a frontispiece of Apollo presenting him with what looks to be the text of the book under a Latin quotation which suggests that Ogilby will be the legislator of the roads.

19 Flamsteed's commission as cited by Francis Baily, *Account of the Revd. John Flamsteed* (London, 1835), p. 111.

20 Like Newcourt's map of 1658, Norden shows compass points and cross lines, but not meridians. He describes his work as 'chorographicall', though its text is mostly historical.

21 '*Periplum*' means literally 'circumnavigation' but metaphorically 'a spiritual journey'.

22 See Gwyn Williams, *Madoc, the Making of a Myth* (London: Eyre Methuen, 1979).

23 'Inventing America', pp. 483, 484, 489. Boelhower describes the soldiers of Ralph Hall firing on the Indians of Virginia as 'topophobia', i.e. the attack of definitive geography on descriptive chorography.

24 See Lucia Nuti, 'The Mapped View by Georg Hoefnagel: The Merchant's Eye, the Humanist's Eye', *Word and Image*, 4 (1988), p. 553.

25 Hollar's 1660 map of London was never published. The map by him published in 1673 is an aerial view, but one on so small a scale that no individual features of it can easily be distinguished.

26 Stow's 1604 dedication refers to his having 'consecrated myselfe to the search of our famous Antiquities'. *Survey*, ed. C. L. Kingford (London: Oxford University Press, 1908), p. lxxxi.

27 Ibid., pp. 286, 392, 394.

28 See especially his explication of Drayton's *Poly-Olbion* in the chapter 'The Land Speaks' in *Forms of Nationhood*, pp. 105–147.

29 Pope's celebration of the unfettered life of the forest in *Windsor Forest* (1713) is part of a debate about commons and nature and the imposition of legal authority. Most attention to this controversy has been focused on the infamous 'Black Act' of 1722, in which the ancient rights of the common people to hunt and gather wood were criminalized. See below, Ch. 5. See also E. P. Thompson, 'Windsor', in *Whigs and Hunters* (Harmondsworth: Penguin, 1977), pp. 27, 115, and Christopher Hill, 'The Norman Yoke', in *Puritanism and Revolution* (London: Panther, 1968), pp. 58–125. Evelyn's acquaintance, Richard Richardson, on the other hand, wrote a long poem, *De Cultu Hortorum* (London, 1699), in praise of William III, political liberty, and gardens.

30 See the discussion of this in Maynard Mack's note to Epistle I, 6–16, *An Essay on Man* (Twickenham edn, London: Methuen, 1950), Twickenham iii. 1, p. 11.

31 In Tony Kushner's play, *Perestroika*, Belize accuses his friend Prior of being 'up in the air ... too far off the earth to pick out the details', and associates this with America's love of the abstract at the expense of the particular (New York: Theatre Communications Group, 1994), p. 96.

32 *The Road to Botany Bay*, p. 305.

33 Similarly, French-influenced estates of Restoration England employed aerial perspective, whereas the landscape gardens created in reaction to them in the early eighteenth century employed ground-level discovery, choice, and mistake as part of their meaning.

34 See James Turner, *The Politics of Landscape* (Cambridge, Mass.: Harvard University Press, 1979).

35 *The Cosmographicall Glasse* (London, 1559), fo. 7.

36 See Petrus Ramus, *Dialecticae Institutiones* (1543), and Walter J. Ong, *Ramus, Method and the Decay of Dialogue* (Cambridge, Mass.: Harvard University Press, 1958).

37 *Religio Medici, The Works of Sir Thomas Browne*, ed. Geoffrey Keynes (London: Faber and Faber, 1928), i. 19. In his edition of *The Major Works*, C. A. Patrides notes Browne's consistent opposition to definition (Harmondsworth: Penguin, 1977), p. 70. See also John Mulder, '*Religio Medici*: Aristotle *versus* Moses', in *The Temple of the Mind: Education and Literary Taste in Seventeenth-Century England* (New York: Pegasus, 1969), pp. 54–62.

38 For a history and discussion of this subject see Walter J. Ong, *Ramus, Method and the Decay of Dialogue* (Cambridge, Mass.: Harvard Univ. Press, 1958) and Sister Miriam by Joseph, *Shakespeare's Use of the Arts of Language* (New York: Columbia: Studies in English and Comparative Literature, 1949).

39 *Spiegel der Zeevaerdt*, trans. by Sir A. Ashley as *The Mariner's Mirror* (1588). In spite of what the *OED* says, it seems to me that the word 'navigator' refers to 'land navigator' and is far older than canal building. Boelhower suggests that there is a correlation between kinds of map and stages of contact with new territory. The 'portolan' he identifies with the activity of colonization. 'Inventing America', p. 480.

40 Ibid., p. 477.

41 I am indebted here to J. B. Harley, 'Meaning and Ambiguity in Tudor Cartography', in *English Map-Making 1500–1650*, ed. Sarah Tyacke (London: British Library, 1983) pp. 26–9.

42 *Emariculfe by E. C. Esquier 1595* (London: Roxburghe Club, 1881).

43 *Adam's Complaint* (London, 1596), i. 58.

44 *A Fig for Fortune* (London, 1596), i. 507.

45 Spenser in fact only use the word 'map' once, in his translation of Du Bellay's *The Ruines of Rome* (1591). But even there, Rome as a city is identified with Rome as an empire, and both are reflected in 'th'auncient Plot of *Rome*': the map of Rome called the *Forma Urbis Romae* which was carved in stone on the outside wall of the library attached to Vespasian's Temple of Peace. See Sarah Tyacke's discussion of the significance of this map in 'Intersections or Disputed Territory', *Word and Image*, 4 (1988), p. 574.

46 Ch. 76, l. 91.

47 *The Perfect- Cursed-Blessed-Man*, (London, 1628), l. 209.

48 *The First Classis*, stanza 133.

49 Gabriel Harvey refers to 'the great Mapp of Mercator' in *Pierce's Supererogation* (1589), and Sir Henry Slingsby writes from Cambridge in 1619 to ask for a map of Asia that his father had bought in 1612, and to assure his father that he had not 'slightly esteam'd those Mapps you sent me'. *The Diary of Sir Henry Slingsby*, ed. Daniel Parson (London: Longman, 1836), p. 313.

50 In 'Reading Maps', Eileen Reeves cites 'Valediction' as 'one of the closest associations of literature with cartography', but it needs to be noted that Donne-the-lover's geographical discourse would have been incomprehensible to his mistress. *Word and Image*, 9 (1993), p. 53.

51 'A Country life: To his Brother, M. Tho: Herrick', ll. 77–82; 'To His Brother Nicholas Herrick', ll. 2–3, 18. *The Poems of Robert Herrick*, ed. L. C. Martin (Oxford: Oxford University Press, 1965), pp. 34, 330.

52 Sarah Tyacke cites Robert Walton, the first map-seller to produce a catalogue (1655), advertising a map 'of all the remarkable passages, and actions that have happened ever since the Long Parliament in 1640'. With this map the potential purchaser could also acquire a set of prints of the four seasons, the five senses, and the four elements or the Cries of London. 'Map Sellers and the London Map Trade c.1650–1710', in *My Head is a Map*: *Essays and Memoirs in honour of R. V. Tooley*, ed. Helen Wallis and Sarah Tyacke (London: Francis Edwards, 1973), p. 66. There was also a considerable increase in map-selling after the Third Dutch War in 1672.

53 'To my Honoured Friend Mr George Sandys', in *The Poems of Henry King* (Oxford: Clarendon Press, 1965), p. 90.

54 Ibid., pp. 85, 86. Sir Henry Blount's *A Voyage to the Levant* was published in 1636. Travel to Greece and the Near East was not uncommon by the 1630s.

55 *The History of the Down Survey of Ireland*, ed. Thomas Aiskew Larcom (Dublin: Irish Archaeological Society, 1851), p. 17. Boelhower identifies scale maps of the Down Survey sort with the imposition of 'a rational and juridical organization'. 'Inventing America', p. 482.

56 Ibid., p. 494.

57 Cambridge, Mass.: Harvard University Press, 1991, pp. 32, 44.

58 *Here begynneth a ryght frutefull mater: and hath to name the boke of surveyeng and improvmentes* (London, 1543), Ch. 19. Fitzherbert's method of measurement is also very similar to Whitlock's.

59 A perch or rod is 15½ ft in length. Whitlock probably refers to the square of that measure as a parcel of land.

60 London, 1654, p. 200.

61 Ibid., p. 554.

62 *Discipline and Punish: The Birth of the Prison* (London: Allen Lane, 1977); see especially Ch. 3.

63 Ibid., pp. 195 ff. Boelhower writes, 'The scale map as panopticon is the result of the line's achievement of an absolute and closed system no longer dependent on the local perspectivism of the image.' 'Inventing America', p. 496.

64 *Duty of a Steward*, p. 86.

65 In much of rural Italy land is still bought and sold by this older method. Vendor and purchaser walk the bounds and agree the parcel. See also J. M. Neeson, *Commoners: Common Right, Enclosure and Social Change in England 1700–1800* (Cambridge: Cambridge University Press, 1993).

66 Roland Barthes, *The Empire of Signs*, trans. Richard Howard (New York: Hill & Wang, 1982), pp. 33, 36.

67 *Moll Flanders*, ed. G. A. Starr (Oxford: Oxford University Press – World's Classics, 1987), p. 192.

68 In his *New Arabian Nights* (1882), Robert Louis Stevenson saw London as a mysterious eastern city full of courts and intrigue.

69 Review of A. N. Wilson, *The Faber Book of London* (London: Faber, 1993), in *The Times Literary Supplement* 4735 (31 Dec., 1993), p. 28. Keates's contrast of London's 'astonishing recklessness' with 'the frowzy, formal monotony of central Paris' is consonant with the contrast between the post-Fire plans and the actual survey that I am making below.

70 *Trivia* (London, 1716), ii. 77–82, in *John Gay: Poetry and Prose*, ed. V. A. Dearing and C. E. Beckwith (Oxford: Clarendon Press, 1974), i. 45. Gay also describes a pursuit of a thief similar to what Moll imagines for herself in iii. 51–76.

71 *The Character of England* (London, 1659), p. 60.

72 This is the world that Waller's poem 'St. James's Park' vainly attempted to rectify. Compare Lady Booby's use of Hyde Park as a place to be seen with her servant Joseph in *Joseph Andrews* i. 4.

73 *Trivia* iii, 267–98, in *John Gay: Poetry and Prose*, i. 168.

74 'A Description of London', 13–16, in *The New Oxford Book of Eighteenth Century Verse*, ed. Roger Lonsdale (Oxford: Oxford University Press, 1984), p. 275.

75 'The Second Epistle of the Second Book of Horace Imitated by Mr. Pope', 88–91.

76 *Gulliver's Travels and Other Writings*, ed. Ricardo Quintana (New York: Modern Library, 1958), p. 347.

77 *Sculptura* (1662). Evelyn was writing about Hollar's earlier plan of 1660, but such is also the inspiration of both his and Wren's post-Fire plans for the city.

78 Evelyn's plans for rebuilding London after the Fire are contained in *London Revived*, ed. E. S. De Beer (Oxford: Clarendon Press, 1938). He complains of the effects of sea coal in London in *A Character of England* (pp. 29–30) and elaborates this criticism in his *Fumifugium* (1661).

79 John Bender, *Imaging the Penitentiary: Fiction and the Architecture of Mind in Eighteenth-Century England* (Chicago: University of Chicago Press, 1987), pp. 81, 76. Bender cites 'the refiguration of the authority latent in cities ... as *The Journal*'s elemental concern', p. 76.

80 *Moll Flanders*, ed. Starr, p. 86.
81 For an account of Virginia in this period, see Ruth Bourne, 'John Evelyn, the Diarist, and his Cousin Daniel Parke II', in *The Virginia Magazine*, 78 (1970), and Louis B. Wright, *The First Gentlemen of Virginia* (Charlottesville, Va.: University of Virginia Press, 1964).
82 Compare Paul Carter's description of the 'fabrications' that Australian convicts created as 'strategies for constructing a believeable space'. *The Road to Botany Bay*, p. 296.
83 *The Illustrated Journeys of Celia Fiennes 1685–c.1712*, ed. Christopher Morris (London: Macdonald & Co., 1982), p. 32.
84 A. W. Secord has illustrated Defoe's familiarity with contemporary cartography in *Studies in the Narrative Method of Defoe* (Urbana, Ill.: University of Illinois Press, 1924), pp. 114 ff.
85 Joan Parkes, *Travel in England in the Seventeenth Century* (London: Oxford University Press, 1925), p. 84.
86 Ibid., p. 93.
87 Book ii. 3 and i. 12, ed. Martin Battestin (Boston: Houghton Mifflin – Riverside, 1961), pp. 82, 41.
88 British Library 816. MS 12 (162). The pamphlet is undated.
89 Ibid. From the 1670s until the reign of George I Hackney coachmen in London, concerned that their trade was being encroached upon by coaches coming from outside London and stealing their trade, were petitioning Parliament to limit the number of hackney coaches licensed in the capital. See British Library 816. M. 12 (151–160).
90 See Linda Colley, *Britons* (London: Yale University Press, 1992), p. 39.
91 J. B. Harley points out that Tudor estate plans fostered 'an almost poetic sense of attachment to place while simultaneously reinforcing concepts of lordly power over the peasant communities where these estates extended'. 'Meaning and Ambiguity in Tudor Cartography', p. 38.
92 He may also be referring to the Earls of Dorset at nearby Knole.
93 *The Country House Poem*, p. 21.
94 *The Cecils of Hatfield House* (London: Constable, 1973).
95 Add. MS 28104, fo. [21v]. Passages in bracketed parentheses come from Add. MS 4229. Place-names suggestive of all three names are to be found in Shropshire and Derbyshire. William Wotton is the modern scholar abused by Swift in *The Battle of the Books*.
96 Ogilby's *Tables of His Measur'd Roads* (1676) was licensed by Henry Oldenburg (1615?–77), the Secretary of the Royal Society.
97 *London Survey'd: or, an Explanation of the Large Map of London* (1677). In fact, Ogilby's map showed two post-Fire mercantile projects that were never built: a new set of wharves on the Thames, and a canalizing of the Fleet River, with wharves and storehouses.
98 Tyacke, 'Map Sellers', pp. 65.
99 Sir Herbert George Fordham, 'John Ogilby (1600–1676). His *Britannia* and the British Itineraries of the Eighteenth Century', *The Library*, 8 (1926), p. 161.
100 *England Exactly Described*, which first appeared in 1715, was advertised as 'according to Mr Ogilby's Survey . . . being made fit for the Pockett'.
101 *The Diary of John Evelyn*, ed. E. S. De Beer (Oxford: Clarendon Press, 1955), iv. 301.
102 *Colonel Jack*, ed. S. H. Monk (London: Oxford University Press – World's Classics, 1989), p. 94.
103 'The Life of Christ. An Heroic Poem', *The Life of Our Blessed Lord and Saviour* (London, 1693), ll. 620–35.

104 See G. R. Crane, *Maps and Their Makers* (London: Dawson – Archon Books, 1978), p. 87.

105 This poem was attributed by Waller to Prior, but R. W. Chapman subsequently identified it as by Clay. See 'A Poem Attributed to Prior', *Review of English Studies*, 1 (1925), pp. 92–3.

106 Herman Moll, *Thirty Two New and Accurate Maps of the Geography of the Ancients* (London, 1732). Moll's work is extensively indebted to the work of the French geographer du Val, but it uses Laurence Eachard's *Classical Geographical Dictionary* (1715) to correct du Val, and adds a map of Asia after Noah's Flood by the noted antiquary William Stukeley. The British Library's copy was owned by the great botanical explorer Joseph Banks.

107 'Reading Maps', *Word and Image*, 9 (1993) pp. 55–62. Ogilby employed two other surveyors, Gregory King and John Holwell. Holwell's *Sure Guide to the Practical Surveyor* (1678) was, in fact, almost impossible for the ordinary man to understand.

108 *System of Geography*, p. 26.

109 In 1736 Edward Cave published *A New Method of Representing the General Geography of Solar Eclipses*.

110 *The Hermit* by Philip Quarll (Pierre Longueville), a reworking of the Crusoe story in which the hermit has no desire to leave the island, was published in 1746 'with a curious map of the island, and other cuts'. Herman Moll's maps were used to illustrate Defoe's *Tour Through the Whole Island of Great Britain* in 1927.

|3|

Earth's Distant Ends:
Travelling and Classifying

Mapping is inextricably bound up with travelling, and the ability to map the known world from the sixteenth century onwards led to a vastly increased literature of travel, from the publication of Hakluyt's *Principall Navigations* in 1589 (enlarged in 1598–1600) onwards. But what travellers describe is as much a reflection of their own culture's prejudices and preoccupations as of what they actually see. In Tom Stoppard's play *Travesties*, the central character, Henry Carr, is astonished by the information that books in English are kept under 'foreign literature' in the public library of Zurich. 'What a novel arrangement,' is his response.[1] Carr's ludicrous Anglo-centrism is only an extreme example of the Eurocentrism with which the rest of the world was re-ordered and re-named from the seventeenth century onwards. It none the less went hand in hand, at least in some cases, with the recognition that the cultural values of Europe might only be part of the larger cultural story of the world.

Stoppard wrote *Travesties* in the wake of our seeing ourselves for the first time from the point of view of outer space. The most recent production of his play occurred while the Hubble telescope was showing us previously invisible galaxies in an expanding universe that is almost beyond our comprehension. Something like this – a revolution in our sense of ourselves and our place in the universe – happened geographically during the late seventeenth century.

Roger Ascham, Queen Elizabeth's tutor, wrote in condemnation of continental travel, '*Inglese Italianato e un diavolo incarnato*',[2] although he himself had travelled abroad. But the Grand Tour of the continent was not really possible until the early seventeenth century, and it finds its most famous commendation in Francis Bacon's essay 'Of Travaile':

> Let Diaries, therefore, be brought in use. The Things to be seene and observed are: The Courts of Princes, specially when they give Audience to Ambassadours: The Courts of Justice, while they sit and

heare Causes; And so of Consistories Ecclesiasticke: The Churches, and Monasteries, with the Monuments which are therein extant: The Wals and Fortifications of Cities and Townes; And so the Havens and Harbours: Antiquities, and Ruines: Libraries; Colleges, Disputations and Lectures, where any are: Shipping and Navies: Houses, and Gardens of State, and Pleasure, neare great Cities: Armories: Arsenals: Magazens: Exhanges: Burses; Ware-houses: Exercises of Horse-man-ship; Fencing; Trayning of Souldiers; and the like: Comedies; Such whereunto the better Sort of persons doe resort, Treasuries of Jewels, and Robes; Cabinets, and Rarities: And to conclude, whatsoever is memorable in the Places, where they goe.[3]

Even as late as 1656, however, Francis Osborne could warn his son that travel frequently added 'Affectation to Folly, and Atheisme to the Curiosities of many not well principled by Education'.[4] A few years later, the Marquis of Argyll also warned his son against the 'taking vanities of forraign Countries', but he recommended travel none the less as preferable to book-learning:

He that hath nothing to venture but poore, despicable and solitary Parts may be so farre from Improvement, as he hazards quite to loose and bury them in the externall *Levity* of *France*, *Pride* of *Spaine*, and *Treachery* of *Italy*.[5]

What continental travel represented, however, was a breaking of English (Protestant) isolationism: a reassertion of the cultural union of Europe in the topography of a revived classicism. Inigo Jones travelled with Lord Arundel, correcting his copy of Palladio and bringing back with him the architectural vocabulary with which to build a palace of Solomon, Whitehall, founded on the principles of the Roman architect Vitruvius. Milton, like many others, went in search of Virgil and found near his tomb the landscape of the hell of *Paradise Lost*. Similarly he found in the gardens of the Medici the landscape features of Eden, and in Italian opera and poetry the structural material of his epic.

The culture of Italy (and to a lesser degree France) became the text to be translated into English, whether on the ground (in gardens and buildings), in the visual arts (in painting and sculpture), or in literary texts such as Milton's, incorporating both literal and figurative transpositions of Italian sources. One of the famous epic similes in *Paradise Lost* is the comparison of the fallen angels to a hive of bees. In a sudden reversal of perspective the gigantic becomes tiny:

Behold a wonder! they but now who seemd
In bigness to surpass Earths Giant-Sons
Now less then smallest Dwarfs, in narrow room
Throng numberless.

(I. 777–80)

A little more than a decade before Milton's visit to Rome, where he was entertained at the Palazzo Barberini, Prince Federico Cesi published a partial encyclopaedia of natural history that dealt largely with bees, the symbol of the Barberini family. The accompanying illustrative plate by Francesco Stelluti is the first to use a subject observed through a microscope, and its subject is bees.[6] Through the reverse of Galileo's 'Optic Glass' the papal grandeur of the Barberinis is reduced to the microscopic. In a complex simile, Milton plays with this metamorphosis, reducing in the process one of the famous images of epic imperial grandeur (the building of Carthage in *The Aeneid*) to Satanic absurdity.

Charles I, who had himself travelled across France to Spain on an abortive quest for the hand of the Infanta, married his French bride, Henrietta Maria, a Medici who brought with her all the tastes of Italy – even culinary ones. And not only did Charles use the painter Rubens to acquire the Duke of Mantua's huge collection of paintings, but he brought to the English court such Italian painters as Orazio and Artemesia Gentileschi, who in turn promulgated the very taste for 'darkness visible' which Milton was to employ in his description of the Satanic host. From the continent also came the new learning: Galileo's and Brahe's astronomy, Bumaldo's and Ferrari's botany, Gassendi's physics – all of them revolutionary in their refashioning of the old Aristotelian world picture into the 'new philosophy' of doubt and scepticism which made possible both Milton's two cosmologies and the foundations of the Royal Society.

But English travelling also served the imperial interests of the newly established Great Britain. If *The Tempest* is an Italian metaphor for British empire-building, it also exemplifies the way in which the text of the New World was being inscribed within the old. Hardly a century after Columbus, the settlements of Virginia and New England reflected new models of 'out there': the 'fresh woods and pastures new' of millenarianism and speculation. The founding of the Massachusetts colony, and the establishment of the Hudson's Bay Company some 30 years later, represent rival myths of domination and appropriation which, for example, Marvell takes on in 'Upon Appleton House'. Out of this came a whole new vocabulary, visual, scientific and literary, for apprehending the world. In the process, fiction, which had consisted largely of romance, came to reflect the very empirical observation that Bacon recommended: the inventorying of experience on which, for example, Defoe's *Robinson Crusoe* relies. Indeed, it is the very inability to name the wild beasts of Africa that makes them the more terrifying in his novel *Captain Singleton*.

Out of all this diversity came also what Carlos Fuentes has called the 'nostalgia for analogy'[7]: the desire for a system that would contain an increasingly diverse world. Bishop Compton's chaplains in America sending home a wealth of new botanical material made necessary John Ray's first attempts at taxonomy, a text to contain the disorder of empirical discovery. The circumnavigation of the globe and the new trade routes in its wake required a new cartography where the old names – Boston, New Amsterdam, Kingston – could assert a new order, and the myths of lost white tribes of European 'Indians' could legitimate conquest.

My father grew up in a town in Ontario named Madoc, after the twelfth-century leader of a band of Welshmen who sailed to America to found a settlement. In fact, that Canadian town was named after the poem on the subject by the Romantic poet, Robert Southey: a poem which reinscribed the continuing potency of this myth in the settlement of America. But even the word 'Canada' is an ambiguous signifier. Does it mean 'nothing there' in Portuguese, or 'village of small huts' in an Amerindian language? There is strange power in names, not least in an empire like the British one, where words like 'bungalow' and 'verandah' find themselves far from their Indian origins. 'Welcome to our Sepoy town' say the signs outside Lucknow, Ontario; but the Lucknow of the Sepoy Mutiny in India was itself named after Lucknow in Ireland. Such mythography is essential to the emplacement of empire.[8]

In 1713 Pope published his long poem *Windsor Forest*, which had been in gestation for nearly a decade. Drawing on the traditional identification of British forests with British freedom, Pope concluded the poem with an extended image of the trees turned into ships and navigating the previously unknown world. His paean, spoken in the voice of the River Thames, concludes:

> Thy Trees, fair *Windsor*! now shall leave their Woods,
> And half thy Forests rush into my Floods,
> Bear *Britain*'s Thunder, and her Cross display,
> To the bright Regions of the rising Day;
> Tempt Icy Seas where scarce the Waters roll,
> Where clearer Flames glow round the frozen Pole;
> Or under southern Skies exalt their Sails,
> Led by new Stars, and born by spicy Gales!
>
> (385–92)

But Pope also imagines the nations of the world coming to Britain and admiring its strangeness: the sort of cultural confrontation that Swift was to immortalize in *Gulliver's Travels* 13 years later no less ambiguously.

> Earth's distant Ends our Glory shall behold,
> And the new World launch forth to seek the Old.
> Then Ships of uncouth Form shall stem the Tyde,
> And Feather'd People crowd my wealthy Side,
> And naked Youths and painted Chiefs admire
> Our Speech, our colour, and our strange Attire.
>
> (401–6)[9]

The rhyme of 'admire' with 'attire' suggests the superficiality of both, and underlines the ambiguity of the verb. Is it transitive or intransitive (as it first appears), and is its admiration 'wonder' or 'respect'? In the poem English culture looks in a constructed mirror of foreignness to affirm its own cultural values.

For all his subsequent hope that 'Conquest cease, and Slav'ry be no more,' Pope's narrative seems very much like the sort of epic historical painting associated with the later course of empire: Benjamin West's late-eighteenth-century canvas of 'The Death of Wolfe', for example, with its admiring Indian brave looking in wonder at the saintly heroism of imperial martyrdom.[10] These lines in *Windsor Forest* may look back to the pastoral canvas that tells 'a Stuart reigns' (32–42), but they also look forward almost to the end of the poem, to lines describing a different sort of Stuart canvas, Rubens's ceiling for the Banqueting Hall at Whitehall (413–22). Charles I may have intended to celebrate a reign of peace in that painting; but Terror, Vengeance, Faction, and Rebellion had the last word. The king walked to his execution from that room, as surely none of Pope's readers would have forgotten.[11]

Whatever the irony of Pope's poem, however, Edward Young's *Imperium Pelagi. A Naval Lyrick* (1730) leaves no doubt about the legitimacy of the expanding trade that Pope describes so ambiguously. But it does so without the lingering echoes of Stuart greatness that sound so elegiac in Pope's poem. For Young, '*Commerce* brings Riches, Riches Crown | Fair *Virtue* with the first renown', in a world where '*Merchants* o'er proudest Heroes reign' and America with its 'Womb of Gold' offers Britons the chance to 'call Wonders forth from *Nature*'s lap'.[12]

Joseph Addison treated the presentation of four Iroquois chiefs to Queen Anne in 1710 as an occasion to write about English culture looking at itself in the mirrored eyes of foreign observers. Swift had already played with this joke in the introduction to *The Mechanical Operation of the Spirit* (1704), where his persona invites his correspondent to convey his respects 'to the *Iroquois Virtuosi*'.[13] Like Gulliver explaining Britain to the Lilliputians, Addison's faux-Iroquois give an ironic account of English politics:

> The Queen of the Country appointed two Men to attend us, that had enough of our Language to make themselves understood in some few Particulars. But we soon perceived these two were great Enemies to one another, and did not always agree in the same Story. We could make a Shift to gather out of one of them, that this Island was very much infested with a monstrous kind of Animals, in the shape of Men, called *Whigs*; and he often told us, that he hoped we should meet with none of them in our Way, for that if we did, they would be apt to knock us down for being Kings.
>
> Our other Interpreter used to talk very much of a kind of Animal called a *Tory*, that was as great a Monster as the *Whig*, and would

treat us as ill for being Foreigners. These two Creatures, it seems, are born with a secret Antipathy to one another, and engage when they meet as naturally as the Elephant and the Rhinoceros.[14]

Although John Butt uses the word 'visited' to describe this occasion,[15] however, it seems unlikely that the Iroquois chiefs came entirely of their own free will on a European tour. In his account 'Of the interest of the *French* and *English* in North *America*' (1693) the French soldier La Hontan remarks of the Iroquois, 'To alledge that these Barbarians have a dependence upon the *English*, is a foolish Plea; their Respect for the *English* proceeding meerly from the occasion they have to make use of 'em.'[16] And Stephen Greenblatt has pointed out that such accounts as we have 'of Indian responses to the Europeans in the earliest years of contact are precious, but principally because they provide unusually candid and self-revealing access to the European's own self-conception'.[17]

The exoticism of elephant and rhinoceros in Addison's description, moreover, gives the game away; Iroquois would not have known of either. Addison's mock description is a kind of satire called 'Menippean': one in which a 'world in the moon' setting may be used as a critique of the familiar. In this case, though, Addison's use of real inhabitants of a new continent is an interesting blurring of the discourses of satire and exploration. Such writing was to become a sub-genre within English literature, especially the sort of periodical literature of which Goldsmith's 'Chinese Letters' (in *The Citizen of the World*, 1760) are probably the best-known example.

Swift's 'Account of the Empire of Japan' (1728) also uses just such a device to satirize the court of George I: 'Regoge [George] was the thirty-fourth Emperor of Japan and began his reign in the year 341 [1714] of the Christian aera, succeeding to Nena [Anne], a Princess who governed with great felicity.' The Prime Minister, Lelip-Aw (Walpole), and his party have ousted the Yortes-faction (Tories) and so changed the constitution that Regoge's son (George II) no longer has to govern but only to 'appear sometimes in council' and leave the rest to his Visirs (ministers).[18]

Oriental exoticism, whether of the near or far east, was also the staple of much fiction of the later eighteenth century. Like gothicism, however, with which it had close links, orientalism could be either pastiche decoration or imaginative reworking: what rhetoric (and literature) called '*elocutio*' (style) or '*inventio*' (thought).

The decorative arts and customs of Japan and China began to enter English culture as early as the 1650s. In 1664 the diarist John Evelyn wrote of seeing a collection 'sent from the *Jesuites* of *Japan* and *China* . . . with the East *India ships*' of 'prints of Landskips' and 'Pictures of Men, and Countries, rarely painted on a sort of gumm'd *Calico* transparant as glasse'.[19] And in 1671 John Ogilby published three works on Japan and China: his translation of Arnoldus Montanus's *Atlas Jappanensis* (1671) and *Atlas Chinensis* (1670), and Jan Nieuhoff's account of the Dutch East India Company's history there, *An Embassy to China* (1669).

In terms of the change in English social habits in the Restoration period, the advent of both tea and coffee had a great impact. In 1688 the botanist John Ray claimed that there were more coffee-houses in London than there were in Cairo.[20] In spite of a royal attempt to prohibit them, the social life of fashionable men came to be focused there, to be satirized in turn in *The Tatler* and *The Spectator*, and ultimately to be seen as places of virtue's ruin in *Joseph Andrews* (1742). By 1700 Congreve could depict the tea-table as the centre of female society in *The Way of the World*; by 1711, in the second edition of Pope's *The Rape of the Lock* (1714), the whole consumerist aesthetic of China and Japan had become a metaphor for vanity and moral fragility. The sacraments are tea and coffee served on 'the shining Altars of *Japan*'; and lost sexual honour is like 'rich *China* Vessels, fal'n from high', that 'in glittering Dust and painted Fragments lie'.[21]

The significant impact of the orient on English culture, however, was not in terms of porcelain, screens, and fabric, or even tea and coffee, but in the rethinking of such basic concepts as 'nature' and 'art'.[22] Sir William Temple explained the principle of irregularity in Chinese gardens[23] ('*sharawadgi*') and thereby provided a non-Cartesian way of thinking about nature. Published 2 years after the first part of Locke's *Essay Concerning Human Understanding* (1690), his work also provided a philosophical basis for the predominant garden aesthetic of the early eighteenth century. Moreover, it endorsed a model of human nature that was not merely ratiocinative, the very model that his one-time secretary, Swift, was to employ in *Gulliver's Travels*.

If Temple's concept of wild nature was like the unfallen nature of *Paradise Lost* ('wilde above Rule or Art; enormous bliss'), it was also that celebrated by Pope in *An Essay on Criticism* (1711). Like the compiler of *The Arabian Nights Entertainment*, first published in English between 1705 and 1708, this was a nature that Pope also found in Homer.[24] Indeed, the preface to the 1714 translation of these tales seems almost an echo of the Homeric claim for Ulysses that he had seen many nations. 'Here is no Heap of extravagant Ideas collected together,' wrote the editor, 'but the Manners of several Nations . . . In short we may look upon these Tales, as the Relations of Travellers.' At least one of the Sindbad stories from *The Arabian Nights* also found its way into the story of Gulliver's escape from Brobdingnag in Book II of the *Travels*. And of course the taste for oriental fiction engendered by this collection of tales is partly responsible for the vogue of such works as Johnson's *The History of Rasselas, Prince of Abyssinia* (1759).

More important than its individual adventures, however, the structure of *The Arabian Nights* as a whole offered a new mode of narrative, one in which the narrator was duplicitous and the structure itself delusory. Both were central to the role of the narrator and the use of time in Fielding's *Tom*

Jones (1749), and both were a challenge to a 'high priori'[25] literature indebted to the rules of art outlined by Boileau and exemplified in the work of Molière and Racine.

By the time that Dr Johnson wrote about viewing the world 'from China to Peru' (in 'The Vanity of Human Wishes', 1748),[26] a massive travel literature on just such a subject had been compiled for over a century. Awnsham Churchill's six-volume anthology of such journeys and voyages was first published in 1704 and augmented in 1732. Its earliest items are from the beginning of the seventeenth century, but most of them were written from the mid-century onwards and reflect the great expansion of the European known world in that period.

Churchill's collection begins with 'An Introductory Discourse concerning the History of Navigation' by Edmund Halley, the astronomer, which is both dismissive of the late sixteenth-century work of Hakluyt and celebratory of the expanding universe. Hakluyt, however, says Richard Helgerson, had first of all 'to reinvent both England and the world to make them fit for one another'.[27] One of the consequences was that, partly through representations such as his, England became a more commercial nation, committed to the reinvention of the world from European perspective. And this is just the world that Halley celebrates:

What was cosmography before these discoveries, but an imperfect fragment of a science, scarce deserving so good a name? When all the known world was only *Europe*, a small part of *Africk*, and the lesser portion of *Asia*; so that of this terraqueous globe not one sixth part had ever been seen or heard of. Nay, so great was the ignorance of man in this particular, that learned persons made a doubt of its being round; others no less knowing imagined all they were not acquainted with, desart and uninhabitable. But now geography and hydrography have received some perfection by the pains of so many mariners and travellers, who to evince the rotundity of the earth and water, have sailed and travelled round it, as has been here made appear; to shew there is no part uninhabitable unless the frozen polar regions, having visited all other countries tho' never so remote, which they have found well peopled, and most of them rich and delightful; and to demonstrate the *Antipodes* have printed them out to us. Astronomy has received the addition of many constellations never seen before. Natural and moral history is embellished with the most beneficial increase of so many thousands of plants it had never before received, so many drugs and spices, such variety of beasts, birds and fishes, such rarities in minerals, mountains and waters, such unaccountable diversity of climates and men, and in them of complexions, tempers, habits, manners, politicks, and religions. Trade is raised to the highest pitch, each part of the world supplying the other with what it wants, and bringing home what is accounted most precious and valuable; and this not in a niggard and scanty manner, as when the *Venetians* served all *Europe* with spice and drugs from *India* by way of *Turky* and the *Red Sea*; or as when gold and silver were only drawn from *European* and *African* mines; . . . To conclude, the empire of *Europe* is now extended to the utmost bounds of the earth where several of its nations have conquests and colonies.[28]

Halley's preface is an instructive document of the new geographical scientism. Situating itself in opposition to a past of ignorance and superstition, it celebrates the expansion of knowledge allied to trade and leaves little doubt as to the virtue of 'the empire of Europe'. Where James Howell had attributed Venice's survival primarily to the fact that 'she hath bin allwayes an enemy to change',[29] Churchill saw her as an obstacle to the expanding trade and empire that Pope was to celebrate in the original draft of *Windsor Forest*:

> Let Venice boast her Tow'rs amidst the Main,
> Where the rough Adrian swells and roars in vain;
> Here, not a Town, but spacious Realm may have
> A sure Foundation on the rolling Wave.[30]

Pope's poem was published 2 years after the flotation of one of the greatest stock-market speculations in English history, the South Sea Company. Seven years later, in 1720, the year after the publication of *Robinson Crusoe*, the South Sea Bubble burst. In its time, this stock-market collapse was as sensational as the 1929 crash. Like the world of F. Scott Fitzgerald's *The Great Gatsby*, the South Sea speculation had thrived on the myth of a fantasy America of inconceivable riches, a myth that Fitzgerald characterized as 'the orgiastic future that year by year recedes before us'.[31] Even before the bubble burst, Swift was scathing about its never-never land of mariner's tales:

> So by a Calenture misled
> The Mariner with Rapture sees
> On the smooth Ocean's azure Bed
> Enamell'd Fields, and verdant Trees;
>
> With eager Hast he longs to rove
> In that fantastick Scene, and think
> It must be some enchanted Grove
> And in he leaps, and down he sinks.[32]

Herman Moll's *A View of the Coast, Countries and Islands Within the Limits of the South-Sea-Company* established the scenario in 1711, the year of the South Sea Company's charter. The book's purview was itself virtually a metaphor. It would treat, said Moll, all of South America from the 'River

Aranoca to Port Desire', and it offered 'a View of the General and Coasting
TRADE-WINDS' as well as a 'Chart from England to the River Aranoca etc.'.
Moll makes the point that such earlier writers as Dampier, Wafer,
Narbrough, Sharp, and Cowley did not properly describe the nature of the
east coast of the South American continent. There is no doubt in his mind,
moreover, that the motivation of travel is empire and commerce:

> When the Publick Welfare of these Kingdoms depend [sic] so much on
> the Success of the *Company* newly Establishd to carry on a Trade to
> the *South Seas*, it cou'd not but excite the Curiosity of all who wish
> well to it, to know what are the *Countries*, *Commerce*, and *Riches*
> which are the Subject of our present *Views* and *Expectations*.[33]

This, then, is the geography that *Robinson Crusoe* metaphorically inhabits,
a world where Crusoe takes his place 'in an un-inhabited Island on the
Coast of AMERICA, near the Mouth of the Great River of OROONOQUE'. Like
Captain Singleton, published the next year, which was thought to be a
factual account by its first readers, Crusoe finds his literary place also
amongst the accounts of '*English* Pirates, Freebooters, and bold
Adventurers'.[34] Included in these would have been the 'voyages' that Moll
dismisses when he writes:

> the Relations of Seamen are generally dry, consisting chiefly of
> Accounts of Winds, Storms, strange Animals, Trees and Vegetables;
> and that for want of Judgment, Knowledge and Curiosity, many
> excellent Observations, both as to History and Trade, are omitted, and
> the whole confounded with so much Sea-Jargon, that they could
> neither be so useful nor diverting as a Treatise selected from old
> Authors, and made perfect Intelligence for judicious Persons interested
> and conversant in these matters.[35]

Narbrough's account of his travels to the Magellan Straits is a good example
of this sort of 'dry account', but his justification for such a journal is very
Crusoe-like: 'the Improvement of *Geography*, *Hydrography*, *Astronomy*,
Natural and *Moral History*, *Antiquity*, *Trade*, *Empire*, etc.'. 'Few books,' he
says of such travel-writing, 'can compare with them for Profit or Pleasure.'[36]
Perhaps more interesting to the reader of Defoe, however, is the sense of
mystery and inexplicability that frequently haunts these narratives:
Dampier's account of the city of Nombre de Dios on the island of Blanco
that simply disappeared without trace, for example, or Cowley's story of
hearing the voice of a drowning man though none of the crew was missing.
Like Crusoe with the inexplicable footprint, Cowley was driven to a wild
speculation: that 'It was the Spirit of some Man that had been drowned at
that Latitude by accident.'[37]
   In this yet-to-be-charted world there is a continuous sense of wonder that
resists the ratiocinative models of trade and commerce, based as they are on
the model of a scientific geography.[38] This sense of wonder suggests a

survival of the imaginative and dangerous world of Caliban and Ariel, whose island Shakespeare probably based on accounts of islands like Crusoe's in the Caribbean. Wafer offers an account of the the power of Indian magic ('Pawawing') in the isthmus of Panama that is plainly as terrifying as Crusoe's vision of the devil. What is it, Crusoe also wonders, that defines the human? This too is Miranda's question about Caliban, and Dampier's about the inhabitants of western Australia (New Holland). Like Gulliver encountering the Yahoos, Dampier raises the question that George Orwell identifies with Nazism: 'Setting aside their Humane Shape, they differ little from Brutes.'[39]

Not all of the writers of travels and voyages were pleased by the overlapping of ostensible truth with fiction, however. One of the most 'factual' of these writers was Captain Richard Falconer, and the preface to the 1734 edition of his *Voyages* leaves little doubt about his attitude to the rise of fiction:

> it is very rueful to behold the Quill-Drivers of the present Age, so - egregiously triumphant over those of the Last; for now *Shakespear*, and *Ben Johnson*, must give way to *Robinson Crusoe* and Colonel [sic] *Jack*; as well as *Dryden* and *Otway* to *Moll Flanders*, and *Sally Salisbury*: And I myself am terribly afraid that the Voyages and Adventures of Captain *Richard Falconer*, must in a short Period of Time strike [give way] to Sir *John Mandeville*'s lying Travels, and Mademoiselle *Beleau*'s [Defoe's *Roxana*] unheard-of intrigues.[40]

Falconer does not mention Aphra Behn, whose *Oroonoko* (*c*.1688) was published well before Defoe began writing fiction and preceded him in incorporating the apparently documentary world of the Caribbean into fiction. Behn's mythologizing of the South American continent also precedes Churchill's *Voyages* and Moll's *A View of the Coast*, though not the voyage and travel accounts on which those works rely. One of these might have been Ogilby's *America* (1671), which includes Mexico and Peru 'with the several European plantations in those parts'.[41] Her diction, moreover, is the paradisal language of the Eden of Milton's *Paradise Lost*, a poem published in its present form only 14 years before the publication of *Oroonoko*:

> 'Tis a continent whose vast extent was never yet known, and may contain more noble earth than all the universe besides; for, they say, it reaches from east to west, one way as far as China, and another to Peru. It affords all things both for beauty and use; 'tis there eternal Spring, always the very months of April, May and June.[42]

Behn's supposedly factual novel was published in 1688 and transformed into a play by Thomas Southerne in 1695. She herself, on the other hand, led a life that itself seems frequently fictional. Her novel is set in Surinam, a country that she had visited and one that probably included Crusoe's desert island. *Oroonoko* raises the questions of primitive innocence and the slave trade, both dealt with in Defoe's novels. Captain Singleton, for example, understands the nobility of the 'Black Prince' whom he first captures, but he has already decided to 'quarrel with some of the Negro Natives, take ten or twelve of them Prisoners, and binding them as Slaves, cause them to travel with us, and make them carry our Baggage'.[43] His 'religious thoughts' on the occasion go no further than thanking God for his superior intellect and reflecting 'how happy it was, that I was not born among such Creatures as these, and was not so stupidly ignorant and barbarous'.[44]

Singleton is more representative of contemporary attitudes than is the moral relativism of Robinson Crusoe or Aphra Behn. In Isaac Watts's *Divine Songs for Children* (1715), the most popular collection of poems for children ever published, pious nonconformity puts the following stanzas into the mouths of children to 'beautify their Souls':

> LORD, I ascribe it to thy Grace,
> And not to Chance, as others do,
> That I was born of *Christian* Race,
> And not a *Heathen*, or a *Jew*.
>
> I would not change my native Land
> For rich *Peru*, with all her Gold;
> A nobler Prize lies in my Hand,
> Than *East* or *Western* Indies hold.[45]

'Children of high and low Degree, of the Church of *England* or Dissenters, baptized in Infancy or not,' says Watts, 'may all join together in these songs.'[46]

It needs, then, to be stressed how exceptional *Oroonoko* is in moral attitudes and characterization. It uses the exotic setting of a Caribbean island through which to look at European moral and imaginative issues.[47] Put another way, it refigures Eurocentrism in what seems a feminist way by looking at an exotic place which in turn looks back to Europe. And in this Behn may have been indebted to the romance tradition that led back to Joseph Hall's *Mundus Alter et Idem* (1607), in which the women-ruled country of Viragina is more or less where *Oroonoko* is also set, i.e. Surinam.[48]

Oroonoko is a captured African prince who, because his name is 'barbarous, and hard to pronounce', is renamed 'Caesar': a name appropriate, it seems, to one whose 'nose was rising and Roman instead of African and flat'.[49] Moreover, his story is narrated in the context of romanticized primitivism where 'Nature is the most harmless, inoffensive and virtuous mistress.'[50] Into a literature overshadowed by *Paradise Lost*, Behn introduces a prelapsarian nature in a postlapsarian world.

Suggestive of Milton's elegiac description of Surinam 20 years earlier as 'yet unspoiled Guiana', her narrative takes its place between Adam's last

vision of a world almost like his own (in *Paradise Lost* XI. 410) and the one
which Pope rewrites in *Windsor Forest*, where 'the freed *Indians* in their
native Groves I Reap their own Fruits, and woo their Sable Loves.'[51] This is,
of course, a reconstructed Arcadia. George Warren (one of Behn's probable
sources) used terms for it that directly invoke the language of the second
book of Virgil's *Georgics*: 'A happy people in relation to this World, if they
but knew their own good fortune.'[52] This happiness, however, is fragile: as
fragile as Milton's vision of an unfallen world from the perspective of a
world of rapacious trade already in full swing when he wrote. Two years
after the publication of *Oroonoko*, the English sailor Edward Barlow
reflected:

> But for nations to come and plant themselves in islands and countries
> by force, and build forts and raise laws, and force the people to
> customs against the true natures and people of the said places without
> their consent, how this will stand with the law of God and the religion
> we profess, let the world judge.[53]

Given Behn's involvement with Dryden's heroic play on this subject (*The
Indian Queen*, 1664), it is not surprising that Oroonoko himself speaks in a
diction that the dramatist Thomas Southerne came to think should be cast
in the blank verse of heroic drama. He also speaks in the artificial diction of
late-seventeenth-century European romance, one of the discourses used in
Margaret Cavendish's strange mixture of fiction, science, and philosophy
called *The Blazing World* (1666). It is not surprising that French romance
was very popular with such Royalist exiles during and after the
Commonwealth, many of whom spent their time of exile in France. But even
Dorothy Osborne, who lived in England throughout this period, spends
several of her early letters to her future husband, Sir William Temple,
discussing French romances and memoirs. Indeed, she writes of one of her
unwanted suitors as 'a most Romance Squire' who wants to 'goe in quest of
some inchanted Damzell'. In one letter she writes about reading Robert
Ashley's *Almansor* (1627), a translation of a Spanish romance by a fictional
Arabian author, which was to be used in another Dryden play, *The
Conquest of Granada* (1670).[54]

Oroonoko's speech is very similar to the diction of the sort of French
romance represented by Honore D'Urfé's *Astrée*, a work from which Behn
took her soubriquet, 'Astrea'. The account of Oroonoko's falling in love
with Amoinda long before Behn's supposed contact with the prince is in the
declamatory discourse of theatrical romance:

> And he often would cry, 'O my friends! Were she in walled cities, or
> confined from me in fortifications of the greatest strength; did
> enchanters or monsters detain her from me, I would venture through
> any hazard to free her.'[55]

How is this cultural inversion related to Crusoe's response to cannibalism?

In spite of Montaigne's dismissal of cannibalism as a European superstition – 'they are savages at the same rate, that we say Fruits are wild'[56] – its fetishizing was in full swing by the late seventeenth century. It is a subject thoroughly described, for example, in John Ogilby's account of the rescue of a native Caribbean from the cannibals in his *America* (1671).[57] Robinson Crusoe takes place, afer all, in a demonized geography; the very name 'Caribbean' is the root of the word 'cannibal', and cannibalism entered the journal of Columbus's second voyage. Crusoe's recognition that he has no right to pass judgement even upon the cannibals who come to his island, however, is certainly a great step beyond the mere horror of Ogilby's account:

> I debated this very often with myself thus: How do I know what God Himself judges in this particular case? It is certain these people either do not commit this as a crime; it is not against their own consciences reproving, or their light reproaching them. They do not know it be an offence, and then commit it in defiance of divine justice, as we do in almost all the sins we commit. They think it no more a crime to kill a captive taken in war, than we do to kill an ox; nor to eat humane flesh, than we do to eat mutton.[58]

The interpenetration of the familiar and the exotic, or of supposedly universal values and particular variables, is a consistent motif in Defoe's 'foreign' novels. Like Robert Boyle's careful experimental method in chemistry, however, Crusoe's consideration of the issue owes much to the tradition of casuistry, or the examination of cases of conscience, from earlier in the seventeenth century. Crusoe, after all, was born in 1632, and his early youth in the 1640s would have been spent during the time when such matters were everywhere the subject of public debate and private self-examination.[59]

Moreover, this interchange or internal moral dialogue in the novel is an analogy of the struggle between writing and experience, author and subject. For all the inventoried world of fact in *Robinson Crusoe*, it is at such moments of moral crisis that the novel most comes alive: the selling of Xury, the apparition of the devil, the footprint in the sand. One of the common objections to much of Defoe's fiction is that it is apparently disorganized or accords with no established structure or genre. And yet its structure surely reflects the inchoate nature of the experience being recounted: mapped and unmapped, known and unfamiliar, wondrous and horrific.

In the latter part of *Captain Singleton*, there are two occasions when apparently extraneous narratives are introduced. Both of them are about Europeans who have got lost or have been ensnared in other cultures. The first is the story that William the Quaker hears from a Japanese priest about English sailors marooned on the north side of Japan. The priest has with him a slip of paper on which one of these Englishmen had written '*We came from Greenland, and from the North Pole.*'[60] Here, then, is a text within a text within a text: the scrap of paper about a mythical polar route, the story of the lost sailors, and the pirate-world of Defoe's novel. But *how* do all these 'texts' mean, individually and in the context of one another? The inability of Singleton's crew to unravel the text they are presented with, or to rescue the sailors, stays in the novel as an analogy of the fiction at large, about how we are reading it.

The story of the lost men is compounded by William's fear that these men may never be rescued and may, perhaps, 'some time or other be murdered by the barbarous People [the Japanese], in Defence of their Idolatry'.[61] This story of apprehended barbarity, cruelty, and enslavement by treacherous foreigners returns to haunt Singleton's crew in the subsequent interpolated story of Captain Knox who, with his men, was deluded into coming ashore on what is now Sri Lanka. Separated from his crew and from his son, who escapes to tell the tale 20 years later, Knox represents (in William's citation of his story) a direct analogy of the danger in which Singleton's crew find themselves having run aground on that island. But the full story of Captain Knox is not interpolated in Defoe's text until after Singleton's crew have escaped the danger. This subsequent interpolation is a footnote to William's story, one that Singleton hears from a friend long after the events of the novel are over, and so is doubly interpolated. Moreover, Captain Knox's story takes up ten pages of the novel and concludes only a few pages before Singleton, in the novel's narrative sequence, resolves to give up his life of piracy and return to England.

This narrative, first published in 1681 and reprinted in John Harris's collection of travel writing, *Navigantium* (1705), is itself indebted to older forms of narrative, primarily the stories of exemplary and suffering piety represented in John Foxe's *Book of Martyrs* (1554) and its successors in nonconformist literature. Indeed, it seems not unlikely that Harris's narrative is indebted to another work derived from this tradition, John Bunyan's *Pilgrim's Progress* (1678).

What does all this mean? And how are we to understand the meaning of Captain Knox's story not only in the context of *Captain Singleton* but in relation to the contemporary story of Crusoe's isolation in the Caribbean? (Knox's capture happens in 1657; Crusoe is marooned in 1659.) Certainly both works exist in the context of what Edward Said calls 'orientalism'[62] – European demonization of the abroad – and both inhabit the melding of description and narration that had been a convention of travel writing since the sixteenth century.[63] But in both *Captain Singleton* and *Robinson Crusoe*, what is going on is more complex than that, whether in the ultimately inscrutable moral problem of cannibalism in *Crusoe* or in the dense narrative intertexuality of *Singleton*.

Crusoe's reflection raises moral questions that are not simply multi-cultural, but also reflect on the right of Europeans, even Englishmen, to pass judgement on one another. The two issues that he combines exemplify the extent of the moral dilemma: 'They think it no more a crime to kill a captive taken in war, than we do to kill an ox; nor to eat humane flesh, than we do to eat mutton.'[64] Whereas Europeans did not indulge in military cannibalism, it was not uncommon (though against military convention) for them to kill captives taken in war. These are just the issues that Montaigne had already raised in his famous essay on the subject written in the 1570s. What, then, is the narrative and moral effect of Crusoe's placing the killing of captives and cannibalism side by side? Here, too, we are a long way from the 'high priori road' either of Cartesian rationalism or the theoretical sciences which, after 1680, began to dominate the activities of the Royal Society. Ten years after *Crusoe*, Swift could turn the subject of cannibalism on the heads of European hypocrites by suggesting ironically, in *A Modest Proposal*, that the reasonable way to deal with the problem of over-population in Ireland was to eat the children.

Certainly with Defoe and Swift we are a long way from the sort of cultural triumphalism espoused by James Thomson in *The Seasons* in 1744. There the world of 'the branching Oronoque' is one blasted by a tyrannical sun that

<blockquote>
gives the gloomy hue
And feature gross – or, worse, to ruthless deeds.
Mad jealousy, blind rage, and fell revenge
Their fervid spirit fires.
</blockquote>

Thomson will have none of Behn's romantic idealism, Pope's tropical pastoralism, or even Crusoe's doubt:

<blockquote>
Love dwells not there,
The soft regards, the tenderness of life,
The heart-shed tear, the ineffable delight
Of sweet humanity: these court the beam
Of milder climes.
</blockquote>

<blockquote>
('Summer', 887–94)
</blockquote>

Crusoe's world, on the other hand, is one where nature, if fallen, is certainly less than damnable. 'So Nature rejoicing has shown us the way with innocent revels to welcome the day,' Purcell writes in his 'Birthday Ode for Queen Mary'[65] published in 1694, midway between the events of *Robinson Crusoe* and its publication. In Crusoe's casting up of his shipwrecked situation, positive outweighs negative as goodness does evil in Adam's vision in Book XII of *Paradise Lost*. Although island nature does not provide Eden's 'wilderness of sweets', it none the less offers 'abundance of cocoa trees, orange, and lemon, and citron trees'.

Within the same part of the Caribbean, the Bay of Campeche where Captain Singleton also eludes pursuit by the English navy, Behn had discovered a host of new butterflies and exotic woods 'of different colours, glorious to behold'. One of these woods was *Haematoxylon Campechianum*, commonly called 'logwood', a wood that provided a strong red dye and which was imported as a tree into Britain within 5 years of the publication of *Robinson Crusoe*.[66]

Even before *Oroonoko*, on 27 September 1681, John Evelyn wrote to William London in Barbados asking about 'an *Orange* of the most prodigious size' and inquiring about sugar, cinnamon, cloves, indigo, and nutmeg. Evelyn had himself had some foreign and exotic flower seeds which he had 'sowed and set, but with very little success' the previous spring.[67] Many of these imported trees and shrubs from America (North and South) changed the face of the English landscape: not simply such showy shrubs as the first rhododendrons (*Kalmia latifolia*), but trees on the scale of the white pine (*Pinus strobus*) and the tulip tree (*Liriodendron*). The famous botanical Bishop of London, Henry Compton, whose diocese included the whole of North America, introduced the first magnolia (*Magnolia virginiana*) and Dogwood (*Cornus amomum*) to be grown in England.[68] With such trees, gardens ceased to be an affair of walled enclosures and became instead the large landscapes (what Virgil called *ingentia rura* in *The Georgics*) which Marvell praised in 'Upon Appleton House' and Pope in his 'Epistle to Burlington'.

Gradually the wilderness (Milton's 'wild above rule or art') became the model for the garden, rebuking not only what Milton called 'nice Art | In Beds and curious Knots', but the notion that nature's profusion was not part of the garden. In the Preface to his *History of Plants* (*Historia Plantarum*, 1688), the pioneering botanist John Ray marvelled at the enormous botanical variety of the world which exploration was revealing. 'Who would believe that there is a botanical Europe in the middle of tropical India?' he wrote: mountains where on one side are palms, pepper and sugar cane, and on the other oaks, elms and pines. Here, in effect, was the material of his most famous work, *The Wisdom of God Manifested in the Works of Creation*, published in 1691.

This new nature suggested the possibility, pursued by many royal and noble menageries, as well as by Crusoe himself, of reconstructing Eden by assembling all the living things of the world.[69] Multitudinous beyond the ability of the old systems of botany and zoology to account for it, however, the nature of the new world also demanded a revised and expanded taxonomy. An enormously expanded botanical vocabulary could no longer simply be attached to familiar European classes or families of plants, although that is what John Ray was forced to do in the second volume of his *History of Plants*. Forty years later, James Thomson was still describing 'the living herbs, profusely wild' as 'beyond the power | Of botanist to number up their tribes'.[70]

Ray's inevitable Anglocentrism was compounded by his own isolation in rural Essex from many of the things that were happening in botanic gardens elsewhere in the country. He was not aware, for example, that the larch and the cedar of Lebanon had already been introduced into England. But he was also severely hampered by the confusion of names for plants among botanical writers; the old systems of classification had become virtually unworkable. Ray's contemporary, the legendary merchant-pirate Dampier, exemplified this problem when he wrote in the Far East: '*Esquisetum Novae Hollandiae frutescus foliis longissimis*, 'tis doubtful whether this be an *Esquisetum* or no.'[71] Even as late as the 1740s, what Linnaeus was to call '*Pinus strobus*' (white pine) was still known as '*Pinus Americana quinis ex uno folliculo setis longis tenuibus triquetris ad unum angulum per totam longitudinem minutissimis crenis asperatis*' ('The American pine with five long slender needles from a single triangular pod that comes to an angle along its entire length with extremely small uneven points.')[72]

Among the curiosities that fascinated Ray was the 'Jesuit's Tree', as Quinine (*Chincona*) was called, although he still thought of it as like a plum or a pomegranate, nor could he have foreseen how essential it would be to the further exploration of the malarial parts of the world.[73] Not all the materials of this brave new nature, however, came from North and South America. In the late seventeenth century Mary Capel, Duchess of Beaufort cultivated many exotics which had been imported from Africa and the Far East. So did her brother Henry, and Bishop Compton, who had contact with the East India Company and raised Chinese Sumac (*Rhus chinensis*) from seed sent to him. Many of these exotics came initially from the Dutch East India Company via Holland, but by the 1680s the popularity of such a work as the *Hortus Malabaricus* indicates the obsession with exotics of all kinds, as do the increasing reports of exotic botanical rarities in the *Philosophical Transactions* of the Royal Society.

Ray's account of his trip to the continent of Europe in the early 1660s, written just as Milton was finishing *Paradise Lost*, only comes alive in his lists of new genuses and species that he finds there. Like other contemporary botanists, Ray was confused about the correct names of many plants. At Messina, for example, he found a plant called *Fenugraeco sylvestri* (fenugreek) which others had called *Vicia Sesamacea Apulia*, but which he thought ought to be called *Glaux peregrina annua*.[74] His continental tour was an opportunity both to encounter a much greater range of plants than he had previously known and to enter the scientific world of the continent. 'I must confess,' he writes of the Philosophical Academy of Virtuosi in Naples,

> that I was not a little surprised to see such a Company of Learned Men, in a place, where I was of opinion, they would scarce allow a reasonable Latitude of Judgment; and I must give them their due, that they were not only acquainted with the best and most refined Authors of the immediately preceding Age, such as *Galileus à Galileo, Des Cartes, Gassendus, Harvey, Verulam* [Bacon] etc but also with those surviving in the present Age.[75]

Despite much that has been written about it, then, the Grand Tour of the late seventeenth and early eighteenth centuries was not simply about paintings, sculpture, and buildings. The indebtedness of such travel accounts as John Evelyn's to continental guides stressing the visual arts[76] has tended to obscure the many other things which interested travellers: political economy, law, medicine and anatomy, land management, plants, and the curiosities of science generally.[77] This is what Montaigne had recommended in his *Essais*, a recommendation which, in Charles Cotton's translation of 1685, sounds like a rebuke to the itineraries of many later English travellers:

> Conversation with men is of very great Use, and Travel into Foreign Countries is of singular Advantage; not to bring back (as most of our young Monsieurs do) an Account only of how many Paces *Santa Rotonda* is in Circuit; or of the Richness of *Signiora Livia*'s Attire; or, as some others, how much *Nero*'s Face, in a Statue in such an old Ruine, is longer and broader than that made for him at such an other Place: but to be able chiefly to give an Account of the Humours, Manners, Customs, and Laws of these Nations where he has been.[78]

John Locke's account of his tour to Paris in the late 1670s reflects this wide-ranging curiosity; it is full of accounts of mechanical inventions, medical experiments, and even of seeing a model of the moons of Jupiter. Excited though he was by the gardens of Versailles, he was more interested in the cabinets of curiosity and libraries of learned men.[79] Two decades later the famous hygienist, Martin Lister, was even more interested in gardens than Locke, but his travel account comes alive in the dissecting room:

> I went up, with my Lord Ambassador's Retinue, to see Mr. *Bennis*, who was in the dissecting Room, working by himself upon a Dead Body, with his Breast and Belly gutted ... And indeed, a private Anatomy Room is to one not accustomed to this kind of Manufacture, very irksome, if not frightful. Here Basket of Dissecting Instruments, as Knives, Saws *etc.* And there a Form with a Thigh and Leg flayed, and the Muscles parted asunder: On another Form an Arm served after the same manner: Here a Trey full of bits of Flesh, for the more minute Discovery of the Veins and Nerves; and every where such discouraging Objects.[80]

Lister was a physician, but his interest in the anatomy and the workings of the body was shared by a wide range of continental travellers. John Ray's travelling companion, Sir Philip Skippon, lists the British travellers whom he encounters, and the list is very extensive. Skippon seems as startled as Ray by the wide intellectual interchange already extant between English and Italian learning: that the Professors of Anatomy at Naples and of Humanities at Rome are English, and that the Professor of Law at Padua is a Scot. He also gives an account both of the Physic Garden at Padua, founded in 1545 and famous as a botanical resource, and of the work of

Aldrovandus at Bologna where he 'saw ten folio's of plants, curiously painted ... with other plants not described, [which] this apothecary intended to print in his catalogue of plants in his garden'.[81]

Just such paintings and prints of plants John Evelyn had seen in Rome in 1644, work which was to be assembled by the great Jesuit botanist, Giovanni Battista Ferrari, in his *Hesperides* (1646). Illustrated by engravings from works by Pietro da Cortona, Andrea Sacchi, Poussin, Guido Reni, and Lanfranco, *Hesperides* not only represents a considerable advance in botanical taxonomy but places the study within the world of humanism and the arts.[82] This Roman world of learning is also the one that Milton encountered. Ferrari's earlier work, *De Florum Cultura*, had been published in 1633 with the assistance of Francesco Barberini, one of the cardinals who were Milton's hosts in Rome in 1638. John Ray's visit to Italy was no less fruitful. Nearly half a century after Milton's trip, in his *History of Plants* (1686), he was to incorporate trees he had found on the continent that he had still not seen in England: the Venice sumach (*Rhus Cotinus*), the Judas tree (*Cercis Siliquastris*), which he had seen on the hills of Rome, the laburnum, which he had seen near Geneva, *Phillyrea Latifolia* (mock privet), which he had seen in Tuscany, and the oleander which he remembered finding on Mount Etna.[83]

Such gardens and catalogues not only required a wholesale rethinking of the nature of the plant world: they questioned the very concept of nature itself. In that sense, their effect was as disquieting as the astronomical discoveries of Kepler and Galileo earlier in the seventeenth century. A late-seventeenth-century reviewer of a book on the physic garden at Amsterdam expresses just this sense of wonder:

> This Work is none of the least *Specimens* of Modern Magnificence and Improvement in the History of Nature, which though she opens such Mines and Treasures, yet is never like to be exhausted. The *Art* of *Calcography* [engraving] has given to these Studies a new sort of life and Perspicuity; the Beauty and Graces whereof, have drawn many Illustrious Persons abroad, into a kind of Emulation who should excel in this Noble and most useful Ornament: What the *English* want in this Part, they have made up in their Critical Methods in their Discoveries of *Non Descript Species*, and in their judicious References to the Synonimous Names of various Writers, whereby the terrible Vices of Confusion and Multiplicity have been very much corrected.[84]

When Pope (in the *Essay on Criticism*) recommends that the writer 'follow nature', then, what his culture means by 'nature' is something radically different from the nature who 'paints her colours' in Book V of *Paradise Lost*. What Pope elsewhere calls 'the green myriads in the peopled grass' is the infinitely expanding nature of Pascal and Fontenelle.[85] A change in quantity has become a change in kind.

Pope's revisions of his concept of order – whether of man, his subject, or of his own poem – also reflect one of the radical impacts of continental travel: the concept of what constituted a garden. In *An Essay on Man*, where he first proposed 'a mighty maze of walks without a plan', he came instead to write, 'A mighty maze! but not without a plan.' Here, as in his prefatory remarks to *The Iliad* or in *An Essay on Criticism*, nature and Homer are the same, and the schoolboy confusion of *The Odyssey* and theodicy (a work demonstrating the attributes of God) is no longer a joke. In the 'wild nature' of the former, as in *Paradise Lost*, may be seen the manifestations of the latter.

By the early 1740s, when Pope was composing the fourth book of *The Dunciad*, the Grand Tour had become a travel agent's joke: a parade of brothels and operas and palaces where the young milord

> Dropt the dull lumber of the Latin store,
> Spoil'd his own language, and acquir'd no more;
> All Classic learning lost on Classic ground;
> And last turn'd *Air*, the echo of a sound.
>
> (IV. 319–21)

Classic ground was not, however, a joke for Joseph Addison when he went on his continental tour in 1701. Published as *A Letter from Italy* in 1703, Addison's poetic account is largely a search for just that classic ground, an attempt to read classical texts in the context of their original locations. He cites Claudian, Livy, and Lucan on the Apennines as if they had taught him to appreciate the beauty of those mountains. The Alps are the text in which sublimity can be read:

> Fired with a thousand raptures I survey
> Eridanus through flowery meadows stray,
> The king of floods! that rolling o'er the plains
> The tow'ring Alps of half their moisture drains.
>
> (15–28)[86]

Such a stance is a significant departure from his immediate predecessor in this genre, Gilbert Burnet. Not only did Burnet find the greatest Medici garden, Pratolino, 'no pleasure to walk in', and the Villa Borghese in Rome merely like 'an English Park', but he found the mountains only horrific: 'the vast ruines of the first World, which at the Deluge broke here into so many inequalities'.[87]

In this he was representative of most late seventeenth-century travellers, whose transit of the Alps was vertiginous to say the least. John Clenche, a decade earlier, had been similarly uninterested in Italian gardens; but his account of Mount Cenis (the usual point of crossing the Alps) shared Burnet's inability to see sublimity in landscape that was 'troublesome and horrid in respect of the rude Rock and Stones which lye as if there thrown and tumbled down the Hill'.[88] And William Bromley, crossing the much less formidable Apennines, wrote in 1692 of 'nothing but climbing Precipices, and dangerous craggy Hills to pass'.[89]

This attitude to what Shaftesbury was to call 'the horrid Graces of the *Wilderness*' was a commonplace one well into the eighteenth century; but Milton's phrase about Eden – 'wild above Rule or Art' – suggests that an aesthetic change was beginning to take place long before that. This change was rooted in the discovery of the concept of sublimity as outlined by the Greek writer commonly called Longinus. Even before his Italian trip in 1638, Milton had probably encountered Longinus through the work of his friend, the art historian Francis Junius;[90] but Longinus was not to become widely known in England until Boileau's translation into French of 1674. And even then, Boileau's sense of what Longinus meant by 'sublimity' was largely as a matter of style or even inspiration rather than something inherent in the subject itself.[91] Indeed, Pope's satire, *Peri Bathous, Or the Art of Sinking in Poetry* (1728), was an attack on the stylistic excesses that this rhetorical sort of sublimity inspired, as in Swift's 'Oratorial Machines' in *A Tale of a Tub*.

So it is not surprising that neither Celia Fiennes nor Daniel Defoe in their respective accounts of tours of England are enthusiastic for the sublimity of wild landscape as a subject. For Fiennes, the earlier account, 'the great hills interposeing' are at best a nuisance and at worst 'very terrible'.[92] And Defoe, even in his later tour, published in 1742, still sees mountains as the ruins of nature, as he had seen them 'dismal and frightful' in the earlier tour of 1727. 'Nothing can be more surprising of its Kind,' he writes of Chatsworth in Derbyshire in the later tour,

> to a Traveller, who comes from the North, when, after a tedious Progress thro' such a dismal Desart, on a sudden the Guide brings him to this Precipice, where he looks down from a comfortless, barren, and, as he thought, endless Moor, into a delightful Valley, and sees a beautiful Palace, adorn'd with Gardens.[93]

With respect to the wild terrors of mountainous landscape, Fiennes and Defoe might well have taken their cue from Charles Cotton's *Wonders of the Peake* (1681), a catalogue of marvels and horrors in the same Peak District of Derbyshire which concludes, similarly, with a contrasting description of Chatsworth. Cotton is in no doubt as to the grotesque discourse appropriate to such a tour:

> A *Country* so deform'd, the *Traveller*
> Would swear those Parts *Nature's Pudenda* were:
> Like *Warts* and *Wens*, Hills on the *one side* swell,
> To all but *Natives* Inaccessible.[94]
>
> (7–10)

It was for Pope's friend, the classicist Joseph Spence, to 'translate' into the English landscape from the continent the concept of sublimity, not as elevated thought or high style, but as subject. Mountains and wild places became, for him, Pope's 'grace beyond the reach of art': a concept that Shaftesbury and Addison had only glimpsed, and that most seventeenth-century travellers would have greeted with horror.

Although Spence's first visit to Italy in 1731 involved a frightening passage through the Alps, he was none the less able, unlike Burnet and Clenche, to imagine the mountain pass in terms of a ruined 'town with broken pillars and arched windows in a thousand parts of it' in which 'the cathedral of this town was built by nature'. Less than a decade later, in 1739, the Alps were for him no longer 'the formidable things they were when I was first acquainted with them' because the road had been improved; and crossing the Apennines in the following year, Spence (unlike Bromley) could rejoice in the 'fine remains of the Deluge' and write of the passage in almost magical terms:

> though I had some pains in it, 'twas fully made up in the pleasure I had of experiencing what it is to travel among the clouds, more strongly than ever I did before, either in the Apennines or the Alps.[95]

'Rocks and precipices beautiful when properly situated,' he was to write in 1752; and, probably recollecting the 'steep wilderness' and 'insuperable highth' of Eden in *Paradise Lost*, was to quote a friend's remark: 'God could never have been so bad a gardener as to have made Eden all on a flat.'[96] Inspired both by Pope's translation of the *Odyssey* (for which he wrote the notes) and by the mountainous vistas of Italy and engravings of the imperial Chinese garden at Yuan-ming-yuen,[97] Spence came to see wilderness not as it had been previously (something created artificially in a garden) but as something necessarily untamed, 'wild above rule or art'. Not only did he set about to incorporate views of a barren hill from his own garden into Miltonic 'woodie Theatre | Of stateliest view', but he wrote in 1752 of the landscape of Matlock in Derbyshire – 'an Alpine View of Rocky and Woody intersperst' – in a way that Defoe's *Tour* of a decade earlier would have found inconceivable.

Already by this time, however, others had echoed his preference for natural sublimity. In 1744 Joseph Warton contrasted the 'tortured waters' of Versailles to

> some pine-topped precipice
> Abrupt and shaggy, whence a foamy stream,
> Like Anio, tumbling roars.[98]

Five years later Burke was to publish his famous *Philosophical Inquiry into the Sublime and Beautiful*, a work that established major categories of aesthetic discourse for late-eighteenth-century thought. Like Hogarth, who published his *Analysis of Beauty* in 1753, however, Burke was not a pioneer in aesthetic theory. Hogarth's sense that all beauty consisted in the tension between geometric shape and serpentine line had been inscribed in the landscape gardens of England for nearly half a century before he canonized it as a precept. Similarly, the literal groundwork preceding Burke's recognition that sublimity consisted (among other things) in the unmeasurable and awesome had been discovered in Italy in the early eighteenth century and recognized even in the English landscape.

The year 1753 was also the date of publication for Linnaeus's *Species Plantarum*, the final keystone in the taxonomic building erected by Linnaeus over nearly half a century. More than anything, it represented the emplacement of system. In 1757 Sir John Hill, an eminent scholar of mosses and fungi, published his book *Eden* to acquaint gardeners and nurserymen with Linnaeus 'and to deliver his Method in such a Manner, that all may comprehend it'.[99] Hill's dedication to the Earl of Bute, the creator of the botanic garden at Kew, was even more grandiose in its ambition to rid the botanic world of folly and error, to plumb all the depths of nature, and to recreate Eden. Not everyone was so enthusiastic, however. The year after the publication of Linnaeus's book, the great amateur botanist, Peter Collinson, wrote to Linnaeus fearing the specialization of knowledge it implied and objecting that 'none but real professors can pretend to attain it'.[100]

Notes

1 London, Faber & Faber, 1975, p. 43.
2 *The Schoolmaster*, ed. Lawrence V. Ryan (Ithaca, NY: Cornell University Press, 1967), p. 66.
3 *The Essayes or Counsels, Civill and Morall* (London, 1625), pp. 101–2.
4 *Instructions to a Son* (Edinburgh, 1661), pp. 74–5.
5 *Advice to a Son* (Oxford, 1656), III. i., ii. pp. 58–9.
6 It is impossible to prove that Milton knew this plate, though his introduction to the Barberini household through its librarian suggests that he was likely to have been shown the more interesting books. A. R. Hall notes that the 'flea glass' was also popular among the members of the Royal Society in the early 1660s just before the publication of *Paradise Lost. The Scientific Revolution 1500–1800* (Boston: Beacon Press, 1966) p. 240.
7 'Cunning Stunts', *Art Forum* 30 (1991), p. 111.
8 See Mary Louise Pratt, *Imperial Eyes: Travel Writing and Transculturation* (London: Routledge, 1992).
9 In ll. 423–31 from 'Summer' (1744) and ll. 118–33 from 'Autumn' (1730), from *The Seasons*, James Thomson echoes this praise of imperial maritime destiny. The edition of Thomson used throughout this book is *The Seasons and The Castle of Indolence*, ed. James Sambrook (Oxford: Clarendon Press, 1991).
10 West's model was Rembrandt's 'Descent from the Cross', and the complexity of the subject is dealt with in Simon Schama's *Dead Certainties* (London: Granta, 1991), pp. 21–39. After 1760 the inclusion of 'Quebec' monuments in the landscaped gardens of England signified the consolidation of the Empire. In the copy of Gray's 'Elegy' that Wolfe had with him, the line 'the paths of glory lead but to the grave' is underlined.

11 Laura Brown believes that Pope's use of synechdoche in this passage 'serves to dismember the problem of imperialism', and that the poem 'consistently translates the political or military components of English mercantilism into "natural", pastoral phenomena'. *Alexander Pope* (Oxford: Basil Blackwell, 1985), p. 30. On the contrary, the 'pastoral phenomena' she refers to underline the hollowness of imperial promises. See also Simon Schama's treatment of the Indian in West's painting in *Dead Certainties*, pp. 31–2.

12 Strain i. 15; iii. 12; iv. 20–2.

13 *Gulliver's Travels and Other Writings*, ed. Ricardo Quintana (New York: Modern Library, 1958), p. 394.

14 *The Spectator*, 27 April, 1711. Simon Schama is wrong to state of the Iroquois in *Dead Certainties* that 'the Augustans saw [them] as repellent barbarity', p. 31.

15 *The Poems of Alexander Pope: A One-Volume Edition of the Twickenham Text with Selected Annotations* (London: Methuen, 1965), p. 210. R. P. Bond has explored this incident at length in *Queen Anne's American Kings* (Oxford: Clarendon Press, 1952).

16 John Harris, *Navigantium atque Itinerarium Bibliotheca* (London, 1705), ii. 928.

17 *Marvellous Possessions* (Oxford: Clarendon, 1992), p. 192, n. 36. English reception of Amerindian culture is not easy to trace apart from John White's early accounts of Virginia. Except for the *Jesuit Relations* (and only occasionally there) there is little European writing about what native peoples themselves believed.

18 'An Account of the Court and Empire of Japan Written in MDCCXXVIII', *Miscellaneous and Autobiographical Pieces, Fragments and Marginalia*, ed. Herbert Davis (Oxford: Blackwell, 1962), p. 99.

19 *Diary*, ed. E. S. de Beer (Oxford: Clarendon Press, 1955), iii. 374.

20 *Historia Plantarum* (1691), ii. None the less, virtually nothing was known of the coffee tree (*Coffea arabica*); in the British Library copy (433. g. 16) the contemporary botanist James Petiver writes, 'The Persians drink much of that Liquor thinking it allays natural heat and hinders the getting of children.'

21 Laura Brown sees this mercantilist catalogue of commodities as an attack on the fetishizing materialism of the Whigs. *Alexander Pope*, pp. 12ff. The disjunction that she notes between the rhetoric of heroic allusion and the triviality of its content could also be found a century earlier in Ben Jonson's poem 'On The Famous Voyage' (1616).

22 There is a danger in loading a vessel so light as *The Rape of the Lock* with more ore than it will bear, but it seems likely that part of Pope's satire is aimed precisely at the substitution of Chinese and Japanese *appearances* for the real question which these cultures raise of the relation between nature and art.

23 His essay 'Upon the Gardens of Epicurus' was written in 1685.

24 The preface to Pope's translation of *The Iliad* (1715) celebrated the poem as a garden untrammelled by the rules of art: 'a wild Paradise, where if we cannot tell the Beauties so distinctly as in an order'd Garden, it is only because the Number of them is infinitely greater' (Twickenham edn, London: Methuen, 1967, vii. 3). Although Pope dismissed Ambrose Phillips's translations of *Persian Tales* in his 'Epistle to Dr. Arbuthnot' (l. 180), they were widely popular as a form. Philips seems first to have been involved with the edition of 1714 called *The Persian and Turkish Tales Compleat*.

25 Pope uses this phrase in *The Dunciad* (iv. 471) to dismiss the mechanism of Descartes and others.

26 In fact the phrase had been used earlier both by Sir William Temple and by Thomas Warton the Elder.

27 *Forms of Nationhood: The Elizabethan Writing of England* (Chicago: University of Chicago Press, 1994), p. 153.

28 *A Collection of Voyages and Travels* (London, 1704), i. p. lxix.

29 *A Survay of the Signorie of Venice* (London, 1651), p. 3. This is also a theme in Otway's play *Venice Preserv'd* (1682).

30 Cited in Robert M. Schmitz, *Pope's Windsor Forest 1712: A Study of the Washington University Holograph* (Saint Louis: Washington University Studies No. 21, 1952), p. 44. Omitted in the 1713 version, these lines follow 'as in the Sea her Streams' (l. 362).

31 New York: Scribner's, 1953, p. 182.

32 'The Bubble', *Poems*, ed. Harold Williams (Oxford: Clarendon Press, 1958), i. 251–2. For Pope, 13 years later, the South Sea speculation was still a metaphor for wealth and ease, 'The Second Satire of the Second Book of Horace Paraphrased', ll. 133–4. The turnip-seller of an anonymous poem of 1720, called 'The Old Tur-p-Man's Hue – And – Cry After more Money', describes the huge fortune 'fled to France or Spain' and 'South-sea, like a treacherous Wh-re, | Cast only Pearls on Foreign shore.' See the thorough account by John Carswell, *The South Sea Bubble*, Stroud: Alan Sutton, rev. ed., 1993.

33 Sig. A2. Over half of John Ogilby's *America* (1671) is also about the Caribbean and South America.

34 Herman Moll, *A View of the Coast* (London, 1711), p. 5. Like many of them, Crusoe in the *Further Adventures* goes on to India and China.

35 *A View of the Coast*, pp. 1–2.

36 *An Account of several* LATE *Voyages and Discoveries* (London, 1711), sig. A.

37 Dampier's 1688 voyage is from *A Collection of Voyages* (London, 1739), i. p. 58. Cowley's 1683 account is contained in William Hacke, *A Collection of Original Voyages* (London, 1699), p. 41.

38 In *The Horse-Hoing Husbandry* (1733), Jethro Tull also claims that his work deals with 'Matters of *Fact* [that] are not like some stories told by *Travellers*, hard to be disproved if they are wrong.' sig. [B2v].

39 Dampier, *Voyages* i. p. 464. Cf. 'the most unpleasant Looks and the worst Features of any people I ever saw' iii. p. 102. Wafer's account of his 1681 expedition, *A New Voyage and Description of the Isthmus of America* is in *Voyages*, iii.

40 *The Voyages, Dangerous Adventures and Imminent Escapes of Capt. Rich. Falconer* (London, 1734). Sally Salisbury (also known as Mrs Sarah Prydden or Priddon) was a courtesan whose trial for murder in 1723 produced a flood of popular literature. The *Travels* of Sir John Mandeville (republished from a correct manuscript in 1725) are full of just the improbable fictions against which Falconer seeks to defend himself. Aware of the danger of criticism's taking on the literature of travel, Falconer tells the great critic of his time, John Dennis, to leave his book alone.

41 Ogilby also published a *Jamaica* in 1671.

42 *Oroonoko, The Rover and Other Works*, ed. Janet Todd (London: Penguin, 1992), p. 115.

43 *Captain Singleton*, ed. Shiv K. Kumar (Oxford: Oxford University Press – World's Classics, 1990), p. 51 Later in the novel, William the Quaker argues with his fellow crew-members to persuade them not to murder a shipload of slaves who appear to have murdered the Portuguese crew of their ship. The Law of Nature, he says, has justified them for 'the Injustice done them, to be sold for Slaves without their Consent', p. 157.

44 Ibid., p. 61. In a classic piece of raw vs cooked discrimination, Singleton observes that the enlightened 'Prince' teaches his men to desist from eating their meat raw.

45 Song VI p. 8.
46 London, 1715, sigs. [A6v], A10.
47 Compare Addison's apparently fictitious story of two 'Negroes and Slaves' whose love for the same woman led them to murder her and commit suicide: a story that supposedly happened in St Kitts c.1699, though no source of it has ever been found. Its function as a narrative seems to have been to illustrate 'what strange Disorders are bred in the Minds of those Men whose Passions are not regulated by Vertue and disciplined by Reason', *The Spectator*, No. 215 (6 Nov., 1711).
48 For a further discussion of the relation between slavery and feminism, and the relation of both to imperialism, see Laura Brown, 'The Romance of Empire: *Oroonoko* and the Trade in Slaves', in *The New Eighteenth Century: Theory, Politics, and English Literature* (London: Methuen, 1987), pp. 41–61, and Moira Ferguson, '*Oroonoko*: Birth of a Paradigm', *New Literary History*, 23 (1992), p. 339. Although I agree with Brown about the use of romance, I do not agree with her conclusions.
49 Caesar – Oroonoko is more than a noble savage. He is what in twentieth-century slang is called an 'oreo': black on the outside and white inside.
50 This is also the world that Ferdinand imagines in *The Tempest*. Francis Sparrey describes a very similar island in his account that precedes Shakespeare's play, *Some Observations on the Island of Trinidado* (1595–1602). Churchill, *Voyages*, p. 711.
51 *Windsor Forest*, ll. 409–10. Cf. the 'poor Indian' of *An Essay on Man* who, like the Indians described in *Oroonoko*, inhabit a 'happier island in the watry waste' (ii. 99–108).
52 *An Impartial Description of Surinam* (London, 1667), p. 23. Virgil's words are '*felix si bona norint*', *Georgics*, ii. 458.
53 *Barlow's Journal*, cited in Rediker, *Between the Devil and the Deep Blue Sea* (Cambridge: Cambridge University Press, 1987), p. 40.
54 Dorothy Osborne, *Letters to Sir William Temple*, ed. Kenneth Roberts (London: Penguin, 1987), letter 21, p. 80, letter 11, p. 62.
55 *Astrée*, p. 86. Much of the subsequent account set in Africa sounds like a combination of *The Arabian Nights* and a fairytale in the manner of Charlotte Bronte's 'Chronicles of Angria'. The controversy in the early 1670s surrounding Elkanah Settle's play, *The Empress of Morocco*, Dryden's attack on it, and the latter's own *Aureng-Zebe*, reflects the interest in oriental and African subjects in the decade before the publication of *Oroonoko* (but after its supposed events). See also Moira Ferguson, *Subject to Others: British Women Writers and Colonial Slavery, 1670–1834* (London: Routledge, 1992), p. 37.
56 *Essays of Michael Seigneur de Montaigne ... New rendred into English By Charles Cotton* (London, 1685), Chap. 30, i. 366. Montaigne's essay as a study in cultural relativism is an interesting precedent for Crusoe's reflections.
57 Ogilby also offers an inventory of Crusoe's domestic life: 'Trees for Dying, Joyners Work and Building', observations on how well barley and rye might prosper, and vine that grows wild and 'yet yields a very fair large grape', p. 436.
58 *The Life and Adventures of Robinson Crusoe* (Harmondsworth: Penguin, 1985), p. 177. Mandeville asserts a similar cultural relativism in his 'Search into the Nature of Society', in *The Fable of the Bees*: 'What Men have learned from their Infancy enslaves them, and the Force of Custom warps Nature, and at the same time imitates her in such a manner, that it is often difficult to know which of the two we are influenced by.' (Oxford: Clarendon Press, 1924), i. 331.
59 See G. A. Starr, *Defoe and Casuistry* (Princeton: Princeton University Press, 1971).
60 *Captain Singleton*, p. 202.
61 Ibid., p. 201.

62 Edward Said, *Orientalism* (New York: Pantheon, 1978).

63 See Mary Louise Pratt, 'Fieldwork in Common Places', in *Writing Culture: The Poetics of Ethnography*, ed. James Clifford and George Marcus (Berkeley: University of California Press, 1986), p. 33.

64 *Robinson Crusoe*, p. 177. As I write this, the newspapers in London raise the issues of a German Captain, Wilhelm Mohnke, who gave just such an order in 1940 (*Independent* 20 Jan., 1994, pp. 3, 19), and the shooting of captured prisoners in the rebellion in Ciapas in Mexico.

65 'Birthday Ode for Queen Mary', ed. Michael Tippett and Walter Bergman (London: Schott & Co., 1951). For a discussion of the changing English response to the natural world in the seventeenth century, see Keith Thomas, *Man and the Natural World* (New York: Pantheon, 1983), though it is a reflection of the Anglocentrism that I have been discussing that Thomas means 'English man' and 'the English natural world'.

66 In the second volume of his *Historia Plantarum* (p. 1737), also published in 1688, John Ray refers to the dye of Logwood as known to all the world.

67 *The Diary and Correspondence of John Evelyn*, ed. William Bray (London, 1859), iii. 258.

68 Among the rare trees in Compton's garden and at the Chelsea Physic Garden in 1684, Sir Hans Sloane listed New England Cedar, Bermuda Cedar, Jerusalem Pine, and Goa Cedar. *The Correspondence of John Ray*, ed. Edwin Lanchester (London: Ray Society, 1848), p. 157.

69 See John Prest, *The Garden of Eden: The Botanic Garden and the Recreation of Paradise* (New Haven: Yale University Press, 1981).

70 'Spring' (1728), ll. 222–4. Ray himself recognized that botanists would continue to have trouble with species of doubtful classification.

71 Churchill, *Voyages* (1729), iii. 111.

72 Although the White Pine had been introduced into England in the early seventeenth century, John Ray was unaware of its existence when he published the second part of his *Historia Plantarum* in 1688.

73 On 8 April 1686 Ray's friend, Tancred Robinson, wrote to Sir Hans Sloane, who was in Jamaica, 'They tell mee Dr Trapham hath the Jesuits Tree in his garden at Port Royall, you can soon clear that up.' British Library, Sloane MS 4036 fo. 32v. John Evelyn had already seen the tree in the Chelsea Physic Garden in the previous July.

74 Ray's *Observations, topographical, moral & physiological; ... with a catalogue of plants not native of England* was first published with the travel journal of his friend Francis Willughby in London in 1673. This version is from Harris, *Navigantium*, ii. 569.

75 Harris, *Navigantium*, ii. 568. For a discussion of the varying discourses of travel writing, see Mary Louise Pratt, 'Fieldwork in Common Places,' pp. 27–50.

76 For a good general account of the Grand Tour in this period, see John Stoye, *English Travellers Abroad* (rev. edn; New Haven: Yale, 1989). See also De Beer's notes in vol. i of *The Diary of John Evelyn*, and Edward Chaney, *The Grand Tour and the Great Rebellion: Richard Lassels and 'The Voyage of Italy' in the Seventeenth Century* (Centro Interuniversitario di Ricerche sul 'Viaggio in Italia', Moncalieri, Italy: Geneva: Slatkine, 1985).

77 For accounts of cabinets of curiosities, see William Schupbach, 'Some Cabinets of Curiosities in European Academic Institutions', and John Dixon Hunt, 'Curiosities *to adorn* Cabinets and Gardens', in *The Origins of Museums: The Cabinet of Curiosities in Sixteenth- and Seventeenth-Century Europe*, ed. Oliver Impey and Arthur MacGregor (Oxford: Clarendon, 1985). Between them, Ray and Skippon mention seeing such cabinets in Rotterdam, Heidelberg, Munich, Altdorf, Basle, Rome, Milan, Lyons, Nimes, and Paris.

78 *Essays of Michael Seigneur de Montaigne . . . New rendred into English By Charles Cotton* (London, 1685), Ch. 25, i. 251.

79 *Locke's Travels in France 1675–1679*, ed. John Lough (Cambridge: Cambridge University Press, 1953).

80 *A Journey to Paris in the Year 1698* (London, 1699), pp. 63–4. Lister went on to describe the dissecting room of Mr Merrie, where 'that which delighted my Curiosity, was the Demonstration of a blown and dried Heart of a *Foetus*'.

81 *An Account of a Journey Made Thro' Part of the Low-Countries, Germany, Italy and France,* Churchill, *Voyages* (1729), v. 531, 560.

82 See David Freedberg, 'Cassiano Dal Pozzo's Drawings of Citrus Fruits', *Il Museo cartacceo di Cassiano dal Pozzo: Cassiano Naturalista (Quaderno Puteani,* n.d.) i. 23.

83 Here, as above, I am indebted to C. E. Raven, *John Ray Naturalist* (Cambridge: Cambridge University Press, 1958), for guidance through the *Historia Plantarum.* Ray also made use of collections of dried plants, though he thought them inferior to living plants.

84 *Philosophical Transactions of the Royal Society,* 20 (1698), v, p. 29. The review of of *Hortus Medicus Amstelodamensis* is by Joannus Commelinus and others, with notes by the English botanist, James Petiver. The art of engraving had been promoted by John Evelyn in his *Sculptura* (1662), but John Ray (whose scrupulous search for plant synonyms is probably referred to here) had been unable to afford plates for his *Historia Plantarum* (1688). Writing to his friend Tancred Robinson in 1684, he complained that a history of plants without illustrations is like a book of geography without maps. *The Correspondence of John Ray,* ed. E. Lankester (London: Ray Society, 1848), p. 164.

85 See A. O. Lovejoy, *The Great Chain of Being* (Cambridge, Mass.: Harvard, 1936), although Lovejoy was indifferent to natural history. In *Man and the Natural World* Keith Thomas addresses this expansion of the vocabulary of the natural world, but not that of an infinitely receding system challenging the very idea of system itself.

86 In 1712, however, a correspondent in *The Spectator* (probably Addison's partner, Sir Richard Steele) deplored taking children abroad for this purpose (28 April, 1712; ed. D. W. Bond, iii. p. 369). Five years later Lady Mary Wortley Montagu was prompted by hearing children playing on reed pipes in Turkey to suggest that Addison might pursue his speculations about ancient instruments there, but not many English travellers went that far east until later in the century. Mary Wortley Montagu, *The Turkish Embassy Letters,* ed. Malcolm Jack (London: Virago, 1993), Letter 31, p. 74.

87 *Some Letters Containing An Account of What Seemed Most Remarkable in Switzerland, Italy etc.* (Rotterdam, 1686), p. 14.

88 *A Tour in France and Italy Made by an English Gentleman, 1675* (London, 1676), p. 24.

89 *Remarks in the Grande Tour of France and Italy* (London, 1692), p. 12.

90 Junius's work on the paintings of classical antiquity, *De Pictura Veterum* (1638), would have instructed Milton in how to approach such 'sublime' sites as Vesuvius and the Alps on his trip in that year, which were to enter his visual imagination and reappear in *Paradise Lost.*

91 Marjorie Hope Nicolson's account of the rise of the concept of sublimity in nature, *Mountain Gloom and Mountain Glory* (Ithaca, NY: Cornell University Press, 1959), cites little before Burke's *Philosophical Inquiry into the Sublime and Beautiful* (1757).

92 *The Illustrated Journey of Celia Fiennes 1685–c.1712,* ed. C. Morris (London: Macdonald & Co., 1982), pp. 167, 168.

93 *Tour Through the Whole Island of Great Britain*, 1742 [?] i. 126 and iii. 93. The *Tour* was first published in 1724–6 and republished after Defoe's death, with expansions, in 1742. A later version in 1753 exaggerates the element of surprise and adds a poem on the subject.

94 *The Wonders of the Peake* (1725: 4th edn), 7–10.

95 *Joseph Spence: Letters from the Grand Tour*, ed. Slava Klima (Montreal: McGill-Queens University Press, 1975), pp. 69, 223, 325.

96 *Observations, Anecdotes, and Characters of Books and Men* (Oxford: Clarendon, 1966), i. 1070, 1078, pp. 409, 411. Spence's friend was rebuking the claim of another Burnet, Thomas (in his *Telluris Theoria Sacra* [*The Sacred Theory of the Earth*], 1681) that the earth at the Fall ceased to be flat and was deformed into mountains.

97 Spence knew Yuan-ming-yuen only through engravings, but even his sense of Italian mountains was modulated by the paintings of them by Gaspar Poussin and Salvator Rosa.

98 *The Enthusiast*, ll. 29–31, in *The New Oxford Book of Eighteenth-Century Verse*, ed. Roger Lonsdale (Oxford: Oxford University Press, 1984), p. 389. Some of the vocabulary of such poems can be found in such poems of prospect as John Dyer's 'Grongar Hill' (1726) or Sir John Denham's 'Cooper's Hill' (1642), to which Pope's *Windsor Forest* was indebted. Such poems, however, have other (frequently political) agendas, like James Thomson's imperial prospect of the world in 'Summer' (ll. 690–783). See also James Turner, *The Politics of Landscape* (Oxford: Blackwell, 1979).

99 *Eden* (London, 1757), p. 3.

100 *Correspondence of Linnaeus and Other Naturalists*, ed. Sir James E. Smith (London, 1821), i. p. 31.

|4|

The Garden of the World
Erewhile: Husbandry,
Pastoral, and Georgic

The myths of discovery and possession that animated the literature of travel were intimately connected with changing attitudes to domestic landscape as well, and not least to the possession of agricultural land and its uses. What Bacon saw as a vast empire of knowledge beyond the Pillars of Hercules contained also the whole arena of learning, including the revived science of agriculture and its significance for the creation of a social utopia.

Adam and Eve's life in Milton's Eden signals the end of the pastoral myth of idle pleasure in English literature. In *Paradise Lost*, even before the Fall, their life consists of agricultural and horticultural tasks; occupations which Adam is prompt to point out to Eve are not 'irksome toil' but 'pleasant labour'. Unfallen Eden is a place for their 'rural work':

> Among sweet dewes and flours; where any row
> Of Fruit - trees overwoodie reached too far
> Thir pampered boughs, and needed hands to check
> Fruitless imbraces: or they led the Vine
> To wed her Elm; she spous'd about him twines
> Her mariageable arms, and with her brings
> Her dowr th'adopted Clusters, to adorn
> His barren leaves.
>
> (V. 212–19)

By the time of the poem's publication (1667), this celebration of husbandry as a spiritual occupation was a commonplace, and it remained so into the early eighteenth century. Samuel Collins entitled his 1717 book about fruit trees *Paradise Retriev'd*; William Ellis wrote of 'the Vegetable World' as 'an elegant Feast to the Soul, as well as to the Senses of Mankind' in 1736;[1] and Richard Neve, writing under the pseudonym 'T. Snow' in 1702, claimed:

That the *Holy - Ghost* himself, has been pleased to Honour this
Science; not only in appointing *Adam* the Practice of it, even when he
was in *Paradice*, Gen. 2. 15. But also in the History of the First
Monarchs of the World, from *Adam* to *Noah*; there is nothing of their
Actions mention'd, but only that they lived so long, and taught their
Posterity Husbandry, *etc.*[2]

Sir Hugh Plat's popular work on gardening and agriculture was called *The
Garden of Eden*. It had been published in 1653, the same year as Ralph
Austen's *A Treatise of Fruit Trees*: a book dedicated to the greatest of the
agricultural reformers, Samuel Hartlib, the man to whom Milton also
dedicated his essay, *Of Education* (1644). Austen was in no doubt about the
connection between fruit-growing and spiritual perfection:

> God, who is wisdome it selfe; says that a *Garden of Fruit-trees* was the
> meetest place upon all the Earth for *Adam* to dwell in, even in his state
> of perfection . . . *Augustin* [St Augustine] is of opinion, that this *dress-
> ing of the Garden*, was as well an exercise of the hand, as of the mind,
> not with toylesomeness and trouble, but with delight and pleasure.[3]

Austen's position here represents more than a strong strain of
Commonwealth piety. It also reflects the position of the group of scholars,
organised in the late 1640s in Oxford, who were later instrumental in the
founding of the Royal Society. Established by John Wilkins, a future bishop,
the group included Henry Oldenburg (the Society's future Secretary),
Robert Boyle, William Petty (the founder of political economy), John Locke,
and Christopher Wren, the future architect. Strongly influenced by the work
of Sir Francis Bacon earlier in the century, they saw the possibility of restoring Eden by reforming agriculture, not least through the cultivation of
orchards. Austen exalts this labour when he says, 'Adam in the time of his
Innocency *was imployed in this part of* Husbandry *about Fruit-trees . . . But
when he had sinned, he was put from this worke to till the ground, a lower
and inferior labour*.'[4]

Austen's position and discourse were shared by a large number of writers
on agriculture in the period, many of them associated with the correspondence exchange organized by Austen's dedicatee, Samuel Hartlib. John
Worlidge, who published his *Systema Agriculturae* the year after *Paradise
Lost*, wrote: 'Mr. *Hartlib* in his Legacy tells you of the benefits of Orchard-
fruits, that they afford curious walks for pleasure.'[5] Hartlib himself, in *The
Reform'd Spiritual Husbandman*, expressed the hope that 'such as reap an
earthly crop by my Communications' may 'contribute something towards
the sowing of a heavenly Seed'.[6] And Adolphus Speed also makes Austen's
point about the pleasure of gardening (a pleasure that Eve does not seem to
understand in Book IX) in his *Adam out of Eden* (1659):

> How excellent and how innocent the art of *Husbandry* is, has been
> sufficiently made out by the best of *Authors*; *God* himself, who chose

out that employment for the best of the Creatures, *Man*, whom he placed in *Eden*, not only to *enjoy*, but to labour, without both which no place can be a *Paradise*.[7]

In his book on herbs, *The Art of Simpling*, William Coles makes similar claims for agriculture as spiritual instruction:

> It was not so much for *Adams* recreation, who at that time was not acquainted with wearinesse, as it was for his Instruction, but to us it will serve for both. There is not a Plant which growes but carries along with it the legible Characters of a Deity, . . . And if the outward senses be so delighted, the inward will be so too, it being as it were, the School of Memory and Fancy. Hereupon it was that the antient Poets did so much extoll the Gardens of *Alcinous* and the *Hesperides*.[8]

In his *Systema Agriculturae* (1675), John Worlidge adopted the discourse of Wilkins's circle – their interest in hieroglyphs and universal signs – to praise these gardens as 'Hyeroglyphically and Philosophically representing unto us the Summary of eternal Atchievements or Enjoyments.'[9] And two years later, like Coles, he claimed that 'the Original of Gardens was from a Divine Hand', and reconciled this in a traditional humanist way to the gardens of antiquity.[10]

Coles was also in no doubt about the relevance of Adam's lesson to his own readers:

> By this time I hope you will thinke it no dishonour to follow the steps of our Grandsire *Adam*, who is commonly pictured with a Spade in his hand, to march through the Quarters of your Garden with the like Instrument, and there to rectifie all the disorders thereof.[11]

Austen, Coles, Plat, Speed, and Hartlib were all part of that movement within the English Revolution which saw the millenium not in terms of the Last Judgement but in the economic and social reform of society. At its most extreme, this position was represented by the Diggers, a proto-communist sect whose appropriation of common land for cultivation was an early form of arable enclosure. In his *A Vindication of . . . Diggers* (1650) Gerard Winstanley wrote:

> First, let every one that intends to live in peace, set themselves with dilligent labour to Till, Digge, and Plow, the Common and barren Land, to get their bread with righteous moderat working, among all moderat minded people.[12]

John Beale, an Anglican clergyman who had been deprived of his parish in the Interregnum, was also in favour of this sort of enterprise. A friend of John Evelyn and a participant in Hartlib's scheme for exchanging agricultural information, Beale wrote in spiritual terms of gardens as part of a larger agriculture:

We do commonly devise a shadowy Walk from our Gardens through our Orchards (which is the richest, sweetest, and most embellish'd Grove) into our Coppice Woods or Timber Woods. Thus we approach the resemblance of Paradise, which God with his own perfect Hand had appropriated for the delight of his innocent Masterpiece.[13]

Eden, in other words, was not a place of idle pleasure but of rewarding labour.

This was the common discourse of the writers whose efforts led to the formation of the Georgical Committee which was very active in the early years of the Royal Society just as Milton was finishing *Paradise Lost*. The language of Milton's Eden, in other words, arises from this georgic discourse. It also participates in the general turning away from a pastoral mythology that had become identified with the corruptions of the Stuart court: a decorative style suitable for seductions. And this is, indeed, just how Milton uses pastoral to describe Satan entering Eden to seduce Eve: as a city gent prepared, like Lady Wishfort in Congreve's *Way of the World*, Marie Antoinette, or some latter-day Laura Ashley, to play at being in the country, but to do so with seductive intent:

> As one who long in populous City pent,
> Where Houses thick and Sewers annoy the air,
> Forth issuing on a Summer's Morn to breathe
> Among the pleasant Villages and Farmes
> Adjoind, from each thing met conceaves delight,
> The smell of Grain, or tedded Grass, or Kine,
> Or Dairie, each rural sight, each rural sound;
> If chance with Nymphlike step fair Virgin pass,
> What pleasing seemd, for her now pleases more,
> Shee most, and in her look summs all Delight.
> Such Pleasure took the Serpent to behold
> This Flourie Plat, the sweet recess of *Eve*
> Thus earlie, thus alone.
>
> (*Paradise Lost*, IX. 445–57)

The contorted syntax and occasionally faltering scansion in this passage reveal the meretricious appeal of ersatz pastoralism. This is also the pastoral that Milton deploys ironically in *Comus*, where the seducer imagines the Lady as a wood nymph and she, deluded by his spells, imagines him to be a 'gentle Shepherd'. But Satan is also like an urban speculator or city moneylender; he sees Eden only as a place of 'narrow limits' in need of development. Associated with a city of 'Houses thick and Sewers', he comes from the world of the urban pollution that John Evelyn had attacked in the previous decade.[14]

Satan is a modern version of the Aufidius of Horace's ironic second epode, 'Beatus ille'. Aufidius knows all the vocabulary of country retirement, but to him it is no more than a fashionable reverie. At the end of the poem he dismisses the notion of buying a farm and puts his money back out at interest. His catalogue of the blessings of the country is as empty as the real-estate jargon of Toad's 'desirable country residence' in The Wind in the Willows. Theirs is a landscape of vignettes: a Disneyland countryside where no real labour appears to be taking place and milkmaids are there for the taking, as Beau Didapper thinks Fanny is at the end of Joseph Andrews.

This, indeed, is the way this pastoral myth continued to survive in many eighteenth-century poems and paintings:[15] the sort of pastoral represented by the poems of Ambrose Philips which Pope mocked. In fact, as Pope must have known, such 'Watteau-pastoralism' had nothing to do with the Virgilian original, where only one of the Eclogues was set in Arcadia, and all of them resonate with the life of a fallen world. In 1653 Dorothy Osborne (the wife of Swift's first patron) went and sat with the shepherdesses on the common adjacent to her family's house, Chicksands in Bedfordshire. Seeing their lives at first hand, she liked to think of them as 'Ancient Shepherdesses' she said, but she found 'a vaste difference there.'[16] between ancient writers and modern practice.

Similarly, Pope's early friend, Lady Mary Wortley Montagu, travelling to Turkey with her husband in 1717, was charmed by what she thought a living pastoral where boys still garlanded their lambs with flowers as they did in the time of Theocritus. In a letter to Pope, she made clear that she had no illusions that this was an appropriate subject for English pastorals. English boys would be more likely to take up 'cudgel playing and football', she observed drily. Her belief that 'Threshing and churning' were the proper subjects for English pastoral[17] cannot have endeared her to Pope, who had stated that pastoral 'consists in exposing the best side only of a shepherd's life and concealing its miseries'. Pope thought Theocritus had erred in introducing reapers into pastoral, and that his swains were 'abusive and immodest, and perhaps too much inclining to rusticity'.[18] The gentility implicit in this stance is even truer of Philips.

Philips sees the pastoral world from a genteel distance. In his 1726 poem to Lord Carteret on his leaving Ireland, he refers to his own verses as 'the voice of nature, undebas'd by skill', but his Pastorals suggest that he had little sense of skill, ironic or otherwise. Addressing the Earl of Dorset at the beginning of his 'First Pastoral', he sets his own deployment of the pastoral mode in just the context of rural excursion that Milton had used so ironically to describe the entrance of Satan:

> If we, O Dorset, quit the city throng
> To meditate in shades the rural song
> By your commands; be present: and, O bring
> The muse along! the muse to you shall sing.[19]

Like many an unskilful imitator of Milton's epic diction, moreover, Philips makes the mistake of using the Latinate inversions of epic in a lyric and often in order to enforce a rhyme.

Marvell's popular spoof of this kind of poetry, 'A Dialogue Between Thyrsis and Dorinda', however, led the way for a number of subsequent parodies of the pastoral.[20] Of these, the best known is John Gay's series called *The Shepherd's Week*, where the realist world of country labour makes short work of the convention; an attack on Philips masquerades as a burlesque of Virgil:

> *Marian*, that soft could stroak the udder'd cow,
> Or lessen with her Sieve the Barley Mow.[21]

There seems little doubt that Gay was also parodying the work of Thomas D'Urfey, a popular-ballad poet whose reduction of the rural to the comic-rustic had also been mocked by other members of the so-called 'Scriblerians': Matthew Prior, Thomas Parnell, and Swift. Indeed, Pope was to identify Philips with D'Urfey in his poem 'Sandys's Ghost Or, A Proper New Ballad on the New Ovid's Metamorphoses'. In this poem the subject of metamorphosis seems an appropriate venue for the way in which D'Urfey has changed into Philips and pastoral has been subverted. Their work, says Pope, 'shall like *Persian* Tales be read, | And glad both Babes and Nurses.' [22]

But even Pope was unable to reanimate pastoral. The subject of rural retirement which he invokes in his first pastoral, 'Spring', to praise Sir William Trumbull is in fact a georgic theme:

> *You*, that too Wise for Pride, too Good for Pow'r,
> Enjoy the Glory to be Great no more,
> And carrying with you all the World can boast,
> To all the World illustriously are lost.
>
> (7–10)

In light of the rumours that clouded Sir William's retirement from public office less than a decade earlier (accusations that he had not resigned but been dismissed), the second line of this passage has an ambiguous irony. In a similar (and possibly earlier) address to Sir William in *Windsor Forest*, moreover, the trope of retirement itself compounds this ironic note:

> Happy the Man whom this bright Court approves,
> His Sov'reign favours, and his Country loves;
> Happy next him who to these shades retires,
> Whom Nature charms, and whom the Muse inspires.
>
> (235-8)

'Happy the man' is Horace's '*Beatus ille*': the opening words of a poem ostensibly in praise of retirement that turns sardonically on its subject.[23] If pastoral was a difficult subject in the first decade of the eighteenth century then, by 1750 pastoral itself was a form that, as Dr Johnson said of Milton's *Lycidas*, had become 'easy, vulgar and therefore disgusting'.[24]

Pope's praise of the country estate in his *Moral Epistles* makes use and fruitfulness central subjects, but it is never entirely clear how they are so in his poems. He deploys the landed mythology of the seventeenth-century country-house poem as a contrast to the vulgarity of the new-made money of Timon or Sir Balaam. His 'Neighbours glad' and 'chearful Tenants' come from the world of Jonson's poem 'To Penshurst' to rebuke the useless fountains and the sterile grandeur of modern luxury. But the argument for the former depends largely on the absurdity of the latter; like the pleasing variety Pope recommends in landscape design, it depends upon a rhetorical heuristics of contrast.

What this process conceals is the radical change in agricultural practice that gives the lie to his use of older agricultural mythology. In the first place, Richard Boyle, Lord Burlington's acres were no more ancestral than Bathurst's; but, more importantly, the rural culture of custom and use and interdependency that Jonson celebrates in 'To Penshurst' had long since been displaced by what Locke had recommended: an agriculture of 'land-lord, capitalist tenant farmer, and laborer, each respectively living on rents, profits, and wages'.[25]

'For Locke or Milton 'tis in vain to look,' Pope wrote of the Gatsby-ish library of Timon, where the bindings were everything and the contents nothing. Given Locke's hostility to commerce and his endorsement of agriculture as the true capitalist model, this is a more significant moment than has been noted. Locke collected nearly a thousand botanical specimens from the Oxford Physic Garden and had a large library of just the seventeenth-century writers on agriculture that I have referred to above. His 'grand tour' of France (1675–9), as noted in Chapter 3, included many observations on agriculture, and he subsequently wrote extensively on the subject. Indeed, he owned vast amounts of land in south-west England, and he put his agricultural knowledge to use at Oates, an estate owned by his friend Lord Masham near London. There, where he spent his last days, he was an enthusiastic gardener and particularly pleased with his apple trees, some of which he gave to Pope's early mentor, Sir William Trumbull.[26] He gave agricultural advice as well to his friend Edward Clarke, for whom he also wrote *Some Thoughts Concerning Education*. For Clarke's estate at Chipley, Locke bought sheep in Holland, and he advised him on planting his walks with trees.

Locke's agricultural economics were not merely theoretical, in other words; his estates were a better example of use sanctifying expense than anything that Boyle or Bathurst (celebrated in Pope's *Moral Epistles*) had done. Both his theory and practice, then, could provide a way of restoring Milton's '*Eden*, vanish'd now so long' (as Pope invoked it at the beginning of *Windsor Forest*) and allowing dispossessed Adam, the tenant-farmer, to return. Pope's neo-georgic takes up the tone of the end of Milton's epic: the possibility of restoration.

In Book X of *Paradise Lost*, Milton's georgic Eden – that 'Fabrick wonderful | Of absolute perfection' – is displaced by the commercial empire of Satan. Like the seventeenth-century military supplier (or 'suttler' – the comparative of an adjective Milton uses of Satan) of the Thirty Years War, Mother Courage, Sin, and Death come as macabre camp-scavengers to a scene of slaughter looking for spoils. And before doing so they build a commercial bridge 'for intercourse | Or transmigration': a building work that involves a 'Mole immense', that is, a huge pier to protect the building works from the sea of chaos.

Just such an immense mole had been built in 1662 to protect the harbour of the port of Tangier – a port which the English had just acquired through Charles II's Portuguese marriage – from Barbary pirates. 'Our main design in putting ourself to this great charge for making this addition to our Dominions,' said the Royal Commission to Lord Peterborough, the first Governor, was 'to gaine our Subjects the Trade of Barbary and to enlarge our Dominion of that Sea.'[27] The instrument of this possession was the navy under the command of Lord Sandwich, a former Parliamentarian now ennobled thanks to his conversion to the royalist cause.

Is it entirely an accident that Satan, another turncoat, is first seen in Book I equipped in the manner of the new navy of Charles II?

> His Spear, to equal which the tallest Pine
> Hewn on *Norwegian* hills, to be the Mast
> Of some great Ammiral, were but a wand.
> (I. 292–4)

Satan's 'wand', in other words, is like the mast of the flagship of the fleet, the sort of ship in which Sandwich sailed. And, like the ships of Charles II's newly reconstituted Royal Navy, it came from Norwegian timber suppliers.

Satan's enterprise is also cast within the discourse of trade. Replete with allusions to eastern riches and in the context of a Turkish assembly ('divan'), Satan offers to his 'Plutonian' host a realm gained by deceit: 'without our hazard, labour or allarme'. And over this 'Infernal Empire' Sin and Death, as mercantile plenipotentiaries, are to 'Dominion exercise', just as the father of Pope's friend, the Earl of Peterborough, did at Tangier.

The conclusion of *Windsor Forest* picks up Milton's lost Eden in its play with the slippage from georgic to commercial and imperial: a slippage that takes the reader from *The Georgics* to *The Aeneid*. And a similar slippage from the 'milky heifer' to 'Imperial Works' occurs in the 'Epistle to Burlington'. William Benson, who had translated two books of *The Georgics* a decade before Pope published his 'Epistle to Burlington', was not alone in thinking *The Aeneid* an inferior work because it had been written only to please the Emperor Augustus. *The Georgics*, on the other hand, seemed to prophesy a constitution like Britain's after the 'Glorious Revolution' of 1688.[28] Where then did this leave Richard Boyle, Earl of Burlington, a man ostensibly associated with the Whig cause of parliamentary democracy but apparently engaged in the 'Imperial Works' of kings?

Windsor Forest's invocation of *Paradise Lost*, in other words, suggests the irony of imperial works, where such works both in Book X and in the building of Pandaemonium in Book I are Satanic. Indeed, the 'straw-built citadel' of the Carthaginian bees at the end of Book I is just the image that Bernard Mandeville was to invoke in *The Fable of the Bees* (1714). 'Private Vices, Public Benefits' was the subtitle of Mandeville's founding work of commercial theory in this post-lapsarian world.

This is the very world that Milton's disconsolate Adam sees more and more despairingly stretching off into future history in the last two books of the epic. The future which Adam sees extends beyond Pope's time to the Last Judgement, but it also includes at least one notable instance of 'imperial works': the building of the Tower of Babel, a passage in which are Michael's memorable words, 'Man over men I He made not Lord; such title to himself I Reserving' (XII. 70–2).

How then are we to read this ostensibly triumphant conclusion to *Windsor Forest*, and what is the force of its echo twenty years later in the conclusion of 'The Epistle to Burlington'? In addressing Lord Burlington, the poetic voice metamorphoses a georgic subject ('the milky heifer and deserving steed'), first into a forest, then into commerce, and finally into 'Imperial Works'.[29]

> His Father's Acres who enjoys in peace,
> Or makes his Neighbours glad, if he increase:
> Whose cheerful Tenants bless their yearly toil,
> Yet to their Lord owe more than to the soil;
> Whose ample Lawns are not ashamed to feed
> The milky heifer and deserving steed;
> Whose rising Forests, not for pride or show,
> But future Buildings, future Navies, grow:
> Let his plantations stretch from down to down,
> First shade a Country, and then raise a Town.
>   (181–90)

But this transformation can only be done by a poetic sleight of hand in which, like the use of the word 'heritage' in our own time, a new wine is poured into an old bottle in order to dress it up. In the process of creating the architecture of a modern commercial empire, Boyle is first invested with the mantle of Jones and Palladio and then becomes like the ancient Roman architect Vitruvius.

> You too proceed! make falling Arts your care,
> Erect new wonders, and the old repair;
> Jones and Palladio to themselves restore,
> And be what'er Vitruvius was before;
> Till Kings call forth th'Idea's of your mind,
> Proud to accomplish what such hands design'd.
>
> (191–6)

Keeping in mind that Satan's first title after the Fall is 'prime Architect', a title given to him by Sin, we might well wonder quite what the resonance of Burlington's intended public works is meant to be, not least in the context of Sin and Death's major public benefaction: the building of the bridge from hell to earth. Pope's 'Arch' and 'Mole' seem ominously close to that founding enterprise 'over the foaming Deep high archt', if indeed the mole does not invoke what turned out to be the disastrous folly of the Mole at Tangier:[30]

> Bid Harbours open, public Ways extend,
> Bid Temples, worthier of the God, ascend;
> Bid the broad Arch the dangerous Flood contain,
> The Mole projected break the roaring Main;
> Back to his bounds their subject Sea command,
> And roll obedient Rivers through the Land:
> These Honours, Peace to happy Britain brings,
> These are Imperial Works, and worthy Kings.
>
> (191–204)

In fact Boyle never became the public benefactor that Pope celebrates. For that matter, even the private things for which Pope seeks to praise him were not true at Burlington's Chiswick estate. Not content with his father's acres, Burlington proceeded to extend his estate: not to provide for 'cheerful tenants', however, let alone to provide grazing for cows or horses. Nor were the woody plantations of Burlington's vast new gardens designed to provide timber for the navy.

Important questions, moreover, go begging in this dazzling bit of transformation. In what mood are these last twenty-four lines: the interrogative, the indicative, the conditional, or the imperative? Coming as they do after the Timon portrait in which squandered wealth becomes the Mandevillean 'charitable Vanity' that clothes the poor and feeds the hungry, these lines make a rather baffling affirmation. If agriculture leads to commerce, how is the former innocent of the vices of the latter or, to put it another way, why is Timon's 'charity' less valid than the idealized landlord of these lines?

And what does the phrase 'you too proceed!' (addressed to Boyle) mean if the preceding ten lines are only a conditional dependent on the somewhat belated word 'let'? Does the 'too' mean that Boyle's 'proceeding' is equally dependent on a series of conditions, conditions that are nowhere spelled out in his case? Does it mean 'like him, you' or 'in like (conditional) manner, you'? The Scheherezade of those 'Persian Tales' to which Pope compared bad pastoral could not have done a better job of concealing while appearing to reveal.

Like Lady Mary Wortley Montagu, who became fascinated by the Persian Tales when she went to Turkey in 1717,[31] Swift was also attracted by them and plundered them for *Gulliver*. Like her, he was also an affirmer of agricultural values. In fact, he understood more about the subject than Pope, and wrote a number of pamphlets dealing with the reform of agriculture in Ireland.[32] Indeed, Swift's relentless attacks on D'Urfey only make sense if D'Urfey signifies the reduction of the serious subject of the georgic to the comic stuff of tavern ballad. In the hands of Gay, though, georgic came to mean one thing for the landowner and another for the labourer. In his *Rural Sports* (1713) , Gay turns away from the 'Swains with fainting hands' to lay his limbs 'on the Mossy Couch' shaded by beech and oak. His is still the privileged world of pastoral prospect.

James Thomson's *The Seasons*, composed between 1726 and 1730, comes out of this revised georgic tradition. Written very much in the shadow of *Paradise Lost*, its 'epic' subject is the landscape, and especially the working landscape of agriculture that was, for him, part of national destiny. But Thomson's descriptive and didactic blank verse has none of the dramatic irony and complex prosody of Milton's, let alone the implosive (and elusive) force of Pope's couplet. Milton, moreover, sees his theodicy from the point of view of fallen nature; the georgic harmony of Eden is 'since wild'. For Thomson, however, the idyll of Virgil's georgic world is recoverable through industry and co-operation; the poet, like unfallen Adam, is one of 'the observers of a prospect, in which others are merely objects'.[33] Even the master's 'luxury profuse' (*Autumn*, 356) can be reconciled to a myth of progress: one in which 'georgic' has come to mean what Gay means by it.[34]

In the two years preceding the publication of *Winter* (the first of Thomson's *Seasons*), William Benson published his translation of the first two books of the *Georgics* under the title *Virgil's Husbandry, or an Essay on the Georgics*. Among other things, Benson's work was an attack on Dryden's translation of Virgil's poem, a translation that Benson thought had misunderstood and debased the original by gentrifying and abstracting it.

In fact, Benson's book was part of a larger debate about Virgil and agriculture that went back to the mid-seventeenth century and that continued to animate such novelists as Fielding and Smollett in their descriptions of the English landscape. One of the central Virgilian texts, *laudato ingentia rura exiguum colito* ('praise a large landscape but cultivate a small one') is used in the dedication of John Worlidge's *Systema Agriculturae*. It is also cited by Robert Child, one of Samuel Hartlib's correspondents in his *Husbandry* in 1655. And the image of the 'poorest Cottager . . . encompassed with

Orchards and Gardens' of which John Beale was so fond is derived from the portrait of the old man of Taranto in the fourth book of the *Georgics*.[35]

The *Georgics* remained a potent authority in the period in which Thomson's *Seasons* was published. '*Virgil* his *Georgicks* is reckon'd the Master-piece of that celebrated Poet,' William Mackintosh wrote in his *Essay on Ways and Means for Inclosing, Fallowing, Planting etc Scotland* (1729). Indeed, for Mackintosh, Virgil, Cicero, and Varro represent true learning, '*practical Agricules*, and not speculative philosophick ones'. Like Pope, who began to write *An Essay on Man* in the following year, Mackintosh has no place for the airy speculations of astronomy and mathematics: 'I have no Hopes, our *learned philosophical Speculists* will ever show us a Leaf of a Tree, or a Fish, out of any of the Forests or Seas, their *Telescopes* have pointedly discovered, and they given names to.'[36]

Whether Virgil's recommendations were practical or even correct became a matter of dispute, but Virgil none the less remained the authority to be dealt with in matters of husbandry.[37] For Mackintosh, as for Jethro Tull, the inventor of the cultivator and the seed-drill, the authority of the ancients was not above question, however, especially when that authority seemed to be allied with modern speculative science of the kind which Swift mocks in the third book of *Gulliver's Travels* or which Thomas Shadwell had mocked fifty years earlier in his play *The Virtuoso*. Mackintosh speaks with Tull (whose *Horse-Hoing Husbandry* was first published in 1733) when he writes:

> a great Number of excellent Carpenters, a great Number of ingenious Websters, are much more useful and necessary in a Nation, than so many very learned *Aristotelians*, so many very learned *Cartesians*, *Gassendians*, or even *Newtonians*.[38]

This had been a common subject among many of the early members of the Royal Society too. John Locke expressed an equal dislike of 'the long and elaborate discourses of the ancients' which had both tied the hands of modern science 'with fine but useless speculations, and diverted their enquiries from the true and advantageous knowledge of things'. In husbandry, he believed, there was more to be discovered from the experience of the dull ploughman and unread gardener than the profound philosopher or acute disputant. Speaking very much in the voice of Bacon, he wrote:

> Let not any one be offended that I rank the cook and the farmer with the scholar and the philosopher; for, speaking here of the knowledge of natural bodies, the end and benefit whereof can be no other than the advantages and conveniences of human life, all speculations in this subject, however curious or refined, or seeming profound and solid, if they teach not their followers to do something either better or in a shorter and easier way than otherwise they could, or else lead them to

the discovery of some new and useful invention, deserve not the name
of knowledge, or so much as the waste time of our idle hours to be
thrown away upon such empty, idle philosophy.[39]

Both Tull and Mackintosh were also 'sons of Bacon' in their dislike of
Aristotle and 'the schools'. 'Such Freedom is given now-a-days in
Speculations in *Natural Philosophy*,' Tull writes ironically in support of
common sense and experiments, 'that 'tis common to see People even in
print maintain that there are *Antipodes*, that the Earth moves round the
Sun, and that he doth not set in the Sea.'[40] And if it had not been for such
practical knowledge, Mackintosh writes, Plato's 'philosophick Nation and
King must have been of short Duration, and, in a few Days after their being
instituted, all starved to Death'. Moreover, whereas he allies natural
philosophy and agriculture with true knowledge, he condemns 'the wandering Star-gazing Shepherd' of the debased pastoral to the cloud-cuckoo-land
of astronomy.[41]

In 1759, John Mills, the translator of Duhamel du Monceau's *Traite sur
la cultivation des terres* (first published in 1750), cited the *Georgics* on the
title page but went on to praise Lord Townshend's improvements in
husbandry, and chiefly his promotion of turnip cultivation as part of crop
rotation. Like Swift, he claimed that such improvements were 'the genuine
and original source of the wealth and power of this Island, as well as of its
ornament and security'. And he went on to cite Francis Home, a botanist
who became the first Professor of Medicine at Edinburgh, who claimed that
agriculture was as much a part of natural history as medicine and chemistry
and as such should be 'reduced to a regular system, by the means of experiments.'[42] This, of course, had been Tull's position as well.

Tull soon found himself caught up in controversy with a periodical called
The Practical Husbandman and Planter, whose chief writer was Stephen
Switzer. As the primary apologist for 'the extensive way of gardening' (i.e.
'*ingentia rura*') in his book *Ichnographia Rustica* (1718), Switzer regarded
himself as the keeper of the Virgilian flame, and sprang to the attack. Tull,
however, was not easily cowed. He quoted one ancient against another:
Seneca's remark that '*Virgil did look not upon what might be spoken most
TRULY, but what most GRACEFULLY; and aimed more at Delighting his
Readers, than at instructing Husbandmen.*'[43] Moreover the translation he
cited was by Abraham Cowley, a poet famous for his introduction into
English of the Pindaric ode, a free form which Addison cited as the model
for his style of 'informal' gardening.[44]

By citing Benson's attack on Dryden's earlier translation of the *Georgics*,
Tull managed to marginalize this debate as one on style 'which the Criticks
themselves differ about'. So far as content is concerned, Tull remarks, Virgil
was born a farrier and can only have known as much about ploughing as
ploughboys do. His further knowledge can only have come from reading
'Authors who lived when Agriculture was in its most imperfect State'.

VIRGIL was *born* a Poet, and undoubtedly the best (of the Latins) that ever wrote; but neither he nor any other, I believe, was ever *born* a Farmer: Talents in Husbandry must be acquired by long Experience and diligent Observation thereon; and he that will make any Improvements therein, must sometimes deviate from the old beaten Road ... by Way of Trial.

Tull also cites Benson's claim that '*There is more of Virgil's Husbandry put in Practice in* England *at this Instant, than in* Italy *itself.*' But he does so not only to get the better of Switzer but to expose the absurdity of following Virgil for Virgil's sake. So far as Tull is concerned, the Augustan age which Virgil celebrated introduced 'perpetual Slavery upon the bravest People in the world'. Moreover, Virgil's husbandry 'has not stood the Test even in VIRGIL's own Country, but is there much disus'd; and, I believe, if the Matter were full enquired into, it would appear, that it never was much practised or approved of about *Rome*, or any other Part of *Italy*.'[45]

What was 'practised and approved' in Italian agriculture had already been noticed by English travellers. Three years before Tull wrote *Horse-Hoing Husbandry* Pope's friend, the gardener and classicist Joseph Spence, had been in Italy, where he remarked on the 'Fields, going from Rome to Venice'.[46] These he came to think of as a possible model for the idea of a *ferme ornée*: a landscape garden in which, as for John Beale, horticulture was part of agriculture. Seventy years earlier John Ray wrote of the same Italian agricultural landscape (Lombardy) as the 'garden of Europe', a phrase, he remarked, that was true only of Lombardy and the Campania.

'I took the first Hints of my *Horse-hoing* Culture from the plowed *Vineyards* near *Frontignon* and *Setts* [Seté] in *Languedoc*,' Tull was to write in 1740.[47] But in the early 1660s Ray gives a fuller account of what Tull probably saw, an account contemporary with Milton's description of the 'marriageable arms' of the vine in Eden's garden:

Corn-fields planted with Trees as thick as our Orchards, against each tree being planted a Vine, the branches of which draw from Tree to Tree in rows, and make a sort of Hedge.[48]

It was not until the early eighteenth century, however, with the advent of the *ferme ornée*, that this combination of beauty and usefulness was to be put into practice; and it is this combination which Pope praises (however inappropriately) in his 'Epistle to Burlington' (1731). Because it is 'Use alone that sanctifies Expence', the sterile horticultural vanities of Timon's estate are condemned to extinction by a fruitful agriculture:

Another age shall see the golden Ear
Imbrown the Slope, and nod on the Parterre,
Deep Harvests bury all his pride has plann'd,
And laughing Ceres re-assume the land.

(173–6)

In his *The Practical Farmer*, published the next year, William Ellis described just the mixture of beauty and use (Horace's *utile dulci*) that Pope espoused. Fields, he wrote, might be divided by 'baulks' 40 feet wide on which would grow lines of fruit trees separated by a cart track from the hedges next to the ploughed fields:

> What a charming sight is a large Tree in Blossom, and after that, when loaden with Fruit enough perhaps to make a Hogshead of Cyder or Perry! A Scene of Beauty, and Hopes, and Profit, and all![49]

Ellis was writing half a century after John Beale, but he noted in 1733 that there was 'so great a difference ... between the present and the former practices of Agriculture, as made an old sagacious Farmer, ... now living, say, that he thought he had been asleep these forty Years past.'[50]

Arable agriculture of any sophisticated kind came late to England. If Richard Weston (a Royalist Catholic who was educated in Flanders and wrote during the Commonwealth) is to be believed, there was not much of it before the early seventeenth century:

> About fifty years ago, about which time Ingenuities first began to flourish in *England*, this Art of Gardening began to creep into *England*, in *Sandwich*, and *Surrey*, *Fulham*, and other places.
> Some old men in *Surrey*, where it flourishes very much at present, report, That they knew the first Gardeners that came into those parts, to plant *Cabbages* and *Cauliflowers*, and to sow *Turnips*, *Carrots*, and *Parsnips*; to sow *Raith* (or early ripe) *Rape, Pease*; all which at that time were great rarities, we having few or none in *England*, but what came from *Holland* and *Flanders*.[51]

Publishing Weston's book in 1742, Thomas Harris claimed that it was still an important and relevant work because so many works on agriculture were still theoretical and not practical. Men, says Weston, have 'beaten their brains about the Perpetual Motion and other curiosities when they ought to have invented a better plow.'[52] In fact there were some improvements in agricultural implements before Jethro Tull's seed-drill and cultivator, but the chief problem seems to have been the low esteem in which husbandry was held and the need to accord it a respectable status.

One of the 'modern Authors' whom Harris abused was Richard Bradley, the first Professor of Botany at Cambridge; but Bradley's *Monthly Register of Experiments and Observations in Husbandry and Gardening* (1722) was not a theoretical undertaking. Like Hartlib's *Husbandry* nearly 70 years earlier, it was intended as an interchange of information in which Bradley was to be 'rather as a Secretary, than as a Director'.[53] When he wrote in *The Country Gentleman and Farmer's Monthly Director* that a farmer 'ought to be a Philosopher', he did not mean a metaphysician but a 'natural philosopher': one who should 'study the Nature of every Soil ... to know how to improve one sort by another'.[54] Indeed, Bradley's explanation of crop rotation faces an engraving of Ceres presiding over a field full of harvesters.

For Bradley, the best writers of antiquity provided an example not for mere speculation but for practice. Writing in hope that farmers might have 'a School for their Information ... as soon as a Physick Garden is compleated in Cambridge', he cited the example of the ancients where

> we find that Husbandry was accounted a study so extremely beneficial to the Commonwealth, that Persons of the highest Rank and figure did not only promote the Practice and Improvement of it amongst the Common People, but took a Pride to distinguish themselves by such new Inventions and Contrivances as might add anything to an Art of so general Advantage.[55]

Like John Locke, William Mackintosh also thought that 'the Children of Indigent People' should be taught 'Agriculture and Pasturage' along with their letters and the Protestant religion. Indeed, he set out a curriculum of classical authors on husbandry while warning against over-educating boys by sending them to Latin schools.[56] His Scots compatriot, Robert Maxwell, was even more ardent in *The Practical Husbandman* (1757):

> You see the wise *Socrates* was perswaded, That Agriculture is the Parent and Nurse of all other Arts: that they flourish when it is rightly pursued, and that it should never be neglected, because then every Thing goes to ruin by Land and by Sea ... And had not [Columella] and the best writers on Husbandry since his Time great Reason? seeing Agriculture, I believe, had never a Professor appointed for it by any Government, tho' it is the Preservation of all Mankind; yea, *the King himself is served by the Field.*[57]

One of the recurring themes of many agricultural writers is one that exercised Pope and Swift as well: the disdain for agriculture on the part of the nobility and gentry and their consequent ignorance and neglect of their own estates. The situation in Ireland was even worse. Philip Skelton, writing in Ireland in 1741, claimed that many of them regarded agriculture as if it were a crime, and paid no attention to it.[58] Absentee landlords, who were either ignorant of or hostile to tillage, consigned their land to grazing. The consequent unemployment of farm labourers who ought to be working on agricultural improvement was in fact one of the major causes of the poverty of the Irish population. Like Pope, Swift believed that the true wealth of a monarchy 'ariseth from the Rents and Improvements of Land,'[59] and this could not be done by absentee owners or those who had no interest in agriculture.

This is a theme that Swift also takes up in the second book of *Gulliver's Travels*, where the benign King of Brobdingnag speaks with Swift's own vehemence against what Swift elsewhere called 'Party Rage':

where Gentlemen, instead of consulting the Ease of their Tenants, or cultivating their Lands, were worrying one another, upon Points of *Whig* and *Tory*, of *High Church* and *Low Church*; . . . While *Agriculture* was wholly discouraged, and consequently half the Farmers, and Labourers, and poorer Tradesmen, forced to Beggary or Banishment.[60]

By contrast to this, and as a result of what Gulliver thinks a deplorable ignorance of political science, the King (like Locke) was more interested in husbandry than politics and

gave it for his Opinion; that whoever could make two Ears of Corn, or two Blades of Grass to grow upon a Spot of Ground where only one grew before; would deserve better of Mankind, and do more essential Service to his Country, than the whole Race of Politicians put together.[61]

Swift put his reflections on these and related concerns most succinctly in his poem 'Ireland', where he imagines a spokesman arguing against the position that he himself adopted in *The Drapier's Letters* and many of his other tracts:

> Next for encouragement of spinning,
> A duty might be laid on linnen
> An Act for laying down the Plough,
> England will send you corn enough.
> Another act that absentees
> For licenses shall pay no fees.
> If England's friendship you would keep
> Feed nothing in your lands but sheep
> But make an act secure and full
> To hang up all who smuggle wool.
> And then he kindly give[s] me hints
> That all our wives should go in Chints.[62]

What needs to be reiterated is that Swift was not alone in these interests, but that they were central to the ideal of classical humanism that he and other Irish writers espoused. Only two years after the publication of Swift's poems the Irish bishop-philosopher, George Berkeley, wrote a series of 'queries proposed to the consideration of the public':

Whether an Irish lady, set out with French silks and Flanders lace, may not be said to consume more beef and butter than fifty of our labouring peasants?

Whether there be any country in Christendom more capable of improvement than Ireland?[63]

Swift's was a classicism that, paradoxically, argued for modern improvement. For him the story of Ajax's mistaking a flock of sheep for his enemies was a parable of the way that sheep-grazing was destroying Ireland in his own time. For Philip Skelton, Varro and Columella taught that agriculture was a learned art requiring schools for its instruction, Tacitus revealed the folly of a country relying upon imported food (as Ireland did on America), and Virgil demonstrated in the *Georgics* that 'the ancient notions of the garden of Eden' and modern agriculture were the same.

Lecturing in Edinburgh in 1756, Robert Maxwell both commended the foundation of the Society of Improvers in the Knowledge of Agriculture in Scotland in 1723 and linked their work to the similar Dublin Society with which Swift was loosely involved.[64] One of these was Alexander McAulay, whose *Some Thoughts on the Tillage of Ireland* (1737) comes with a commendatory letter from Swift; certainly its arguments for tillage and against mere pasturage are consonant with Swift's own. Swift's famous *Answer to the Craftsman* (*c.* 1730) indulges in the usual Swiftian technique of arguing for the opposite case and making it farcical by gross exaggeration. Instead of contending, like McAulay, that an increase in tillage would mean an increase in 'the Number of our labouring Hands', he argues that 8,400 families would be enough to manage the grazing of the country and that (except for 200,000 to cultivate potatoes) the rest of the population could be spared for foreign armies. In the teeth of McAulay's (and his own) belief that linen manufacture would prosper as a result of land cultivation, he argues that all clothes should be imported from England. Samuel Madden, arguing for an experimental farm near Dublin in his *Letter to the Dublin Society* (1739), claims that the neglect of tillage is 'a satyr on the Politicks of Ireland'. Swift's ironic commentary on this is to argue for the worst of the status quo: that 'owners of these Lands should live constantly in *England*, in order to learn Politeness' (and, by implication, nothing about agriculture).[65]

Stephen Duck, the poor thresher who became a poet, was patronized by Queen Caroline (wife of George II), was ordained, and eventually committed suicide, is an instructive example of the problems that such polite education posed. Indeed, the sad history of Duck is not unlike that of the Romantic poet John Clare a century later. Both men were deeply divided between the rural cultures which they knew and the fashionable society that adopted them. Like Marie Antoinette at the end of the eighteenth century, this society liked to play with georgic myths while retaining a genteel control over the working landscape.

Duck's early patron, Joseph Spence, wrote of the impossibility of Duck's ever being 'improved' without the assistance of learning. But Duck's education was not to be of the kind which Tull and the agricultural improvers generally recommended. And even Pope, who affected to think of him as harmless, seems in fact to have to have thought of him as a sort of D'Urfey.[66] None the less, the subscription list to his *Poems on Several Occasions* (1736) contains an astonishing diversity of influential and interesting people. Not only does it include the present and future prime ministers, but many of the landscape 'improvers' of the period. Pope is not there, but his landlord in Twickenham is, and so is Swift. Seized upon as a georgic natural phenomenon and eventually carted off to live in the Hermitage at Kew, Duck was a sort of forerunner of the poet John Clare, driven mad by gentrification at the hands of his supposed benefactors.

Duck's early poem, 'The Thresher's Labour' (1730), was considerably revised during his lifetime, but not at the expense of the realities that underlie the georgic ideal. To the shepherd who may well 'tune his voice to sing', Duck contrasts the din of the threshing that makes song impossible; and the 'dull and melancholy scene' drives away the world of pastoral:

> No fountains mumur here, no lamkins play,
> No linnets warble, and no fields look gay.[67]

This is a world of master's curse and physical exhaustion, an exhaustion reiterated by Duck's contemporary, Mary Collier, a poet who had no such subscribers as he had until later in her life. Collier, however, took exception to Duck's dislike of female labourers; echoing his lines with italics, she pointed out that this labour was even greater for the women who had to take their babies with them to work and then go home to prepare their husbands' evening meal:

> but 'tis not worth our while
> Once to complain, or *rest at ev'ry Stile*;
> We must make haste, for when we home are Come,
> Alas! we find our Work but just begun.[68]

Similarly Mary Leapor, whose father was a head gardener, knew whereof she wrote when, in her 'Essay on Women' (written in 1746), she warned young women that one possible fate was that of 'Cordia in her filthy sty' who feasts 'on stewed potatoes or on mouldy pie'.[69]

All of this is a long way from the pleasurable toil celebrated in the georgic discourse of such poems as James Thomson's *The Seasons*. His lubricious description of haymaking in *Summer* sounds more like Milton's Satan than the dirty exhaustion of Duck's thresher:

> Now swarms the village o'er the jovial mead –
> The rustic youth, brown with meridian toil,
> Healthful and strong; full as the summer rose
> Blown by prevailing suns, the ruddy maid,
> Half naked, swelling on the sight, and all
> Her kindled graces burning o'er her cheek.
>   (352–7)

These lines, added to the poem in 1730, are an example of that curious fusion of georgic with pastoral that became a dominant poetic mode by the mid-century. They reflect both the co-option of georgic by gentility and the power implicit in this third-person poetry of prospect. There is a lingering echo of Satan's sight of Eve, 'the fair virgin' of the countryside that in turn echoes Satan's early vision of Paradise where, like a cormorant, he perches on the tree of life:

> nor on the virtue thought
> Of that life-giving plant, but only used
> For prospect, what well used had been the pledge
> Of immortality.
>
> (IV. 199–201)

Satan's view dominates the landscape as forcefully as the contemporary vista from Le Nôtre's Vaux-le-Vicomte or the radiating avenues of the Duke of Beaufort's Badminton. What ought to be the life-giving centre becomes a metaphor of possession and the inscription of the dominant power of looking. Only from the point of view of this gentrified spectator does discord become harmony, and Thomson's use of the passive voice underlies his privilege:

> while heard from dale to dale,
> Waking the breeze, resounds the blended voice
> Of happy labour, love, and social glee.
>
> (368–70)

Thomson's diction is Miltonic, but what is missing is Milton's sense of loss and the irony implicit in his description of Eden.[70] Thomson, like the gentlemen to whom his poems are addressed, looks from the prospect of rural retirement. The manure and the sweat are too far away to notice. When he celebrates the virtue of work, he chooses as exemplary Peter the Great's rather dubious English 'Grand Tour' in 1697–8, supposedly to familiarize himself with trades.[71] There is a strange discrepancy between the championing of toil in Thomson's later poem, The Castle of Indolence (1748), and the easeful prospect from which the world of The Seasons is viewed. Even in The Castle of Indolence it is not a farmer, or even an owner, but a 'bard' who celebrates the georgic work of the farm labourer as if it were a combination of a rural health farm and an escape from urban vices:

> Better the toiling swain, oh happier far!
> Perhaps the happiest of the sons of men!
> Who vigorous plies the plough, the team, or car,
> Who houghs the field or ditches in the glen,
> Delves in his garden, or secures his pen;

> The tooth of avarice poisons not his peace;
> He tosses not in sloth's abhorréd den;
> From vanity he has a full release;
> And rich in nature's wealth, he thinks not of increase.
>
> (Canto II. st. lv)

All of this is a long way from Duck and Collier, who have little enough opportunity to worry about thinking of 'increase'. It is also a long way from Lady Booby's more characteristic assessment of the countryside as being full of brutes in *Joseph Andrews*. It is a long way from Jethro Tull's *Horse-Hoing Husbandry* as well. Tull may have been an educated man and no friend to idle labourers, but he did not sentimentalize manual work. Writing of his farm-workers, he says:

> These Weeders are the same sort of People that Mr. *Duck* describes as *Haymakers*, their Tongues are much nimbler than their Hands; and unless the Owner, or some Person who faithfully represents him, (and is hard to be found) works constantly amongst them, they'll get their heads together half a Dozen in a Cluster, regarding their *Prattle* more than the Weeds.[72]

John Barrell has written of the embarrassment felt by early eighteenth-century poets in the georgic mode at the 'the freedom permitted to it of describing mean tasks in detail'.[73] The result was not so much that such poems came to 'toss the dung about with an air of gracefulness' (in Addison's phrase),[74] as the absence of the dung altogether, and all the other terracultural aspects of husbandry with it. The cultivation of turnips as a manuring crop was one of the agricultural innovations of the period, as important to the agricultural revolution as fallowing, crop rotation, new strains of clover, and the seed-drill.[75] But turnips were at best a poetic joke in the genteel georgic poem of the period. John Wolcot's abuse of the famous botanical explorer, Joseph Banks, later in the century is indicative of the inability of georgic poetry to take the real business of agriculture seriously:

> Then to your turnip fields in peace retire:
> Return like Cincinnatus, country's squire.
> Go with your wisdom and amaze the boors
> With appletree, and shrub, and flow'r amours.[76]

Barrell has argued that *The Fleece* (1756) by the Welsh poet John Dyer is an exception to this georgic problem, but the poem reflects the same fastidious-ness that Dr Johnson expressed in his *Preface* to the *Dictionary* (1755) when he declined the 'fugitive cant' of the language of trades. Cumbered with the diction of nymphs and swains, and needing even to translate Wales into the ancient 'Siluria', Dyer's work also suffers from gentrified prospects. His rural landscape is one of 'wide airy downs, | And health's gay walks to shepherd as to sheep.'[77]

John Philips's poem *Cyder* (1708), is also often cited as the first English georgic, but the similar discrepancy between its subject and its expression defeats its ostensible purpose:

> Now turn thine eyes to view Alcinous' groves,
> The pride of the Phoaecian isle, from whence,
> Sailing the spaces of the boundless deep,
> To Ariconium pretious fruits arriv'd:
> The Pippin burnish'd o'er with gold, the Moile
> Of sweetest hony'd taste, the fair Permain,
> Temper'd, like comliest nymph, with red and white.[78]

More successful in this vein was Thomson's friend, Richard Savage. Clarence Tracy has written of Savage that 'scattered about in his work are evidences of a feeling for language and genuine poetical power',[79] and in his long poem *The Wanderer* we can see what led Pope (as Johnson says) to read the poem three times over. In the last canto of that poem, Savage frees himself from the generalizing and elevated diction of Thomson and gives a picture of an agricultural landscape almost as fine as that in the poetry of John Clare:

> Here swelling Peas on leafy Stalks are seen,
> Mix'd Flower's of red and Azure shine between;
> Whose waving Beauties, heighten'd by the Sun,
> In colour'd Lanes along the Furrows run.
> There the next Produce of a genial Shower,
> The Bean fresh-blossoms in a speckled Flower;
> Whose morning Dews, when to the Sun resign'd,
> With undulating Sweets embalm the Wind.
> Now daisy Plats of Clover square the Plain,
> And part the bearded from the beardless Grain.

This has all the mixture of pleasure and use, horticulture and agricultural knowledge that Pope asked for in the 'Epistle to Burlington'. Savage's descriptions show his recognition of the importance of rotation and crop mixture as well as his delight in the almost painterly beauty of it, and yet he neither falls into the bathetic dullness of some of the georgic poets nor into the elevated anaemia of others. Among the latter is Thomas Warton the younger, imagining in post-Miltonic language 'the mower blithe' who 'with new-born vigour grasps the scythe', or regretting his confinement to college:

> Thro' the deep groves I hear the chaunting birds
> And thro' the clover'd vale the various-lowing herds.[80]

The task of writing Georgic poetry was not impossible in English. Milton celebrates 'the tann'd Haycock in the Mead' in *L'Allegro*, and Marvell's mower inhabits 'sun-burn'd Meadows' and regrets a love that is like 'Thistles sow'd' there. As the sweat of the 'Mower's wholesome Heat' in his *Upon Appleton House* indicates, this georgic world is not viewed from the prospect of privilege. Written half a century before John Mortimer's *Art of Husbandry* (1707), it captures the same language of the fields without embarrassment. Its diction is at one with the diction of Mortimer's husbandry:

> As soon as your Grass is mown if there is plenty of it, that it lie thick
> in the Swath, so as that neither the Air nor Sun pass freely through it,
> cause your Haymakers to follow the Mowers and to cast it abroad
> (except you fear wet: if you do, let it lie upon the Swath) this they call
> *Tedding* of it.[81]

For Milton, after all, the landscape of Eden could be compared to 'the smell of grain, or tedded grass, or kine'. And it is this world of agricultural labour that Marvell celebrates as 'the garden of the world erewhile' in *Upon Appleton House*. For Marvell's persona in that poem, the 'luckless' England of the Civil War has tasted the apple of dissension and fallen from a world of agricultural bounty. Even as late as Purcell's *King Arthur* (1691), Dryden's libretto balances the harvesters' georgic voices who 'merrily Roar our Harvest Home' with Venus's more famous pastoral celebration of 'Fairest Isle, all Isles Excelling'. Here the labourers answer the mythologizing voices of power. 'Comus' is the chief of the harvesters: not Milton's seducer, but a voice of rural radicalism urging his fellows in a country dance to refuse their tithes to a parson who is a 'Booklearn'd Sot' and a 'Blockhead'.[82]

A host of neglected early eighteenth-century poets are more legitimately the heirs of Milton and Marvell than Thomson and the Wartons. Compare, for instance, George Farewell's description of a summer morning with a similar description by Thomson:

> The crunking crane heard high amongst the clouds
> Alarums up the peasant, whilst the cock,
> Strutting most stately with a towering comb,
> Closing his wings proclaims th'approach of day.
> He rouses up his fellow-labourers;
> All at the crowing put together on
> Their coarse patched coats upon their shivering backs,
> And then their hats, and clumsy thick-soled shoes.[83]

This is the language of *L'Allegro* and *Upon Appleton House* as well as the discourse of real husbandry. Thomson's diction, by contrast, is elevated and abstract, nor is there any sense of the back-breaking toil to which Duck and Collier refer:

> Music awakes
> The native voice of undissembled joy;
> And thick around the woodland hymns arise.
> Roused by the cock, the soon-clad shepherd leaves
> His mossy cottage, where with peace he dwells,
> And from the crowded fold in order drives
> His flock to taste the verdure of the morn.[84]

Similarly, compare the vignette jollity of what Thomson in his *Winter* calls 'the smoothest stream of rural life' to Nicholas James's *The Complaints of Poverty*. Thomson's village winter is a place where

> Rustic mirth goes round –
> The simple joke that takes the shepherd's heart,
> Easily pleased; the long loud laugh sincere;
> The kiss, snatched hasty from the sidelong maid
> On purpose guardless, or pretending sleep;
> The leap, the slap, the haul; and, shook to notes
> Of native music, the respondent dance.
> Thus jocund fleets with them the winter-night.
>   (622–9)

Like Farewell's labourer, James's, on the other hand, sustains 'parching heat' in summer and 'freezing cold in winter'; his winter evening has none of the scenic festivity of Thomson's:

> When winter's rage upon the cottage falls,
> And the wind rushes through the gaping walls,
> When ninepence must their daily wants supply,
> With hunger pinched and cold, the children cry;
> The gathered sticks but little warmth afford,
> And half-supplied the platter meets the board.[85]

I referred earlier to the curious fusion of pastoral and georgic; but in fact what was happening in the work of Thomson and the Wartons was the subjugation of georgic to a re-invented pastoral that gentrified its ostensible subject and made it part of the poetry of prospect. In effect what Thomson did was to take the argument of the seventeenth-century Diggers and stand it on its head. Winstanley's notion of the law of contract was that in over-throwing the 'Norman Yoke' of Stuart authority, the victorious gentry and nobility in the Civil War should share the spoils of that victory with the common people. Thomson, by contrast, appropriates the georgic world of the common labourer to the world of his patrons (and thereby to himself). His point of view is that of the gods who inhabit the upper portion of the engravings by William Kent which accompany each book of *The Seasons*; they look down upon the little rural tragedies and griefs, but are untouched by them.

This, surely, is the irony of Tom Jones's interest in a 'charming prospect' in Fielding's novel. Writing at a time when the Wartons, Young, Akenside, and Thomson had turned the 'thoughtscape' of *Il Penseroso* into a scenario for melancholy, Fielding places Tom's desire for the 'solemn gloom' and 'melancholy thoughts' that such prospects offer alongside the more intelligible scepticism of Tom's companion, Partridge. It is Partridge who detects that Tom's real melancholy is for home, not mere prospects; and when the two men look over the fashionable prospect of 'a vast and extensive wood' what they find is Ensign Northerton trying to rape Mrs Waters.[86]

There is right prospect in *Paradise Lost* too, but it is earned, not appropriated. Adam and Eve are rural labourers, not landowners or employers or overseers, let alone property speculators or visiting poets. They look out from Eden's wide prospect into a landscape that they enjoy as active participants, not as spectators. When Eve, by contrast, is taken up by Satan in her dream, her sudden 'high exaltation' is compared by Satan to 'the gods life there': a curious prefiguring of just what Kent depicts (without a trace of irony) in his illustrations to Thomson's *Seasons*. In Milton's *Comus* there are no 'super-masquers' descending from courtly omniscience to set the world to rights. The agent of redemption, Sabrina, is a water-nymph, and even the Attendant Spirit is a familiar of the woods.

In the court entertainments of the early seventeenth century that preceded *Comus*, however, pastoral was subjected to prospect; the members of the court usually descended at the end of the masque from their Olympian stations to rescue pastoral arcadians from violence and barbarism and to restore order. In the festivities for the marriage of James I's daughter, Elizabeth of Bohemia, in 1613, the masques of Chapman and Beaumont and Campion employ just this device. What is interesting is that *The Tempest*, which was performed as part of the same series of entertainments, undoes Prospero's similar Olympian privelege. This undoing, moreover, begins to happen during a masque within the play itself: a masque of reapers who come not from the pastoral world but from the georgic.

> You sunburn'd sicklemen, of August weary,
> Come hither from the furrow, and be merry:
> Make holiday; your rye-straw hats put on
> And those fresh nymphs encounter every one
> In Country footing.
>
> (IV. i. 150–5)[87]

At that moment Prospero remembers Caliban's plot, and the cold blade of mortal realism that scythes into the play is prophetic of the mortal realism that re-enters the georgic subject in the work of Gray and Goldsmith after the mid-eighteenth century. Neither poet completely abjures the elevated diction of the Thomson tradition; but although the world of darkness of the 'Elegy Written in a Country Churchyard' (1751) may be one of melancholy withdrawal, it is not one of elevated prospect. And, in spite of Gray's celebration of cottage life, the real pain of the 'short and simple annals of the poor' places the poem in a georgicized pastoral which is neither Olympian nor condescending. Gray's labourer, though ignorant of the 'ample page' of knowledge, is not sentimentalized into the merely pictorial. He feels penury and cold, and his labourer's lot is to withstand 'the little tyrant of his fields': Stephen Duck's grasping farmer.

Notes

1 *New Experiments in Husbandry* (London, 1736), p. 124.
2 *Apiroscopy: Or, A Compleat and Faithful History of Experiments and Observations*, sig. *g2.
3 *Treatise*, sig. [B2v].
4 'To the Reader', Ibid., sig. [4]
5 *Systema Agriculturae*, 2nd edn, (London, 1675), sig. [R4].
6 *Husbandman* (London, 1652), sig. A3.
7 *Adam out of Eden* (London, 1659), 'To the Reader'.
8 *The Art of Simpling* (London, 1656), sigs. [F9v–F10], [F11].
9 *Systema Agriculturae*, sig. [Dv].
10 *Systema Horti-culturae* (London, 1677), sig. [Bv].
11 *The Art of Simpling*, sig. [Gv].
12 *A Vindication of those whose Endeavours is only to make the Earth a Common Treasury, called Diggers* (1650), in *The Works of Gerard Winstanley*, ed. George H. Sabine (Ithaca, NY: Cornell University Press, 1941), p. 402.
13 *Herefordshire Orchards* (Dublin, 1724), p. 23. Beale's work was first published in 1657. See also my discussion of Beale '"Wild Pastoral Encounter": John Evelyn and the Renegotiation of Pastoral in the Mid-17th Century', in *Culture and Cultivation in Early Modern England*, ed. M. Leslie (Leicester: University of Leicester Press, 1992), pp. 173–94.
14 See *A Character of England* (London, 1659).
15 See John Barrell, *The Dark Side of the Landscape: The Rural Poor in English Painting 1730–1840* (Cambridge: Cambridge University Press, 1980).
16 Dorothy Osborne, *Letters to Sir William Temple*, ed. Kenneth Parker (London: Penguin, 1987), Letter 24, p. 89.
17 Mary Wortley Montagu, *The Turkish Embassy Letters*, ed. Malcolm Jack (London: Virago, 1993), Letter 31, p. 74. In the same letter Lady Mary also has some interesting observations on the problems of translating metaphors that sound simply 'burlesque' in English.
18 'A Discourse on Pastoral Poetry', *The Poems of Alexander Pope*, ed. John Butt (London: Methuen, 1984), pp. 120–1.
19 *A Supplement to the Works of the Most Celebrated Minor Poets* (London, 1750), Pt II, p. 65.

20 In 'Georgic and Pastoral: Laws of Genre in the Seventeenth Century', Alastair Fowler observes that 'one of the largest and most significant changes during that period [the Augustan period] was the displacement of pastoral by georgic.' Georgic, he notes, climbed from being only just recognizable as poetry at the end of the sixteenth century to being near the top of the hierarchy of genres at the end of the seventeenth. *Culture and Cultivation in Early Modern England*, ed. Michael Leslie and Timothy Raylor (Leicester: Leicester University Press, 1992), p. 84.

21 'Tuesday: Or, the Ditty', ll. 11–12. *John Gay: Poetry and Prose*, ed. V. A. Dearing and C. E. Beckwith (Oxford: Clarendon Press, 1974), i. 101. John Barrell reads this as a mockery of the poor themselves (*The Dark Side of the Landscape*, p. 56), a reading I do not agree with. Realistic pastoral, though popular in the early seventeenth century before the court appropriation of the genre, was only laughable in the eighteenth.

22 In 'An Epistle to Dr. Arbuthnot', ll. 179–80, Pope also aligns 'pilfer'd Pastorals' with turning 'a *Persian* Tale for half a crown' (Twickenham iv. 109). For a thorough discussion of this, see William Ellis, 'Thomas D'Urfey, The Pope-Philips Quarrel, and *The Shepherd's Week*', PMLA 74 (1959), pp. 203–12.

23 It seems unlikely that Pope, who corresponded with Sir William about the allegorical (and political) import of classical texts, would be unaware of this irony. See his letter to Sir William Trumbull, 16 Dec. 1715, in *The Correspondence of Alexander Pope*, ed. George Sherburn (Oxford: Clarendon, 1956), i. 323–4.

24 'Life of Milton', *Selected Poetry and Prose*, ed. F. Brody and W. K. Wimsatt (Berkeley: University of California Press, 1977), p. 426. Johnson clearly did not understand the way in which *Lycidas* wrested pastoral away from amatory triviality and replaced it where Spenser had left it, in the realm of ideas.

25 Neal Wood, *John Locke and Agrarian Capitalism* (Berkeley: University of California Press, 1984), p. 19. I am also indebted to Wood for the survey of Locke's agricultural interests in the following paragraph.

26 Trumbull sent six small trees of these 'Lock apples' down to be planted at his estate (Easthampstead in Berkshire) on 25 February 1697. British Library, Trumbull MSS. Stubbes File IV.

27 Cited by Robert Latham in *The Diary of Samuel Pepys* (London: Bell & Hyman, 1983), x. 409.

28 William Benson, *Virgil's Husbandry, or an Essay on the Georgics: Being the Second Book ... with notes Critical and Rustick* (London, 1724), p. xii. See also Annabel Paterson, *Pastoral and Ideology: Virgil to Valery* (Oxford: Clarendon, 1988), p. 153.

29 See 'Hearts of Oak and Bulwarks of Liberty?' in Simon Schama, *Landscape and Memory* (Toronto: Random House, 1995).

30 Latham says of the Tangier Mole, 'No engineering project of such a size had ever been attempted before by Englishmen.' *Diary*, x. 415. After the Moors' siege of the town in 1680 the Mole, which had never been completed was blown up with great difficulty and the port was abandoned.

31 *The Turkish Embassy Letters*, ed. Malcolm Jack (London: Virago, 1993), p. 54.

32 It may be that Swift's concern for the agricultural poor in Ireland was in part a legacy of his awareness that his own family, like the Boyles, 'were part of the army of occupation of landless gentry who took advantage of that act of arbitrary power by which the whole territory of Ireland was declared confiscated' after the Cromwellian Settlement. David Nokes, *Jonathan Swift: A Hypocrite Reversed* (Oxford: Oxford University Press, 1987), p. 7.

33 See John Barrell, *The Birth of Pandora and the Division of Knowledge* (London:

Macmillan, 1992), p. 50 and 'The Morality of Improvement', in *Poetry, Language and Politics* (Manchester: Manchester University Press, 1988).

34 See John Barrell's treatment of this in his chapter on Gainsborough in *The Dark Side of the Landscape,* pp. 35–88, and his discussion of the tension in *The Seasons* between public statement and private experience, or between idealized panoramic landscape and 'enclosed, occluded landscapes' in *The Birth of Pandora*, pp. 34, 36.

35 *Herefordshire Orchards*, p. 2. See also Chambers, 'Wild Pastoral Encounter', in *Culture and Cultivation in Early Modern England*, pp. 173–94.

36 Edinburgh, 1729, pp. 49, 52–3.

37 On the importance of classical texts to the foundations of English agriculture, see Joan Thirsk, 'Making a Fresh Start: Sixteenth-Century Agriculture and the Classical Inspiration', *Culture and Cultivation*, pp. 18–31.

38 *Essay on Ways and Means*, p. 198. Mackintosh, who says of Newton that 'he was the greatest Lover of Agriculture I ever knew', regrets that he did not write on the subject (p. 197).

39 From an incomplete Locke manuscript called 'De re medica', cited in H. R. Fox Bourne, *The Life of John Locke* (London: Henry S. King & Co., 1876), i. 224, 226.

40 *The Horse-Hoing Husbandry: Or, An Essay on the Principles of Tillage and Vegetation* (London, 1733), sig. [Bv].

41 *Essays on Ways and Means*, p. 188.

42 *A Practical Treatise of Husbandry* (London, 1759), p. viii. Although this work contains a number of illustrations, including a 'horse-ho' or cultivator, it does not mention Tull. Nor does Duhamel adopt Linnaeus's reformed system of botanic taxonomy. Home's work is *The Principles of Agriculture and Vegetation* (1756).

43 *A Supplement to the Essay on Horse-Hoing Husbandry* (London, 1740), p. 219.

44 *The Spectator* 477 (6 Sept., 1712).

45 *Supplement*, pp. 220–1.

46 *Observations, Anecdotes, and Characters of Books and Men*, ed. James M. Osborn (Oxford: Clarendon Press, 1966) i. 603, p. 250. Although Spence is commenting on Philip Southcote's previous trip to Venice in the early 1730s, he himself was also in Italy in 1731. It may well be that the fields he refers to are those visible from the Brenta canal from Padua to Venice, the fields surrounding some of Palladio's famous villas.

47 *A Supplement*, p. 255.

48 John Harris, *Navigantium atque Itinerarium Bibliotheca* (London, 1705) ii. p. 505. Ray's travelling companion, Sir Philip Skippon, was similarly impressed with the agricultural landscape near Parma where he noted, 'The furrows of their plowed lands were flatted, and the ridges not so crooked as in *England*, and made like beds in a garden.' Awnsham Churchill, *A Collection of Voyages* (London, 1732), vi. p. 568.

49 London, 1732, p. 144.

50 *Chiltern and Vale Farming Explained* (London, 1733), sig. [A2v].

51 *A Treatise Concerning the Husbandry and Natural History of England* (London, 1742), p. 12: this work, no longer attributed to Weston, is none the less the fullest exploration of this subject. In *The Practical Husbandman* (Edinburgh, 1757), Robert Maxwell outlined a more universal spread of husbandry from the south to the north (p. 338).

52 *A Treatise*, p. 6. Earlier experiments had included a 'setting stick', invented by Gabriel Plattes in the 1630s, and a 'sembrador' that Lord Sandwich discovered in Spain in the late 1660s, but neither was very successful.

53 London, 1722, sig. [A4v].

54 London, 1726, p. ix.

55 *A Survey of the Ancient Husbandry and Gardening* (London, 1732), sigs. [a3v], a3. The work is dedicated to the agricultural reformer Lord 'Turnip' Townshend, and the British Library copy of this was subsequently owned by the eminent botanical explorer, Joseph Banks.

56 *An Essay*, pp. 193–4.

57 *Practical Husbandman*, p. 381.

58 Triptolemus [Philip Skelton]. *The Necessity of Tillage and Granaries* (Dublin, 1741), p. 27. In the 1744 reprint of Thomas Tusser's sixteenth-century classic, *Five Hundred Points of Husbandry*, a successful farmer explains to one who is not the reason for his failure: 'You said the Farmer, say *Go*, and I say *Come*: You bid your Servants go about this or that Work, and I say to my People, come Boys, let's go do this or that' p. 83.

59 *History of the Last Four Years of Queen Anne's Reign* (Oxford: Blackwell, 1951) p. 69. One of the consequences of some agricultrural improvement, however, was the dispossession that Goldsmith addressed in 'The Deserted Village'.

60 *A Memorial of the Poor Inhabitants, Tradesmen, and Labourers of the Kingdom of Ireland, Directions to Servants and Other Miscellaneous Pieces*, ed. Herbert Davis (Oxford: Blackwell, 1959), pp. 22–3.

61 *Gulliver's Travels*, ed. Ricardo Quintana (New York: Modern Library, 1958), p. 104.

62 *Poetical Works*, ed. Herbert Davis (London, 1967), ll. 49–60, p. 333.

63 *The Querist* (1735) Part I p. 150, Part II p. 1, ed. J. M. Hone (Dublin: The Talbot Press, *c.* 1936), pp. 40, 60.

64 *Practical Husbandman*, pp. 387, 391.

65 *Irish Tracts 1728–1733*, ed. Herbert Davis (Oxford: Blackwell, 1955), p. 176.

66 In his 'Of the Poet Laureate' (1729), Pope's account of the 'plain country-man of Apulia' is a satire on Duck. See also the biographical note on Duck in John Butt's edition of Pope's *Imitations of Horace* (London: Methuen, 1939), Twickenham iv. p. 359.

67 *Poems on Several Subjects* (London, 1730). E. P. Thompson suggests that there are 'older collective rhythms' in the 'huzza' that greets the last harvest-load home in Duck's poem, but (as one who can recollect how back-breaking this sort of harvesting was) I think it is as likely a shout of relief and of pleasure in expectation of the harvest feast. *Customs in Common* (London: Penguin, 1993), pp. 360–1.

68 *The Woman's Labour: An Epistle to Mr. Stephen Duck* (London, 1739). The italicized passage is from Duck's poem. In 'The Resignation of Mary Collier', Donna Landry points out that Collier's triple burden of labour, housework, and childcare together with gender ideology 'subverts the georgic more radically than Stephen Duck had done'. *The New Eighteenth Century*, ed. Felicity Nussbaum and Laura Brown (London: Methuen, 1987), p. 102.

69 'An Essay on Woman' (1751), ll. 43–4, in *The New Oxford Book of Eighteenth Century Verse*, p. 409. In *Mary Leapor: A Study in Eighteenth-century Women's Poetry* (Oxford: Clarendon, 1993), Richard Greene suggests that Philip Leapor's family would have enjoyed 'relative security, though certainly not prosperity' p. 7.

70 In *English Literature in History 1730–1850: An Equal Wide Survey* (London: Hutchinson, 1983), John Barrell has pointed out the unresolvable conflict between the myth of the golden age's decline to the iron present and Thomson's celebration of a present (eighteenth-century) golden age. But there is also a tension between the prelapsarian 'culture of the willing glebe' that he celebrates in *Spring* l. 247 and classical mythology, in that tools were not supposed to have been invented until after the end of the golden age.

71 *Winter*, ll. 950–87. John Evelyn, whose garden Peter the Great destroyed by being wheeled through the hedges by a servant, would have given a different account of the future Czar than either Thomson or Defoe.

72 *Supplement to the Essay on Horse-Hoing Husbandry*, p. 226

73 *English Literature in History*, p. 90. Part of the problem resulted from misreadings (such as Dryden's) of the word '*angusta*' as 'mean' rather than 'specialized'.

74 'An Essay on the Georgics', in Dryden's *The Works of Virgil* (London, 1697).

75 Among the advances in husbandry imported from the Low Countries at the end of the sixteenth century, turnip planting (and hence rotation of crops) was also strongly recommended in Hartlib's circle.

76 Peter Pindar [John Wolcot], 'Peter's Prophecy, or the President and Poet, of an Important Epistle to Sir J. Banks', in *The Works of Peter Pindar* (London, 1836), p. 443. Compare John Ellis's condescending gentrification of a supposed epistle by a rural girl in 'Sarah Hazard's Love Letter' (1747), in *The New Oxford Book of Eighteenth-Century Verse*, pp. 412–14.

77 *Poems by John Dyer* (London, 1761), p. 52.

78 *Cyder*, Book I, *Poems* (Glasgow, 1750), pp. 85–6.

79 *The Poetical Works of Richard Savage*, ed. Clarence Tracy (Cambridge: Cambridge University Press, 1962), p. 2.

80 'Ode XI. On the Approach of Summer' (1753); 'Ode VIII. Morning. The Author Confined to College', *Poetical Works* (London, 1802).

81 John Mortimer, *The Whole Art of Husbandry* (London, 1707), p.26.

82 'Prologue, Epilogue and Songs from *King Arthur*', in *The Poems and Fables of John Dryden*, ed. James Kinsley (Oxford: Oxford University Press, 1962), pp. 460–1.

83 'The Country Man', *Farrago* (London, 1733), in *The New Oxford Book of Eighteenth-Century Verse*, p. 264, ll. 1–8.

84 *Summer*, ll. 60–6. Compare Christopher Smart's 'A Morning-Piece, or, An Hymn for the Hay-Makers' (1748), where, though the diction is less elevated, the narrative and characterizations are none the less abstract. *The New Oxford Book of Eighteenth-Century Verse*, pp. 427–8.

85 (1742), *The New Oxford Book of Eighteenth-Century Verse*, p. 343. Like Farewell, James had been to Oxford, but both were non-metropolitan writers, Farewell in Somerset and James (who was born in Wales) in Devon.

86 Book IX, Ch. II.

87 *The Tempest*, ed. Frank Kermode (London: Methuen-Arden edn, 1964), p. 102.

|5|

Th'Amazed Defenceless Prize: Opening and Closing

The mythologies of land are not innocent of politics, and one of the most interesting developments in this period is the slippage in the use of the word 'enclosure'. Primarily thought of during the Interregnum of the seventeenth century as a means of endowing all small farmers with a stake in some land, it came by 1750 to mean the extensive appropriation of common land by large landowners: what we commonly mean by the term today. In the guise of opening the landscape for extensive views (what Virgil called *ingentia rura* in the *Georgics*), agricultural land came increasingly to be closed, demarcated, and privatized.

Probably in the first year or two of the 1650s, when he was tutor to Lord Fairfax's daughter at Nun Appleton in Yorkshire, Andrew Marvell wrote two of the most famous garden poems in the English language. Composed while Milton was writing *Paradise Lost*, they reflect some of the same concerns about the relation between art and nature, man and the natural world as Milton's poem. Marvell does not, of course, speak with his own voice in these poems; it would be absurd for as artistic a poet as he to be deploring works of art as the mower does in his poem 'The Mower Against Gardens'. None the less, the issues with which these poems play so cleverly are serious ones, employing the sort of debate that, for example, his poem 'A Dialogue Between the Soul and Body' also uses.

The mower is not a pastoral figure; he comes from the agricultural world of georgic, and his occupation is associated with mortality. 'With whistling scythe, and elbow strong, | These massacre the grass,' Marvell writes of the mowers in 'Upon Appleton House'. When the mower speaks in this poem, he does so as a figure in judgement on subjects which were to be central to the subject of georgic for the better part of the next century: luxury, enclosure, soil, exotic plants, and grafting. These are also the subjects of Virgil's *Georgics*, and as such are central both to the writings of agricultural reformers and to the literature of a people inventing its own national mythology.

The mower's list of luxurious vices includes not only the 'forbidden mixtures' of grafting and cross-fertilization but the importation of such exotics as 'The Marvel of Peru', a flower now commonly known in England as 'The Four O'Clock' (*Mirabilis Jalapa*). If there is an irony in his deploring doubleness in flowers while the poem itself plays elaborately with the couplet and inverted syntax, there is an even larger irony in suggesting that nature in the fields could be 'most plain and pure'. How can this be so in a fallen world?

Marvell's contemporary, George Warren, encountered a similar dilemma in Surinam. Faced with what looked like the 'eternal Spring' of Milton's unfallen Eden, he was mystified as to why the European apple tree continued to shed its leaves for three months of the year. Were the effects of the Fall only to be felt in the old world? For the answer to this question, he said, he referred himself to 'the virtuosi': the pioneer scientists and improvers of the Royal Society.[1]

The history of the field, as of the garden, is one of improvement and, to some degree, an attempt to restore Eden. At the very time that Marvell was writing this poem, the 'improvers' in agriculture associated with Samuel Hartlib's circle were already at work.

> We have indeed a kind of plodding and common course of Husbandry, [Hartlib wrote] and a kind of peevish imitation of the most, who (as Wise men note) are the worst Husbands, who only try what the earth will do of itself and seek not to help it with such means as Nature hath provided.[2]

One of Hartlib's correspondents, Robert Child, contributed 'A large Letter concerning the Defects and Remedies of English Husbandry', written in 1651, in which he listed many of the new plants available from North America.

> Why may not the Silk-grass of *Virginia*, the *Salsaperilla*, *Sassafras*, *Rattlesnake-weed* (which is an excellent cordial) be beneficial to us, as also their Cedars, Pines, Plumtrees, Cherries great Strawberries, and their *Locusts*, (which is a prickly plant, a swift grower, and therefore excellent for hedges) be useful to us?[3]

Noting that many exotic trees have already been cultivated in and about London, he goes on to deplore most small farmers' ignorance of the different varieties of grain available even in their own country, and he laments the deficiency in agriculture because there is 'not a *Systema*, or compleat book of all the parts of Agriculture'.[4]

Both a general ignorance and a lack of taxonomic system were to be themes repeated many times in the late seventeenth and early eighteenth centuries, frequently in the context of an argument over what the text of Virgil's *Georgics* really meant. A great deal of ink was spilt, for example, over whether the grafts that Virgil describes in Book II were possible or desirable, but most writers were in agreement that the kinds of trees and plants available needed greatly to be expanded if the Virgilian golden age was to be restored.

Charles Cotton echoes John Evelyn's earlier position when he argues that the English might be better occupied in propagating fruit trees than in aping the 'luxurious Kickshaws, and fantastick fashions' that came into the country from France at the Restoration.[5] And nearly 30 years later William Mackintosh makes the classical argument against the folly of imported luxuries to argue that 'good Meat and Drink, for good Fellowship and plentiful living' come from improved agriculture: 'not only an Art, but likewise a necessary and great one'.[6] 'Such a Man,' wrote Richard Bradley, the first Professor of Botany at Cambridge, 'is worthy to be a Farmer, and his Philosophy and Policy may put him upon the same footing with one of the greatest among the antient Philosophers.'[7]

With the growth of the East India trade, both directly and through Holland, came the sense of being able to restore Eden by gathering all the plants of the fallen world into one place. Abel Evans, celebrating the establishment of the Oxford Physic Garden in 1621, praised the first gardener, Jacob Bobart, for being 'not satisfy'd to know, | The *Plants*, that in three Nations blow,' but extending his curiosity to everything that:

> in *Africk, Asia*, shoots
> From Seeds, from Layers, Grafts, or Roots;
> At both the *Indies*, both the *Poles*,
> Whate'er the Sea, or Ocean rolls.[8]

Virgil's text proved problematic on this and other issues, however. A passage in *Georgics* Book I recommended that the farmer should content himself with what would grow best in the soil and climate of his native ground: the position of Marvell's mower. This was a position diametrically opposed, it seemed, to the attempt to cultivate such exotics as pineapples, bananas, citrus fruit, and even potatoes: plants that a number of writers believed could be propagated in England. Claiming that 'we can make things grow here as if we were three degrees nearer the sun', John Houghton affirmed:

> Had I a set of gentlemen that would bear the charges, there should hardly be a *tree, shrub*, or more tender *plant* in *England, Europe*, or perhaps a larger distance, that was likely to prove greatly useful to *England*, but those gentlemen should partake of; for why may we not as well as *flax-seed* from *Eastland, onion-seed* from *Strasbourgh, melon-seed* from *Italy*, and divers others, have *grafts, roots*, and *seeds* from *France, Spain, Italy*, or any other place we trade in the world.[9]

Houghton's recommendation of such new field crops as spurry and madder were more to the point, and his editor, Bradley, continued to be interested in such things as collecting clover seed and improving land by sowing onions. For him 'the true Cytisus of the ancients' was a question not of footnotes to Virgil but practical agriculture:

As to the fixing of the very Sort [of Cytisus] which was the Favourite of our ancient Husbandmen, I know not better how to do it than that which is the *Cytisus Galeni creditus maranthae Cornutus*, or supposed true *Cytisus*, or true *Trefoil* ... the Flowers are of a yellow shinging Colour, like the Blossom of Broom; and the seed grows in crooked Cods. The *Cytisus* is call'd in English, *Milk Trefoil*.[10]

No one was more prepared to call Virgil's husbandry to account than the great agricultural improver and inventor, Jethro Tull. For him, the conservatism that Marvell's mower espoused represented everything that stood in the way of agricultural and economic advance. In 1740 Tull, the inventor of the cultivator, wrote indignantly about a line in the *Georgics* that claimed that a field need be ploughed only twice a season. Tull, who thought even olives might be grown in England, declined to take Virgil's advice when it appeared to fly in the face of experiment and improvement:

None of the Improvements made on any sort of arable Land by Foreign Grasses, or Turneps, could have been introduced into *Britain* without renouncing the *Sat-erit* ['twice is enough for ploughing'] Doctrine of *Virgil*; for they will not survive on any sort of Land without pulveration by Tillage.[11]

The oldest of these subjects in English discourse, and the one that was to prove the most troubling, was enclosure.[12] It was, says Marvell's mower, man's first mistake:

He first enclosed within the gardens square
A dead and standing pool of air.

And yet what the mower sees as the Fall (or at least the first consequence of it) is, in *Paradise Lost*, what Adam describes as unfallen Eden, the Eden of his dream:

A Circuit wide, enclos'd, with goodliest Trees
Planted, with Walks, and Bowers.

(VIII. 304–5)

Milton's enclosure is not Marvell's, however, or rather Adam's is not the mower's. Both poets write in the context of the Civil War, but Milton writes of unfallen Eden, while Marvell's world is a fallen England where the enclosed garden has been shattered forever:

> Oh thou, that dear and happy isle
> The garden of the world ere while . . .
> What luckless apple did we taste,
> To make us mortal, and thee waste. [13]

Milton's enclosed Eden, however, is also a georgic contrast to the un-enclosed world of Satan. What Satan offers is the real-estate salesman's 'spacious views' while plotting eviction, property as possession, not use. In a speech worthy of a travelling salesman, he offers Eve the mountebank's powder of instant transformation:

> That yee should be as Gods, since I as Man,
> Internal Man, is but proportion meet,
> I of brute human, yee of human Gods.
>   (IX. 710–12)

Like many an eighteenth-century landowner, he speaks of calling in a country of boundless vistas while in fact plotting to expel the tenants.

Milton and Marvell knew one another in the early 1650s, but Milton also knew Samuel Hartlib, and dedicated his tract, *Of Education*, to him. Hartlib's circle of agricultural correspondents laid the foundation of the Georgical Committee which was influential in the early days of the Royal Society and which contributed to the general reform of agriculture after the Restoration. These reformers also looked back to Bacon for their inspiration, though they differed from him in their practice.

One example of this reforming spirit was the founding of the first botanic garden in England, the Oxford Physic Garden. And indeed, when Abel Evans celebrates this garden in his poem *Vertumnus* (1713) his praise of the founder, Lord Danby, begins with enclosing:

> 'Twas Gen'rous *Danby* first enclos'd
> The Waste, and in Parterres dispos'd;
> Transform'd the Fashion of the Ground,
> And Fenc'd it with a Rocky Mound. [14]

Marvell's persona in 'Upon Appleton House' comes to see that beyond the fallen garden the world is not waste, that even the harvesters are like the Israelites passing through the Red Sea to the promised Canaan. And he does so in a series of stanzas that draw attention to the way in which art reveals what simple nature cannot; the word he uses is 'landskip' (st. 58), a word meaning a painting of a landscape. In 'Upon Appleton House' the word 'waste' is both an adjective and a noun. (In the first folio 'thee waste' is written 'The Wast'.) The poem is itself an enclosure where the tragic adjective 'waste' becomes metamorphosed into a fertile noun. What many cottagers and smallholders had been doing during the

Interregnum – making waste land arable – is thereby celebrated in the poem.

The word 'enclosure' is commonly associated with the depredations of large landowners after the middle of the eighteenth century, as revealed, for example, in Goldsmith's 'The Deserted Village'.[15] It is therefore surprising to find that many of the proponents of agricultural reform in the Interregnum were in favour of enclosure too. But the enclosure they favoured was on an individual and small scale, 'for Pastures and Improvements daily', as one of Hartlib's correspondents, John Beale, put it in 1657:

> and as a Stranger passeth by our Habitations, by our Fences, Orchards, Pastures, Arable, he may distinguish a well-order'd Housekeeper and a Freholder, from an over-wracked Tenant, and an Unthrift.[16]

Beale's model there is the picture of the old man of Taranto from the fourth book of Virgil's *Georgics*, a man:

> who occupied
> An acre or two of land that no one wanted,
> A patch not worth the ploughing, unrewarding,
> For flocks, unfit for vineyards; he however
> By planting here and there among the scrub
> Cabbages or white lilies and verbena
> And flimsy poppies, fancied himself a king
> In wealth, and coming home late in the evening
> Loaded his board with unbought delicacies.
>
> (127–32)[17]

Just this sort of enclosure was what Beale proposed to his friend John Evelyn as an alternative to 'princely gardens'. It is, he wrote 'that which the incomparable Poet [Virgil] thought worthy to be singled out for the whole argument, which his pen should adorn, when he pointed out the utility of Gardens'. 'I shall here shew,' he wrote in his *Nurseries, Orchards, Profitable Gardens and Vineyards Encouraged* (1677),

> how a younger Brother of ordinary capacities, who hath but so many Acres of his own as belong to every Cottager by Statute, may thence easily and speedily raise a considerable gain, for the maintenance of his Family, and entertain himself with the sweetest and most innocent of Earthly pleasures.[18]

The phrase 'unbought delicacies' (*dapes inemptae*) was to resonate in much of the georgic poetry of the late seventeenth and early eighteenth centuries, associated as it was with sturdy independence and a life free from vanity and luxury. When Pope writes of himself as piddling about on broccoli and mutton[19] in his garden at Twickenham, it is to this argument for simplicity and use that he is appealing. And it was partly upon this concept that he also based his claim to Lord Burlington that use alone sanctifies expense.

Even John Beale's Royalist contemporary, Richard Weston, could argue the same point about enclosure. Why he says, are there 'fewest poor, where there are fewest Commons'? By enclosing two acres of common land a poor man might get a living instead of leaving them to the rich for mere grazing land. Although Weston was plainly nervous about appearing to be encouraging communist takeovers such as the Diggers had effected in the 1650s, he none the less thought that land used only for small-game hunting (by poor and rich alike) was waste land, and he asked 'whether or no these lands might not be improved very much by the husbandry of *Flanders*, *viz* by sowing *Flax*, *Turnips*, great *Clover* grass' and so on.[20]

Many of Weston's proposals sound very like those of one of Hartlib's agricultural correspondents, Robert Child, and certainly Child would have agreed with Weston's observation, 'A little Farm well till'd is to be preferr'd.'[21] In fact, Weston's sentiment there is almost exactly a translation of one of the most invoked texts from the *Georgics*: '*laudato ingentia rura exiguum colito*' (praise a large estate but cultivate a small one). Frequently misquoted by citing only half of the line (praise a large estate), the tag *ingentia rura* came to mean, in effect, 'Praise a large estate by obliterating many small ones.' As such, Virgil's legacy in the eighteenth century was the enclosures that characterized the landscapes later 'improved' by Capability Brown.

A central text in this process was Stephen Switzer's *Ichnographia Rustica*, an expansion in 1718 of a work first published in 1715 as *The Noblemans Gentlemans and Gardeners Recreation*. Taking advantage of a tide that had already turned against the diminutive fastidiousness of the Dutch garden style, Switzer appropriated the French '*grand manier*' of Le Nôtre but recommended naturalizing its 'calling in of the country'. Nonetheless Switzer's recommendation of Lord Bathurst's estate, Riskins, and his designs for Lord Bertie's Grimsthorpe show him still largely attached to domination and prospect. His enthusiasm for fountains, manifested chiefly in his *Hydrostaticks* (1729), also has much in common with the world of regularity that he affected to despise. The corollary of his advocacy of '*ingentia rura*', moreover, was that such 'naturalized' woodlands as Ray Wood at Castle Howard (which he praised) could only be achieved by moving a whole village (Henderskelfe) out of its way.

Switzer knew very little about the interchange of agriculture and horticulture which he advocated; one of his rivals pointed out that he had many designs but no nursery garden. Having made the mistake of attacking Jethro Tull's *Horse-Hoing Husbandry* in his periodical *The Practical Husbandman*, he left himself open to Tull's agricultural rebuke. Accusing him of being a mere fashionmonger and a plagiarist of others' ideas, Tull wrote:

The Practical Husbandman contradicts the *Title* of his Book, when in p. *x* of his *Pref.* to *Aug.* he shews that he doth not *know* Plowing from Harrowing, and it may be thence inferred he doth not know a Plow from a Harrow; as it may be inferred from *p. xxxii* of the same *Preface*, that he doth not know my Drill from *Platt's Setting-stick*, nor my Hoe-Plow from the *Sheim* of *Kent*. His *Title* should have been *The Cockney Husbandman, who never practised* Agriculture *out of the Sound of* Bow-Bell.[22]

In the first two decades of the eighteenth century, however, Virgil's *'ingentia rura'* was still as much a matter for argument as many of the other Virgilian tags over which Switzer and Tull quarrelled. It was used both to vindicate a small estate, such as Pope's 5 acres at Twickenham, and to justify the creation of such large estates as Mr Allworthy's in *Tom Jones*, where the view of 'several villages' and 'meadows' was (as Marvell's mower also would have it) 'owing less to art than to nature'.[23]

Virgil's text was quoted in the dedication 'to the *Gentry* and *Yeomanry* of *England*' prefaced to the most cited book of Restoration husbandry, John Worlidge's *Systema Agriculturae* (1668). Worlidge's work (he also wrote a *Systema Horti-culturae*) reflects the secularized millenarianism that animated much of the agricultural reform in the Restoration. The apocalyptic last trumpet may not sound, but society can be transformed by a new husbandry. If husbandry will not undo the Fall, it may at least mitigate its social and economic consequences.

In 1739 William Warburton published his influential commentary on Pope's *Essay on Man*: a commentary that stressed Pope's sense that the universe, though fallen, is the best of all possible worlds. In the same year, Samuel Madden, writing on the reform of tillage in Ireland, wrote in similarly visionary terms:

> I would wish to have your Farm to be to Husbandry (nay, if possible, to Gardening too) what a Globe or Map is to the Earth, a description, in Miniature at least, of all its Parts [in order to] see all the Secrets of that human Art divine, as *Milton* speaks, laid open to their Eyes and Hands as well as their Ears.[24]

The roots of such visionary discourse, in English at least, can be traced to another period of agricultural unrest and reform, the early sixteenth century. More's *Utopia*, like Swift's *Modest Proposal*, is set in a world where sheep eat up men while enclosures for grazing drive the agricultural peasants off the land. Looking back to this period from the 1740s, one of Swift's Irish compatriots wrote ominously, 'There was so great *poverty* and *discontent* throughout the kingdom on account of the *decay* of *tillage*, and the *inclosing* of lands for *pasture*, that there were many dangerous *insurrections*.'[25]

The printing of More's *Utopia* was supervised by Erasmus, whose own

Praise of Folly (punningly titled *Encomium Moriae*) in turn inspired Swift's satiric method. And it was one of More's contemporaries, John Fitzherbert, who wrote *The Boke of Surveying* (1543) that continued to be cited by agricultural writers in the eighteenth century. Like these later agricultural reformers, Thomas Berthelot, who wrote the prefatory poem for Fitzherbert, rebuked the idle luxury of his time and appealed to the ancient agricultural writers. This is a time, he laments, when:

> Some had leaver write of love yea of baudry
> Than to so good a mater tourne their style
> Fonde pleasure and pride do them so begyle
> That slouthe wandreth about in every way
> And good busynesse is falling in decay.

By contrast, the ancients were concerned about the improvement of their country:

> The worthy Caton that excellent romayne
> Columella Varro and Vergilius
> Of husbandrie to write had in no disdayne
> Nor many other eloquent and famous
> Thought it nat a thyng inglorious
> Such mater to write wherby they might avaunce
> The common welth. And thyr countre enhaunce.[26]

Richard Bradley was one of those eighteenth-century agricultural reformers who looked back to Fitzherbert, chiefly for arguments in defence of enclosure. Like Berthelot, he also cited the precept of the ancients:

> We find that Husbandry was accounted a Study so extremely beneficial to the Commonwealth, that Persons of the highest Rank and Figure did not only promote the Practice and Improvement of it amongst the Common People, but took a Pride to distinguish themselves by such new Inventions and Contrivances as might add anything to an Art of so general Advantage.[27]

One of Bradley's many publications was a reissue in 1727 of John Houghton's late seventeenth-century *Collection for the Improvement of Husbandry and Trade*, a work similar to Hartlib's *Legacy* in being the vehicle for a number of agricultural correspondents. 'Hartlib's *Legacy* is never to be forgotten,' Houghton writes in 1682 of a man who improved all kinds of husbandry at a time then the English were averse 'from all care of improvements.' Houghton, who cites More's *Utopia* as one of the agricultural books in the collection of the Royal Society, writes in 1681 of his hope that the Royal Society will revive its agricultural committee. He quotes the Society's motto '*nullius in verba*' ('by experiment not reading') in favour of experimentation, and hopes that England may become 'the garden of the world'; but he becomes positively messianic when he writes about enclosure:

'tis inclosure will make *our yoaks easy, and our burdens light*; and it is this will improve our lands and mines, and bring in the linen manufacture; ... it is this may find out some new discoveries, and increase and encourage our old plantations ... For it is not to be doubted, but that land *enclos'd* and *till'd*, yieldeth a far greater increase to the husbandman than lands *open* and *untill'd*.[28]

Houghton there echoes Worlidge's *Systema Agriculturae* (1668). Published the year after *Paradise Lost*, Worlidge's book outlines an agricultural 'paradise regained' in which 'the most principal way of Improvement' of land is enclosure. Like the Elizabethan agriculturist, Thomas Tusser, to whom he looks back, Worlidge proposes a model of enclosure that is in the common interest. 'It ascertaineth every man his just and due Propriety and Interest,' he says.[29]

Enclosure was not, for Worlidge or Houghton, a matter of one owner enclosing hundreds of acres: what it became later in the eighteenth century after the agricultural revolution, when parliamentary acts for the purpose were commonplace. Indeed, Bradley notes that it is gentlemen who are most often opposed to enclosure because the hedges of many small fields interfere with their hunting.[30] Houghton cites Sir Robert Dallington's *Survey of Tuscany* (1605) as a modern instance of the Virgilian example that Beale also commended; in Tuscany half an acre is enough for a man to feel rich. Like Houghton, Bradley also approves of the publication of letters from agricultural correspondents. He quotes a letter from Colchester in 1724 which is also in favour of enclosure, but not before doing a proper survey of the land as Fitzherbert recommends: 'Where this has been practised we find the Lands of more than double the Value they were before ... and every Tenant better contented [because] ... every Cottager may have his Portion of Ground allow'd him, according to his Rent.'[31]

This was the ideal, but plainly it was increasingly not the practice as the century progressed. What had been conceived as a means of improving the lot of small farmers (freeholders and copy-holders) was appropriated by large landowners (especially new-made men from the city) as a way of creating more manageable estates.[32]

As early as 1727 Bradley observed that the large-scale graziers had used enclosure to take advantage of common land where 'poor people have a bare right to feed a cow apiece'. By so doing, he wrote, they 'partake of the poors rights, but even more than their share would come to, if they were really poor.' Not surprisingly, Bradley recommended that every parish have four separate surveys made to prevent disputes 'about the parceling of the ground', but he still believed that the ordinary farmer would be better off with this sort of enclosure than he was before.[33] So too did Swift, whose angry irony at the lazy and grasping landowners of Ireland is directed against large-scale grazing at the expense of tillage and employment:

> But, why all this Concern for the Poor? We want them not, as the Country is now managed; they may follow Thousands of their Leaders, and seek Bread abroad. Where the Plough has no Work, one Family can do the Business of Fifty, and you may send away the other Forty-nine. An admirable Piece of Husbandry, never known or practised by the wisest Nations; who erroneously thought People to be the Riches of a Country.[34]

Small wonder that many have believed that Goldsmith's much later words about a depopulated and impoverished countryside also portrayed his homeland, Ireland![35] Long before Goldsmith, however, opposition to enclosure for the purpose of large pastures was also beginning to be heard. In 1732 *An Essay, Proving, That Inclosing Commons, And Common-field-Lands, Is Contrary to the Interest of the Nation* was published. Written by John Cowper, it takes a stance that is not unlike that of his namesake, William Cowper, in *The Task*:

> Mansions once
> Knew their own masters, and laborious hinds
> That had surviv'd the father, serv'd the son.
> (III. 746–8)

Now, by contrast, land serves for pleasure rather than use: the vast untilled pastures of Capability Brown's landscapes. The world that Pope described in his portrait of Timon's grandiose but sterile villa is one, William Cowper writes, where 'the country starves'. Cowper's father, a rural clergyman who subscribed to Stephen Duck's *Poems on Several Occasions* (1736) would have known the constraints upon poor labourers first-hand.

This is just the point that John Cowper makes in terms that are as indignant as Swift's:

> In those *Parishes* that have *Commons* belonging to them, the Poor and the Rich have a right of *Commonage* one with another. But when these *Commons* come to be inclosed and converted into *Pasture*, the Ruin of the Poor is a natural Consequence; they being bought out by the Lord of the *Manor*, or some other Person of Substance. For when a *Common*, that has been the main Support of perhaps forty or fifty poor Families, and some of them large ones too, is thus taken from them, they will certainly be thereby render'd incapable of maintaining themselves as usual in that *Parish*: This will put them under a Necessity of forsaking their old Habitations, (which in their mean Circumstances must be a great Loss and Hardship) and wandring about till they can find some other Place, where they may enjoy their

former Priveledges, without which they cannot subsist. But if these *Inclosures* become general, whither must they go? Where will they find a resting Place? Or how will they get their Bread? They must become Vagabonds, be driven from one country to another; be reduced to Beggary or Starving; or be forced to leave their native Land, in hopes of meeting with better Treatment in a strange Country.[36]

The answer to Cowper's questions might have been supplied by the largely silenced voices of Stephen Duck, Mary Collier, and Mary Leapor. 'Let those who feast at Ease on dainty Fare, | Pity the Reapers, who their Feasts prepare,' Duck writes in 'The Thresher's Labour'.[37] These are the very peasantry whose ancient common rights were swallowed up by all-powerful landlords and who became, in consequence, dependent wage-labourers upon large estates. Tenant farmers who had escaped the direct burden of increased taxes in the late seventeenth century came increasingly under pressure from market forces and a desire for efficiency on the part of land-lords. Consolidation (or engrossing) did not depend on enclosure, in the strict sense of the word, to be effective. It could be managed by refusing to renew tenancies. 'The major decline of small owners and of small farmers in general', G. E. Mingay has written, 'must have occurred before 1760, probably between about 1660 and 1750.'[38] This is, of course, the period in which Pope and Thomson were celebrating the georgic ideal of the small farmer while addressing their poems in many cases to the very new landowners who were extirpating this Virgilian ideal by creating large estates through purchase and engrossment: Richard Boyle, Richard Temple, Allen Bathurst, Bubb Dodington, and Spencer Compton.

John Cowper's attack on 'the insatiate Avarice, the pride or the Luxury of the few' was addressed to these engrossing landlords. It was a common com-plaint by the middle of the century, but it was a theme to which William Cowper in particular returned again and again. So does John Cowper. 'One third of all the Land of *England*,' he writes, 'has been inclosed within these Eighty Years' only for the good of the 'Grandure and Magnificence of some.' His attack on the values of trade at the expense of farmers and cottagers is just what the poet Cowper iterates in the third book of *The Task*. The empty luxuries of city life, driven by the 'stir of commerce', would have no attraction:

> were England now
> What England was, plain, hospitable, kind,
> And undebauch'd.
>
> (III. 742–4)

The poet's indignation is exactly what registers in John Cowper's denunci-ation of another clergyman, John Laurence, and his brother (a land surveyor) Edward Laurence.[39] Arguing for enclosure, John Laurence claims that the land is thereby properly cared for, many people are employed in the business, and that it 'encreases the Rent of Land sometimes tenfold'. Given these arguments it is not surprising that he says: 'I cannot but admire [be astonished], the People of *England* should be so backward to *Inclose*.'[40] But Laurence puts his case in a rather shaky argument. No matter whether the land is enclosed for tillage or pasture, he claims, the poor will benefit because of its increased productivity, and open fields and waste land are secured from pilfering and stealing.

His brother's recommendation that stewards of estates should attempt to purchase 'all the Freeholders out as soon as possible, especially in such Manors where Improvements are to be made by *inclosing* Commons and Common-Fields,' however, gives the game away. The poor may be employed 'in planting and preserving the Hedges,' or 'afterwards will be set to work in the Tillage and Pasture',[41] but they will no longer be (at least in part) their own masters. And Cowper is not fooled by the duplicity of the argument. 'Is not this telling us,' he writes, 'that a trusty Steward ought to be divested of all Humanity? Sure Christianity teaches us better Things! Christianity teaches us Compassion and universal Benevolence; and not to watch, to seek for, and to take all Opportunities of supplanting and ruining the *Poor*.'[42]

In fact this process of buying out small tenant farmers had been in train since at least the middle of the seventeenth century.[43] Large landowners faced with a gradual fall in agricultural prices found it increasingly profitable to lease their land to large farmers, not the small copy-holders whose interests John Cowper later had at heart. After 1660, conditions had worsened for small farmers; and even many who had secure leases were forced to sell, often to rising men of commerce like Pope's Timon, who sought to establish themselves as members of the landed gentry by buying up tracts of the country piecemeal in order to create estates.[44] The great deal of attention given by early economic historians to the period between the mid-eighteenth and the mid-nineteenth centuries has somewhat obscured the fact that a real decline in owner-occupied land happened *before* the middle of the eighteenth century, indeed in the late seventeenth century, largely as a result of increased taxation and the fall in agricultural prices.[45]

Pope must have known this perfectly well, both from his early friendship with Sir William Trumbull, who had farms within Windsor Forest, and later from Lord Bathurst. Pope's 'Epistle to Bathurst' examines the use of riches, and praises Bathurst's virtue in pursuing them:

> Not meanly, or ambitiously pursu'd,
> Nor sunk by sloth, nor rais'd by servitude.
>
> (221–2)

Bathurst's ability to join economy with magnificence and splendour with charity is contrasted to the son of a nouveau-riche who, having squandered his fortune on party politics, suffers the very consequence of luxury that William

Cowper later deplored in *The Task*: the destruction of his estate's resources. The contrast of the private vice of 'effeminate' luxury with the heroic ideal of public virtue was a commonplace both of literature and the arts in the period, but it is a contrast that resonates strangely in Pope's poem.[46]

But Bathurst had assembled his great estate at Cirencester in very much the way that many a man of commerce had done. Beginning with a house and grounds that had belonged to Henry Danvers, the creator of the Physic Garden in Oxford, Bathurst proceeded to buy up the estate of one of the old families: Sir Robert Atkyns's Sapperton Manor and Oakley Wood. One of Bathurst's first acts after this purchase was to demolish the Atkyns's Tudor manor, but he also began almost at once to plant what had been farmland with trees. Pope, who lent him money (at interest) to do so and advised him on the plantations can hardly have been unaware of how this was done. In 1743, 10 years after Pope's poem, Bathurst was able to extend his holdings at Sapperton, by acquiring about 190 acres of land in exchange with other owners: land that tenants would previously have farmed.[47]

The 'Epistle to Bathurst' uses the conventional discourse for justifying enclosure when it claims that 'wealth in the gross is death ... but well-dispers'd, is Incense to the Skies': a discourse that would have been familiar to Bathurst's uncle, Ralph, who was a member of John Wilkins's circle of agricultural reformers nearly a century earlier at Oxford. But Pope's poem also touches on the legal discourse of enclosure in the couplet that intro-duces the famous Man of Ross, John Kyrle:

> But all our praises why should Lords engross?
> Rise, honest Muse! and sing the MAN of ROSS.
> (249–50)

Pope could and did use the word 'engross' to mean 'write in large letters' (its first dictionary meaning) or even 'to encompass',[48] but both meanings had, by the early eighteenth century, been largely subsumed in a legal discourse increasingly associated with the acquisition of land: the word's fourth meaning in the *New OED*. This is certainly the way Swift used it in his *An Answer to a Paper* in 1728. Writing about the deleterious consequences in Ireland of turning ploughed land into pasture, he first explains that this came about because of the system of tenancy in which farmers on precarious leases were liable to abuse their land.

> This gave Birth to that abominable Race of Graziers, who, upon Expiration of the Farmers Leases, are ready to engross great Quantities of Land ... Thus, a vast Tract of Land, where Twenty or Thirty Farmers lived together, with their Cottagers and Labourers in their several Cabins, became all desolate, and easily managed by one or two Herdsmen, and their Boys; whereby the Master-Grazier, with little Trouble, seized to himself the Livelyhood of a Hundred People.[49]

What then does the contorted syntax of the first line of Pope's couplet (written only 4 years later) suggest? And how is the word 'engross' a clue to something that can only be said interrogatively? How does its failure to form a true rhyme with 'Ross' suggest that the two halves of the couplet (in spite of the ostensible argument) have little in common either? What have Cirencester and Wimpole (the estates of Bathurst and Oxford, the 'Lords' referred to) to do with the reality of the ideals that the poem espouses? The fortune of Edward Harley, second Earl of Oxford, for example, was based on his inheriting the Nottinghamshire estate of Welbeck (through his marriage to the daughter of the Duke of Newcastle) as well as his main estate, Wimpole itself. But this inheritance had only been achieved through an extremely acrimonious legal suit with his wife's family that dragged on for more than a decade and required an Act of Parliament to settle. Part of this settlement, concluded in 1718, involved the settling of ownership and recompense for the recently enclosed woodland of Clumber Park.[50]

What Harley inherited at Wimpole, moreover, was an estate that had gradually been enclosed throughout the seventeenth century: a park of 210 acres as well as seven tenant farms, the largest of which was 100 acres. Once his inheritance was settled, he began to enlarge the house to contain his already extensive book collection: a collection that attracted many scholars and writers, such as Pope's friend, the poet Prior, who died there in 1721. In 1720 Harley also hired the architect Charles Bridgeman to re-landscape the park, most obviously in the great southern avenue which extends (like something designed by Le Nôtre) for 2½ miles and dominates the estate. Patron of artists, architects, and men of letters, Harley none the less offers little evidence of the public-spirited local good works of the Man of Ross.

Kyrle was certainly no engrosser, but rather a benefactor of his town whom Pope compares to Moses. Far from 'engrossing' in the common legal sense of the word, Kyrle offered to his fellow townspeople an opened landscape where the prospect of the Wye valley and the surrounding countryside from the park he created was not private but available to all. His only act of 'enclosure' was to wall in a reservoir for the sake of the town.

Is Pope's praise of Bathurst's ability 'to ease th' oppress'd, and raise the sinking heart', then, ironic, or at least an instance of what is called in pedagogy 'laudando praecipere' (to instruct by praising)? In what sense is the exemplary tale of Sir Balaam, with which the poem ends, a cautionary shot across the bows to Harley and Bathurst, neither of whom seem to have been notable in succouring the poor? And what is the real import of this poem (Maynard Mack calls it 'a sermon')[51] supposedly on vulgar peculation and new-made City money? If all these abuses of riches canvassed in the poem are to be avoided, what does this say about (or to) Lord Bathurst? City-born and bred, and the son of the Governor of the East India Company, how easily is Bathurst's fortune distinguished from Sir Balaam's City-made wealth, founded in part upon a stolen Indian diamond?

Certainly it seems unlikely that the tenants and smallholders bought out or dispossessed at Sapperton would have thought of Bathurst as easing the oppressed. In his poem on the park Edward Stephens says of Bathurst, 'Your lib'ral Bounty num'rous Poor confess,' but his claim that 'this alludes to the great Number of Hands constantly employ'd on this noble Plan'[52] is an ironic admission of the displacement and dispossession implicit in this available work-force. The word 'poor', as E. P. Thompson has pointed out, is a 'gentry-made term,' wholly undiscriminating of the many different sorts of people thus dispossessed. Moreover, it 'carries the suggestion that the bulk of the working population were deserving of gentry condescension, and perhaps of charity (and were somehow supported *by* the gentry instead of the direct opposite)'.[53]

The villagers of Stowe, who had been cleared away in order to extend Lord Cobham's garden there, would equally have been unlikely choristers of Cobham's praises. Although Cobham did not remove the 'vast Parterres' designed by Bridgeman by 'float[ing] them with a lake', his drowning of the old lake in an even larger one entailed wholesale dislocations. One of the nicer ironies of landscape and garden history is the story of the creation of the 'Elysian Fields' at that time. Designed by William Kent (who also designed the engravings for Thomson's *Seasons*), this 'arcadian landscape', celebrating the connection between ancient virtue and modern Britain, was created at the cost of destroying the old village. What remained, ironically, was what had connected the village to the former seventeenth-century manor, the church; but it was conveniently tidied away into a grove of trees and out of sight of the classical moral scheme of the new gardens.[54]

A great deal has been written about Pope's prescriptions to Lord Burlington (in the fourth 'Moral Epistle') about creating a landscape,[55] but little about the discrepancy between the country-house mythology of traditional landed values and the case at Chiswick itself. Although Burlington's mother did come from an old country family, the Cliffords, and brought with her dowry the estate of Londesborough in Yorkshire, Burlington left the running and redesigning of that estate largely to Thomas Knowlton, his steward there. The Boyle fortune, moreover, was not ancient landed money; it had been acquired in Ireland after the depredations of the Civil War by Roger Boyle, an adventurer who was Burlington's grandfather and whose title, Earl of Cork, Burlington inherited.

Chiswick, moreover, was not really a country estate in the way that Pope's poem might suggest. Far closer to London than Pope's Twickenham, it was more a suburban villa[56]– a showpiece for day-visits to the 'country' – than the working farmstead for which Palladio had designed his buildings. Nor, for that matter, did it have much to do with the agrarian values of the letters of the younger Pliny upon which Palladio's farmsteads and Chiswick were ostensibly based.[57] Indeed, what are we to make of Pope's couplet deploring those who 'Load some vain Church with old Theatric state, | Turn Arcs of triumph to a Garden-gate'?

Burlington himself had re-erected in his garden a Palladian arch designed by Inigo Jones, and his invocation of Jones's neo-Palladian buildings there included a summerhouse involving the portico of Jones's St Paul's in Covent Garden.[58] One of the features of Pope's prescription was that Burlington's own 'Light' in this design was to be of more consequence than 'Jones and Le Nôtre', and yet the radiating 'goose-foot' design of the avenues in place by 1730 took the eye immediately to the very bounds that, Pope said, the true designer should conceal.

Probably the most famous phrase in the 'Epistle to Burlington' is the one about the genius of the place that announces Pope's prescriptions for the ideal landscape:

> Consult the Genius of the Place in all;
> That tells the Waters or to rise, or fall.
> (57–8)

When Pope wrote the poem, Burlington had just begun to create the cascade at the south-eastern end of the canal in his garden, the end nearest to the house. Indeed, the cascade was to be part of a terrace that connected the old garden to a new area which he had purchased west of the canal. Because the natural fall of water was in a southerly direction (towards the Thames), however, the cascade at the southern end was completely against what 'the Genius of the place' had to say about how waters might rise or fall. In fact, it never worked properly. Even the disposition of the grounds as a whole seems contrary to what Pope espouses. Most of the gardens were to the north of the house, and many a visitor must have run the risk of catching cold at its Venetian door.

In fact, Burlington's Chiswick had much more in common with collecting drawings, statues, and coins than the poem pretends to recognize. The estate is more about 'playing at country' (to use Dickens's phrase) than anything that has much to do with agriculture. When Pope introduces his advice about concealing the bounds of the estate, he uses the phrase 'he gains all points': a literal translation of Horace's '*omne tulit punctum*' from *The Art of Poetry*. But Horace writes of combining the sweet or pleasant with the useful, and in spite of the famous line ''Tis Use alone that sanctifies Expence', use is not a dominant feature either of Bathurst's Cirencester or Boyle's Chiswick.

> Who then shall grace, or who improve the Soil?
> Who plants like BATHURST, or who builds like BOYLE.
> (177–8)

The rhyme in the couplet is of 'Boyle' with 'soil', but a closer examination reveals that 'improve the soil' is no more the same thing as 'builds like Boyle' than 'gracing' is the same as 'improving'. What the rhyme suggests the sense denies. The couplet, in other words, works to undo its ostensible closure.

There has been a great deal written by Pope scholars and garden historians about the landscape ideals of the 'Epistle to Burlington' but little about what such 'place-making' cost the inhabitants whose villages and farms were swept away or consolidated elsewhere. Much less again has been written about the discrepancy between Pope's georgic myth of deep harvests, milky heifers, and rising forests on the one hand, and the displacement (at Chiswick) of so-called 'cheerful tenants' by a vast pleasure garden on the other.

Perhaps Pope himself gives us such a description in Satire II of 'The Satires of Dr. Donne Versified.' There the unnamed attorney effects what the 'Epistle to Burlington' never overtly names:

> The lands are bought; but where are to be found
> Those ancient woods, that shaded all the ground?
> We see no new-built palaces aspire,
> No kitchens emulate the vestal fire.
> Where are those troops of Poor, that thronged of yore
> The good old landlord's hospitable door?
>
> $(109-14)^{59}$

Although the georgic myth might have been true of Lord Bolingbroke's consciously agrarian estate, Dawley Farm, it was certainly not true of Chiswick. In Leonard Knyff's drawing of the estate in 1707, the house backs onto kitchen gardens and arable land to the north and is fronted on the south by pasture and orchards and a series of small fields that look like smallholdings or tenancies. Thirty years later, after Lord Burlington's 'improvements', all this has been swept away by radiating avenues, serpentine walks, and 'wildernesses' that even extend across the Thames, leaving no room for the 'yearly toil' of agriculture.

The landscape of Middlesex and Surrey, where Lord Burlington had already established his garden at Chiswick when Pope wrote his poem, was not the empty canvas that Pope implies. The 'Genius of the Place' there would have had to include not simply the natural topography of water, valley, and woods but the demography of agriculture that had been part of this landscape for hundreds of years. Decorative woodlands and the occasional picturesque cow or horse may be consonant with the image of the gentleman farmer, but they do not constitute the working landscape that the georgic implies. Only an anthropomorphic nature that 'plants' and 'designs', as Pope describes it, could so easily gentrify traditional agriculture out of existence and effect an enclosure in the guise of opening the country.[60]

Windsor Forest also addresses a georgic subject, but its opening Latin invocation is pastoral: from the sixth or 'messianic' eclogue of Virgil.

Non iniussa cano: Te nostrae, Vare, Myricae
Te Nemus omne canet; nec Phoebo gratior ulla est
Quam sibi quae Vari preascripsit Pagina nomen.

(Not unbidden I sing: it is of you, Varus, that our tamarisks and groves shall sing. Nor is any page more acceptable to Phoebus [Apollo] than the one that bears Varus's name at the beginning.)

Virgil's text is full of ironies. The lines Pope quotes begin with the sentence, 'not unbidden I sing,' but who is doing the bidding, Virgil's patron or his rustic muse? Is this a subject to order or a subject inspired? Pope chooses an appropriate quotation about trees (*Myricae*, tamarisks), but why does he omit more than a line of the quotation about other readers – 'if there are still any to read my songs, any captivated by the theme of love'? Are not these the same learned readers who surely will be aware that this poem contains the mythological stories of theft, rape, and even the bestiality of Scylla and the incest of Philomel? Can Pope have been unaware, moreover, that the historical context of these poems was 'the forcible transfer of land from the possession of its former owners and tenants into the hands of soldiers demobilized by their victorious commanders'?[61] Do not the readers, absent from his invocatory text but present in the audience of his poem, know that these poems about the supposedly ideal life of the country were to fall on the deaf ears both of the authorities and of the gods?

Windsor Forest has been the subject of considerable scholarly attention focused on another kind of enclosure: the restriction, in the early eighteenth century, of ancient common rights in royal and other forests and the criminalizing of acts associated with them under the notorious Black Act of 1723.[62] Coming as it does well after the publication of Pope's *Windsor Forest*, the Black Act has less to do with Pope's poem than with his later career; and interest in the Act has somewhat diverted attention from the earlier discourse of forest laws and enclosure within which the poem takes its place.

Pope's poem is a georgic set within the tradition of prospect poetry by its poetic model, Denham's 'Cooper's Hill'. As such it is political, and invokes by its very genre the myth of an idyllic Stuart golden age which Denham employs and which Rubens had evoked in apotheosizing James I's reign of peace on the ceiling of the Banqueting House at Whitehall. Maynard Mack has pointed out how Pope's poem picks up the very images of Rubens's painting: a painting commissioned by Charles I in celebration of his father's reign of peace:[63]

Exil'd by Thee from Earth to deepest Hell,
In Brazen Bonds shall barb'rous *Discord* dwell:
Gigantick *Pride*, pale *Terror*, gloomy *Care*,
And mad *Ambition*, shall attend her there.
There purple *Vengeance* bath'd in Gore retires,

> Her Weapons blunted, and extinct her Fires:
> There hateful *Envy* her own Snakes shall feel,
> And *Persecution* mourn her broken Wheel:
> There *Faction* roar, *Rebellion* bite her Chain,
> And gasping Furies thirst for Blood in vain.
>
> (413–22)

Windsor Forest looks back to James I's promise of a universal peace, first through the peace implicit in the unification of Great Britain under another Stuart, Queen Anne, and latterly through the conclusion of the Peace of Utrecht for which Pope completed the poem. Denham's earlier poem, moreover, looks towards Windsor as does Rubens's painting 'St. George and the Dragon'. In that canvas, Charles I as St George rescues a very real princess, his queen Henrietta Maria, from the dragon of faction. But because history turned out otherwise (as lines 319–26 of *Windsor Forest* relate), the myth of Windsor, where Charles I's decapitated body was buried, is all the more a very English myth of a lost Eden: as much a microcosm of England as Appleton House is for Marvell.

'The real Sight of such Scenes and Prospects,' Pope wrote of 'Cooper's Hill', 'is apt to give the Mind a compos'd Turn.'[64] But Pope's poem is also a cultural product of a legal controversy about another aspect of enclosure: forest rights. At the time of the poem's composition, Pope would have been familiar with this controversy because of his youth at Binfield within Windsor Forest and his close friendship there with Sir William Trumbull, one of the 'Verderers' of the Forest, who lived a mile away at Easthampstead.[65] It was Trumbull who encouraged Pope to write and probably lent him books. Certainly it was at this time that Pope acquired his love of the classics and hence his ability to 'read' Windsor Forest in Virgilian terms: terms which included playing off idyllic rustic retirement against the brutality of power. Trumbull's estate was a park within the Forest, and many of his own dealings with servants and tenants had to do with the laws of the forest and the rights of tenants and sub-tenants within and adjacent to it.

For Pope, what William I had done in the New Forest represented the iron age. He had, to use Tacitus's phrase, made a desert and called it peace; the New Forest had become a depopulated wasteland guarded by savage laws.[66] Part of Pope's strategy in his poem involved dissociating the Stuarts from the political discourse of the 'Norman Yoke' with which the revolutionary (and latterly Whig) rhetoric of the seventeenth century had identified them. Stuart willingness to rule without parliament had been traced by political theorists to the overthrow of the English constitution and the establishment of 'Norman' absolutist ideas. These were the very absolutist ideas that, in the late seventeenth century, could easily be identified with the monarchy of Louis XIV which the recently completed War of the Spanish Succession had checked. It is very much to Pope's purpose, then, in celebrating the end of that war under a Stuart monarch, to transform the oak associated with Stuart absolutism into the 'hearts of oak' of the new imperial navy and the vessels of the new commerce.[67]

Windsor Forest has often been criticized as a poem of two disconnected parts: an early idyllic passage up to line 290 and an imperial panegyric to the new Britain after the Peace of Utrecht thereafter. But its politics are all of a piece. Only when the 'Norman Yoke' of the opening sequence can be separated from Stuart mythology can the pastoral myth of a golden age invoked by Pope's opening quotation from Virgil's 'Sixth Eclogue' be established. In a sense Pope gives back to the Stuarts what the Civil War had taken away: a world of masques where kings and gods, Queen Anne and Diana, can inhabit the same enchanted world and from it restore the world of lost pastoral that the anti-masque world of the Civil War ('Intestine Wars') had destroyed.

Pope can then place Windsor Forest in a golden age restored, a place better than 'old *Arcadia*' of Virgil, when commoners enjoyed rights within the forest without legal reprisals:

> Succeeding Monarchs heard the Subjects Cries,
> Nor saw displeas'd the peaceful Cottage rise.
>
> (85–6)

These lines allude primarily to an imagined golden age when, under the Stuarts, the enforcement of forest laws was largely in abeyance, a time when peaceful cottages rose on land that properly belonged to the crown. In fact, such a time only existed under the Cromwellian regime's division of the Forest into farms: tenancies abolished by the Restoration of the Stuarts and the return of what Simon Schama has called 'sylvan gangsterism' in the form of corrupt officials.[68] Perhaps it was in recognition of the instability of that tenure that Pope substituted the phrase 'nor saw displeas'd' for what he first wrote: 'and bade secure'!

It was largely in the imagination of such Tories as Pope that the laws of William III seemed more savage than what had preceded them.[69] What occurred in his reign was a strengthening of existing legislation against deer-stealing: an act against 'lewd, sturdy and disorderly persons' living in or near forests who acted in combination to avoid fines. They were now (1688) to be subject to fines of £20 for attempting the offence and an additional £30 for every deer killed or wounded. But it was convenient for Pope to disregard the fact that it was William III who had decreed in 1698 that 200 acres a year were to be set aside in the New Forest as nurseries for oaks.

Some offence against forest laws seems to have been committed by one of Trumbull's own servants in January of 1706, soon after Pope began to compose his poem.[70] The estate correspondence refers to a fine of £9, a hefty sum given that, for example, Trumbull's gardener in 1706 was only earning £18 a year for food. Such a fine also came with the proviso that if it were not paid, the offender was to be imprisoned for a year without bail. Even for pulling down the pales (fences) of the forest (so that deer would stray into land where it was not illegal to hunt them), convicted offenders could be imprisoned for 3 months.

That this act was passed in the same year as the draconian legislation against Catholics which had forced his father to leave London and move to Binfield cannot have escaped Pope's notice.[71] The law to which his couplet about 'the peaceful cottage' alludes, however, had last been enforced in the supposed golden age of the Stuarts. In the second year of the reign of Charles I (1627), John Gale, a Lord of the Manor in the Forest, had allowed his tenants to build cottages on waste ground. His punishment was a fine, and the cottages were allowed to stand only during the lifetime of those who built them.[72]

In the opening part of *Windsor Forest*, Pope's contrast of the 'tyrannick' rule of William I in the medieval New Forest with the supposedly free, late-Stuart world of Windsor Forest is enacted in a hunt. The startled partridge becomes an analogy of the imperial conquests of the newly unified Britain:

> Sudden they seize th'amaz'd defenceless Prize,
> And high in Air *Britannia*'s Standard flies.
> (109–10)

This is a quite astonishing poetic sleight of hand, for in fact these celebrated hunting scenes from lines 90 to 170 were just what the forest laws inhibited, where they did not outrightly prohibit them to ordinary men. 'If a man do hunt in the Forest, and kill a Hare,' forest law declared, 'the Forester may attach him for the same offence; for the same is a trespass in the Venison of the king's forest,'[73] for which the fine was £1: the equivalent of nearly 3 weeks' wages.

The 'ready spaniel', who 'bounds, panting with hope' in pursuit of a partridge in the autumn scene, might be thankful that it is not Mr Wilson's dog in *Joseph Andrews* which lives in a village where the squire could shoot a spaniel, having 'given notice he would not suffer one in the parish'.[74] Pope's spaniel might also be thankful it is not a mastiff: a dog liable under forest law to be 'expeditated', that is to have its paws maimed so that it could not hunt. But in fact, any dogs could be destroyed if caught hunting, and hunting itself could only be undertaken on the edges or purlieus of the forest and under such restrictive conditions that only the well-off could undertake it.[75]

This section of Pope's poem (90–170) is based on the pattern of contrasting depictions of tyranny and liberty in Virgil's *Georgics*; but Pope's mixture of epic hunt with neo-pastoral arcadia obscures the real georgic alternative: the unmolested life of the small independent farmer. And it was this small farmer whose rights to pasture other people's cattle (agistment), to search for firewood (turbage), and to raise crops unmolested by wandering deer were increasingly restricted by enclosure. The couplet about cottages is succeeded by lines about husbandry:

> Then gath'ring Flocks on unknown Mountains fed,
> O'er sandy Wilds were yellow harvest spread,
> The Forests wonder'd at th'unusual Grain,
> And secret Transport touch'd the conscious Swain.
>
> (87–90)

Well might the forests wonder, as much at mountains in Berkshire as at the 'yellow harvest' that supplanted what Pope had first called 'sable Heaths'. For the destroying of heaths, either for collecting firewood or for the purposes of cultivation was and remained what was called 'an assart' within the forest: 'where a man doth fell and destroy his woods, and convert the soile, wherein the woods did grow, for tillage.'[76] The penalty for this offence was imprisonment until an arbitrary fine was paid, and potential seizure of the land by the crown. Even those who had legitimate right of pasturage in the Forest (agistment) could be fined for committing a 'nuisance' if their cattle did not leave enough for the deer to feed on. Throughout the late 1670s and the 1680s even Sir William Trumbull was concerned with paying levies for privileges within the forest, and in 1691 he was refused permission to cut down a wood which he leased there.[77] Perhaps it was a recollection of this which led him in 1698 to regard more than the letter of the law. 'I thought it might be convenient to leave some few such Trees upon every Acre,' he wrote to his steward, 'more than the Number required of the Statute.'[78]

What Trumbull had was a park, but even a park had by law to be distinguished from the forest that surrounded it by being so fenced that forest animals could not get into it. And much of Trumbull's estate correspondence has to do with keeping these 'pales' in repair. A chase, says Manwood, is like a park, but different in being always open. By the late seventeenth century, however, this distinction was in abeyance; for one of the earliest enclosures (1664) was of Malvern Chase, on the borders of Hereford, Worcester, and Gloucestershire. Even forests were not necessarily royal preserves; they might be granted by the crown, usually to members of the nobility, but offences committed within them were still punishable by forest laws.

As Verderer of the forest, Trumbull must have been well aware of the popular resistance to the increasing restriction of common right. And Pope must have known that the discourse of this resistance was one that stretched back to the legend of Robin Hood. Schama's description of the outlaw would be as true of Pope: 'A passionate and nostalgic conservative who yearns for the restoration of a just personal monarchy and who wants a social order dislocated by rogues and parvenus to be set in its proper ranks, stations and portions.' Is not *Windsor Forest*, as much as the ballads of Robin Hood, 'an elegy for a world of liberty that had never existed'?[79]

In spite of the increasing eighteenth-century tendency of the parson to take the side of the squire on these matters, some notable vicars resisted incursions on common rights. One of these was Henry Goode, the rector of Weldon in Rockingham Forest, who kept up a campaign on the subject for at least 20 years in the second quarter of the century. In this instance grievances over rights to 'lops and tops' from tree-cutting were compounded by grievances about grazing, but in these cases there were often other ancient rights involved as well. In 1744 Goode published a pamphlet encouraging his neighbours to resist the restriction of their rights by the enclosures of Lord Cardigan which had already denied them the right to pasture pigs ('pannage') in one part of the Forest: 'You, and your Fathers before You, have, Time out of Mind, constantly every Year, turn'd your Cattle into the open Woods throughout the Forrest of *Rockingham*, there to pasture and feed.'[80]

Rockingham Forest was a royal forest, but the same provisions applied to other forests. Manwood's *Forest Laws* claimed that 'a subject may be owner of a forest and have a forest': a provison that applied as much to those (like Sir William Trumbull) 'that have Woods within the King's Forests as to those that have woods within the Forests of other men'.[81]

Invoking an ordnance of 1643 that sought to restrict the crown from 'carrying Forrest Laws too high,' however, Goode argued that tenants had 'an equal Right of Common, with those that have Houses and Lands of their own and as good a Right by Custom, and the Laws of the Land, as the King himself.'[82] Citing the famous Charter of the Forest granted by Henry III in 1235, the author went on to urge all the villagers in the areas adjacent to the forest not to be divided in their interest to preserve these common rights. Although a similar episode in Charnwood Forest in 1749 indicated that 'high feeling around common rights, and episodes of disturbance need not wait upon enclosure,'[83] however, the pattern had been set. Although most of the Parliamentary Acts of enclosure were not passed until after the mid-century, the assembling of '*ingentia rura*' at the price of enclosure by purchase, forfeited tenancies, and engrossment was well established.

Forest laws had been established, as Manwood said, so that 'the goodly greene and pleasant woods in a Forest' might be 'greene Arbors of pleasure, for the King to delight himselfe in'.[84] By the late seventeenth century this ideal had spread to the nobility and the newly landed classes, but the corollary was the exclusion of the very labourers on whom it depended. In 1759 the first Lord Harcourt removed the village of Nuneham Courtnay, thereby in all probability occasioning Goldsmith's poem 'The Deserted Village'. Many a village had succumbed to aesthetic ideals long before then, however, thanks not least to the poems of Pope and Thomson.

Notes

1 *An Impartial Description of Surinam* (London, 1667), pp. 27, 28.

2 *Samuel Hartlib his Legacy of Husbandry* (London, 1655), introduction 'Extracted out of the Surveyors Dialogue'. More than a century later the plodding husbandman was still a problem in Scotland. 'The Farmer that does not think deliberately before he acts,' Robert Maxwell was to write, 'may work himself out of Breath and do small service to his Family.' *The Practical Husbandman* (Edinburgh, 1757), p. 403.

3 Ibid., p. 69. Many travellers made similar observations. In *An Impartial Description of Surinam* George Warren suggested that the fruits of the island were an 'abundance of Wilde Trash, which, perhaps if transplanted, might not prove so contemptible as they now are', (p. 15).

4 Ibid., pp. 77, 89.

5 *The Planter's Manual: Being Instructions . . . In Planting and Grafting* (London, 1715), sig. [T8v].

6 Even the much-admired cultivation of Greek culture, he argues, depended upon farming as an art. *An Essay on Ways and Means for Inclosing, Fallowing, Planting etc SCOTLAND* (Edinburgh, 1729), pp. 80, 82.

7 *The Country Gentleman and Farmer's Monthly Director* (London, 1726), p. xvi.

8 *Vertumnus. An Epistle to Mr. Jacob Bobart* (London, 1713), p. 14. Richard Bradley imagined importing songbirds so that 'our Woods would in a short time Rival our Operas; and our Songsters from *America*, put those from *Italy* out of countenance', *The Monthly Register of Experiments and Observations in Husbandry and Gardening. For the Months of April and May, 1722* (London, 1722), p. 48.

9 *A Collection for the Improvement of Husbandry and Trade*, ed. Richard Bradley (London, 1727), iii. 13; ii. 374.

10 *A Survey of the Ancient Husbandry and Gardening* (London, 1725), pp. 285–6. Bradley was probably replying to this question about the Cytisus raised by Stephen Switzer, the influential theorist of gardens and landscape, in his *Ichnographia Rustica* (1718). For all his interest in expanding the repertoire of agricultural botany, however, Bradley was sceptical about writers who 'heaped together a load of Observations from *Varro* and *Pliny*' without considering the difference of soils and climates. *New Improvements of Planting* (London, 1728), 2nd edn, sig. [A4v].

11 *A Supplement to the Essay on Horse-Hoing Husbandry* (London, 1740), p. 218.

12 I am indebted in the discussion of enclosure generally to 'Enclosures, Commons and Communities', in Raymond Williams's *The Country and the City* (Frogmore, St. Alban's, Herts., 1975), and J. M. Neeson's *Commoners: Common Right, Enclosure and Social Change in England 1700–1800* (Cambridge: Cambridge University Press, 1993).

13 'Upon Appleton House', stanza 41. Andrew Marvell, *The Complete Poems*, ed. E. S. Donno (Harmondsworth: Penguin, 1978), p. 85.

14 *Vertumnus. An Epistle to Mr. Jacob Bobart* (London, 1713), p. 21.

15 In *The Country and the City* Raymond Williams points out that in Goldsmith's poem a much older process than an act of parliamentary enclosure is involved. 'The social process is in fact one of clearance, of eviction and evacuation . . . It is based on engrossing', (p. 96).

16 *Herefordshire Orchards* (Dublin, 1724), p. 18. In a letter to John Evelyn on 26 November 1670, Beale writes to recommend to the Royal Society that 'the greatest service that can be done for the public by Agriculture would consiste in these two points. 1 In draining bogues, and excluding the Seas. 2 In reclayming

the Commoners, especially the hortolane enclosures.' British Library, *John Evelyn, Incoming Letterbook*.

17 *The Georgics, Translated into English Verse with Introduction and Notes by L. P. Wilkinson* (London: Penguin, 1982), iv. pp. 127–32.

18 *Nurseries, Orchards*,p. 2.

19 Satire II. ii. l. 138.

20 *A Treatise Concerning the Husbandry and Natural History of England* (London, 1742). pp. 50–6. In *Poetry, Language and Politics* (Manchester: Manchester University Press, 1988), John Barrell observes that 'in the instance of enclosure of open fields and wastes, the imposition of a more productive order on the landscape produced, indeed, a new landscape, and one admired because it was believed to be more orderly – more rectilinear, more rationally divided, more the product of art than nature' (p. 116).

21 *A Treatise*, p. 109. In *An Essay on Ways and Means*, William Mackintosh makes a similar argument for the benefit of this sort of enclosure to the poor: that with it a 'poor Man's few Cattle can feed in the Common without the charge of keepers', (p. 121). This echoes the earlier arguments of two of Hartlib's circle, John Beale and Cressy Dymock, who respectively believed that enclosure would prevent disease in cattle and arguments about common interest.

22 *A Supplement to the Essay on Horse-Hoing Husbandry*, p. 248.

23 *Tom Jones*, ed. Fredson Bowers (New York: Modern Library, 1985), i. 4, p. 43.

24 *A Letter to the Dublin Society, on the Improving Their Fund: and the Manufactures, Tillage, etc.* (Dublin, 1730), p. 44.

25 Publicola [Thomas Rawson and Philip Skelton], *A Dissertation on the Enlargement of Tillage* (Dublin, 1741), p. 34. Like Tull, the authors thought that land-management should be controlled and the amount of land taken in should be limited to what could be tilled, perhaps by dividing it into smaller farms.

26 *The Boke of Surveying*, sig. [a4v].

27 *A Survey of the Ancient Husbandry and Gardening* (London, 1725), sig. a3.

28 These citations are all from either the letter of 8 Sept. 1681 or that of 20 July 1682. iv. p. 80, 3, 4, 17, 144.

29 *Systema Agriculturae* (London, 1668), p. 10.

30 *A Complete Body of Husbandry* (London, 1728), p. 263.

31 *A Treatise Concerning the Manner of Fallowing Ground . . . Scotland* (Edinburgh, 1724). This argument, as E. P. Thompson has pointed out in *Customs in Common* (London: Penguin, 1993), p. 107, was taken up later in favour of parliamentary enclosure of vast tracts of land.

32 John Barrell also points out how the discourse of civic humanism (public good), as it was translated from republican Florence to Britain, came to identify the true interests of society with the ownership of landed property. *The Birth of Pandora and the Division of Knowledge* (London: Macmillan, 1992), p.51.

33 *A Complete Body of Husbandry* (London, 1728), pp. 258–69.

34 *A Memorial of the Poor Inhabitants, Tradesmen, and Labourers of the Kingdom of Ireland, Directions to Servants and Other Miscellaneous Pieces*, ed. Herbert Davis (Oxford: Blackwell, 1959), p. 22.

35 In his edition of *The Poems of Thomas Gray, William Collins, and Oliver Goldsmith*, Roger Lonsdale notes various claimants for the location of the 'deserted village' (London: Longman, 1969), pp. 670–1.

36 *An Essay* (London, 1732), p. 2.

37 London, 1736, p. 25.

38 *Enclosure and the Small Farmer in the Age of the Industrial Revolution* (London: Macmillan Studies in Economic History, 1968), p. 31. For another account of this process, see Neal Wood, *John Locke and Agrarian Capitalism* (Berkeley: University of California Press, 1984), pp. 17–19.

39 The rest of Cowper's title is: *in which some passages in the New System of Agriculture, by J. Laurence, M. A., and in the Duty and Office of a Land-Steward, by E. Laurence . . . are examined.* John Laurence identifies Edward as his brother in *A New System of Agriculture and Gardening* (London, 1726).

40 Ibid., pp.45–6.

41 *The Duty of a Steward to His Lord* (London, 1727), pp. 37–8.

42 *An Essay*, pp. 17–18. Laurence believed that freeholders would turn their enclosed ground into pasture, not tillage, but that seems far more commonly to have been the practice of large landowners.

43 For an account of 16th-century resistance to enclosures, see Roger B. Manning, *Village Revolts: Social Protest and Popular Disturbance in England, 1509–1640* (Oxford: Clarendon Press, 1988).

44 See Nigel Everett, *The Tory View of Landscape* (New Haven & London: Yale University Press, 1994), pp. 21–30.

45 See H. J. Habakkuk, 'La Disparition du Paysan Anglais', *Annales*, 20 (1965), pp. 649–63, and G. E. Mingay, *English Landed Society in the Eighteenth Century* (Toronto: University of Toronto Press, 1963), esp. Chs 2–4; R. C. Allen, *Enclosure and the Yeoman: The Agricultural Development of the South Midlands, 1450–1850* (Oxford: Clarendon Press, 1992).

46 William Kent's design for the garden at Rousham included multiple choices between Venus and Apollo, the sort of choice between vice and virtue that Sir William Chambers found attractive in the gardens of China and that illustrated the fourth edition of Shaftesbury's *Characteristicks* (1727). See John Barrell, *The Birth of Pandora*, pp. 65–6.

47 *Victoria History of the Counties of England: Gloucestershire*, xi. p. 94. In 1685 there had been a 40-acre field in which there were 2 cow-pastures and 48 sheep-pastures.

48 'Epistle to Arbuthnot', l. 18; *Essay on Man* i. 118. In a letter to John Evelyn on 10 May 1669 John Beale writes, 'Doe not too many of our Parliament men engrosee the maine benefit of the excise, and leave his Majesty a small remainder?' British Library, *Evelyn Correspondence, Incoming Letterbook*. 'Engross' could also mean 'to hoard'.

49 *Irish Tracts 1728–1733*, ed. Herbert Davis (Oxford: Blackwell, 1955), pp. 17–18.

50 See A. S. Turberville, *A History of Welbeck Abbey and its Owners* (London: Faber & Faber, 1938), i. Chs 13, 14.

51 *Alexander Pope: A Life* (New Haven: Yale University Press, 1988), p. 513.

52 *A Poem on the Park and Woods of the Right Honourable Allen Lord Bathurst* (Cirencester, 1748), p. 10. As in *Windsor Forest* so at both Cirencester and Stowe, the figure of Queen Anne joined an iconic landscape to imperial victory: 'a due Reward to virtuous Pow'r alone', (p. 7).

53 *Customs in Common*, p. 17. Thompson also points out that there is little firm evidence of the number who held 'their land by copyhold or other forms of customary tenure', (p. 114).

54 In 1680 Cobham's father had been attacked in an anonymous pamphlet called *New News of a Strange Monster Found in Stow Woods* for having 'stoln away the Parsonage-House that the Inchanted Castle might be all of a Piece'.

55 See J. D. Hunt, *The Figure in the Landscape* (Baltimore: Johns Hopkins Press, 1976), pp. 91–100; Peter Martin, *Pursuing Innocent Pleasures: The Gardening World of Alexander Pope* (Hamden, Conn.: 1984), pp. 19–61; and Maynard Mack, *The Garden and the City* (Toronto: University of Toronto Press, 1969), pp. 87–107. Maynard Mack recounts Pope's prescriptions without critique and observes, 'It is only with Timon's villa we need be now concerned' (p. 498).

56 See David Solkin, 'The Happy Rural Life', in *Richard Wilson: The Landscape of Reaction* (London: Tate Gallery, 1982), pp. 1–34.

57 See Denis Cosgrove, *The Palladian Landscape* (Leicester: University of Leicester Press, 1992), pp. 93–138.

58 In *The Palladian Revival: Lord Burlington, His Villa and Garden at Chiswick* (London & New Haven: Yale University Press, 1994) John Harris claims unpersuasively that this building is derived from a brewhouse in Newmarket.

59 I am grateful to Bruce Redford for drawing my attention to this passage. By invoking the 'stately frontispiece of poor' from the opening of Marvell's 'Upon Appleton House', Pope also manages to suggest the poetic tradition of country-house hospitality, here lamentably absent.

60 Not all of the dispossessed went easily. At Studley Royal, the inhabitants dispossessed of their ancient hunting privileges by the creation of Lord Aislabie's garden fought back through arson and vandalism. The records of Richard Boyle's cousin, John, at Marston Bigot in Dorset, suggest that other estates had similar trouble. See my *Planters of the English Landscape Garden* (New Haven: Yale University Press, 1993), p. 78, 149.

61 Virgil, *The Eclogues: The Latin Text with a Verse Translation and Brief Notes by Guy Lee* (London: Penguin, 1984), p. 22.

62 E. P. Thompson, 'Windsor' and 'Alexander Pope and the Blacks', in *Whigs and Hunters* (London: Allen Lane, 1975), pp. 37–118, 270–7. Pat Rogers, 'Blacks and Poetry and Pope', in *Alexander Pope* (Cambridge: Cambridge University Press, 1993), pp. 168–83.

63 *Alexander Pope: A Life*, p. 202.

64 Note to *Iliad* xvi. 466 (London: Methuen, 1967), Twickenham VII. p. 261.

65 Even before Pope's birth one of Trumbull's stewards had been involved in a conflict with one of the Fermors, the family to which the model for Pope's Belinda in *The Rape of the Lock* belonged.

66 F. H. M. Parker demonstrates that the story of post-Conquest devastation in the New Forest was a medieval fiction: 'The Forest Laws and the Death of William Rufus', in *English Historical Review*, 27 (1912), pp. 26–38. It was none the less to Pope's poetic purpose to believe the chronicles he had read. See Simon Schama, 'Hearts of Oak and Bulwarks of Liberty', in *Landscape and Memory*, pp. 153–74.

67 Maynard Mack has challenged the claim that *Windsor Forest* alludes to William III. *Alexander Pope: A Life*, pp. 853–4. That it does so only by allusion and symbology is none the less consonant with Pope's mode of argumentation, which implies a coterie of those who understand.

68 *Landscape and Memory*, p. 148. Schama uses the phrase about medieval abuses, but he makes it plain elsewhere in the book that these also existed under Charles II.

69 Thompson quotes an anonymous poem from Charnwood Forest in North Leicestershire tracing royal impositions on the forest to 'Popish Jemmy', James II, the last Roman Catholic king. *Customs in Common*, p. 105.

70 The letter from John Power, a clergyman who also acted as an estate manager for Trumbull, refers to a man called Humphreys and is dated 7 Jan. 1706. British Library Trumbull MSS.: Power File.

71 See *The Statutes at Large by Danby Pickering* (London, 1765), ix. I W & M Cap. 9. Cap. 26 in the same year establishes the legislation allowing such Roman Catholic owners as the Fermors to be overriden in the appointment to church livings. The statute about deer-stealing is Cap. 10.

72 *Manwood's Treatise of the Forest Laws ... The Fourth Edition, Corrected and Enlarged by William Nelson* (London, 1717), p. 306.

73 Manwood, *A Treatise and Discourse of the Lawes of the Forrest* (1598) fo. [29v].

74 *Joseph Andrews*, iii. Ch. 4, ed. Martin Battestin (Boston: Houghton Mifflin –
   Riverside, 1961), p. 192. The subsequent hunting scene in which Adams
   becomes a hare hunted by a pack of hounds at the behest of another villainous
   squire (Ch. 6) shows hunting in a different light than Pope chooses to paint it.
75 See the extensive discussion of this in *Whigs and Hunters*, pp. 27–54.
76 Manwood, *Forest Laws* (1598), fo. [48v].
77 See the Trumbull Papers: Stubbes Files for this period in the British Library. It is
   an interesting footnote to Pope's subsequent garden taste that Sir William's
   garden at Easthampstead had been laid out by London and Wise at the end of
   the seventeenth century in just the sort of mirrored regularity that Pope was to
   despise in the 'Epistle to Burlington'.
78 British Library, Trumbull Paper: Stubbes File IV, Letter to Richard Stubbes, 28
   April 1698. Stubbes was in fact rector of Easthampstead, but he acted as
   effective steward in Trumbull's absence.
79 *Landscape and Memory*, pp. 150, 149.
80 *A Letter to the Commoners in Rockingham Forest* (Stamford, 1744), p. 3.
81 *Manwood, Lawes of the Forrest* (1598), fo. 17.
82 Ibid., p. 4.
83 *Customs in Common*, p. 104.
84 *Forest Laws* (1598), fo. [33v].

|6|

Childhood's Tender Shoots: Instructing and Imagining

If the mythology of land in this period shifted from stewardship to owner-ship – increasingly of an exclusive sort – so did the mythology of childhood. Locke's central account, *Some Thoughts Concerning Education* (1693), is a document of control, and one that was to be invoked increasingly as an instrument of social change. In the late seventeenth and early eighteenth centuries, childhood was as much a contested territory as common land.

The term 'childhood', like 'nature' or 'primitivism', is a social con-struction: a concept that in this case reflects the adult interests and pre-occupations of those who choose to explore it. What it meant in the late seventeenth and early eighteenth centuries seems almost as difficult to recover as what was meant by the word 'science' at the time. As Keith Thomas has observed, the major difficulty in exploring the subject is 'that there was not one single world of children, any more than there was one of women'.[1] But the search is worth it, for what is meant by 'childhood' provides a biopsy of any culture's sense of itself, then or now.

In the late seventeenth century, arguments over childhood and education were one aspect of the larger argument about the nature of the physical and mental world. Although many of the reforms in education and pedagogy were not new, the belief in them as a universal system was. The discourse of the most influential work of the period, Locke's *Some Thoughts Concerning Education*, for example, is shot through with the concepts of order and obedience. Childhood, and education in particular, had become an aspect of social control.

How this childhood is to be defined, however, is a battleground more fought over than most. For one thing, its history is based upon very scattered and unrepresentative evidence.[2] By definition, there is very little documentation of what the illiterate thought about their children except when they were in trouble with the law. And there is equally very little evidence of what children themselves thought. Even when we do have family records, it is not always clear for what purpose they were kept. That a set of estate accounts contains little about the children, for example, may mean no more than that accounts relating to the children (let alone letters about them) were kept elsewhere and have disappeared. Only rarely do we get a large correspondence, such as the Evelyn archive or the letters of the family of Sir Simon D'Ewes, in which there is continuous evidence of attitudes to children and child care.

The history of childhood, moreover, has many possible beginnings. Jacob Bronowski believed that the Romantics (especially Blake) discovered childhood, but Philip Ariès traced it to Montaigne at the end of the sixteenth century. Others would argue, as Lawrence Stone suggests in *The Family, Sex and Marriage*, that John Locke's concept of the child's mind as a *tabula rasa*, a blank slate on which anything might be written and the child shaped as an ideal citizen, was the ground upon which any definition of childhood rests.[3] But even that concept was much older than Locke and can be traced to the fathers of the early Christian church and further into antiquity.

What is not in doubt is that by the middle of the seventeenth century parents of whatever religious persuasion were attached to their children even in infancy. One of Simon D'Ewes's married sisters wrote to her brother, sister, and sister-in-law over a period of nearly 20 years, frequently about just such subjects. Having herself felt the anguish of child death – 'that bitter cup, whereof I have so often tasted' – she was especially solicitous of her older brother's children and wrote to his second wife a letter about her son's care that is revealing of medical attitudes and paediatric customs:

> I was so troubled with the newes of my nephews ellness [illness] as I could take no rest that night[.] you know if my advice might have prevaled your sweet sonne had never suckt that stale milke[.] I hope you have changed the milke and if it weare mine I would have it in the house where you may see the ordering of it your selfe and feede the nurs at your own trencher [.] pray tamper not with dochters to put the child to any pane or trobell nor let it not be danct nor kept from sleepe or suck which I know has bin the way of very good doctors in this case but let it have a full breast of new milke at command and all the quiet and content may be [.] let it weare a piece of dry castor like the corall and the nurs often put to the childs nose the sent of it being very good against those fits [.] also let some sperit of amber 3 drops at a time be with a warme hand rubed gently in the nape of the neck and pole of the head sometimes when the child is dresed[.] and if it should have any more fits touch the outer part of the nostrells with a littell of the sperit of amber[.][4]

The vast correspondence of the Evelyn family from the mid-century onwards also contains many letters expressing grief and commiseration about infants who died soon after birth. Evelyn dedicated his translation of

Chrysostom's book on the education of children 'to both my Brothers, to comfort them upon the losse of their Children'.[5] Certainly once children had begun to speak and learn, the sorrow at their death was even greater. Evelyn was a man of restrained emotions, but his grief at the death of his 6-year-old son, Richard, is by no means unrepresentative of a middle-class father of the late seventeenth century. Writing to his father-in-law, Sir Richard Browne, in the same year, he speaks first of his garden where, though all is 'now infinitely sweete and beautifull,' the memory of his son is still overpowering: 'There is but one plant, the losse whereof goes to my Soule, and that I must never forgett, because I shall never repaire.'[6] Even a year later, Evelyn's wife, Mary, was still grief-stricken:

> I was in so happy a condition, such a blessing seldom lasts to enjoy a good husband, hopefull Children, and a contented minde: all which I accounted my selfe possessed of when it pleasde God to take away my Juell and the joy of our lives by so sudden and unexpected a Death that without Gods great mercy to mee, I must have sunk under the sorrow, all my constancy being too weak to carry me through.[7]

Ralph Josselin and John Evelyn were on opposite sides in the Civil War; whereas Evelyn was a Royalist and devout traditional churchman, Josselin, a Parliamentarian, was as far from the doctrines of the established church as it was possible for a priest still in that church to be. And yet, like Evelyn's, Josselin's grief for the death of his daughter, coming soon after the death of his son, is only just containable in his address to God: 'Thou art better to mee then sonnes and daughters, though I value them above gold and jewells.'[8]

In the late seventeenth and early eighteenth centuries, however, the subject of childhood assumed an importance and attention that it had not previously possessed. Central to this shift was not simply the reform of education, but an argument about human nature. Both are reflected in the struggle between the claims of reason and the imagination, in which Locke's *Some Thoughts Concerning Education* was the paramount document.

After the restoration of the monarchy in 1660, for example, Evelyn shared in the general reaction against strict Calvinistic beliefs in infant damnation: a reaction that was a strong feature of intellectual and spiritual life. Even before 1650, another Anglican clergyman, Henry Vaughan, could write:

> Happy those early days! when I
> Shined in my angel-infancy.
>   ('The Retreat')

This was a theme that Vaughan's younger contemporary, another clergyman, Thomas Traherne, took up in the 1670s:

> To Infancy, O Lord, again I com,
>   That I my Manhood may improv:
>   My early Tutor is the Womb;
>   I still my Cradle lov.
>   'Tis strange that I should Wisest be,
>   When least I could an Error see.
>   ('The Return')

Such a position was in antithesis to the continuing Calvinist one represented by Bunyan's *A Book for Boys and Girls* (1686) or even Isaac Watts's *Divine and Moral Songs* (1715). Bunyan's little book of emblems adapted for children sees sin in a butterfly and mortality in an ant. And even in Watts the disobedient child is told the reward of his sin in terms that were commonplace in the late seventeenth century too: 'The Ravens shall pick out his Eyes, | And Eagles eat the same.'[9]

But this position is also at variance with the increasingly rationalist attitude to childhood, represented pre-eminently by John Locke's *Some Thoughts Concerning Education*. Locke and Traherne shared the concept of the child as a *tabula rasa*, but Locke could not countenance anything in the mind that did not arise from the five senses.[10] For Traherne and some early writers for children, however, sensuous knowledge did not preclude intuitive knowledge or the imagination.

Children, moreover, had access to an oral tradition of folk-tales, fairy-tales, and poems: an underground literature of popular culture that remained extremely important to the later development of children's literature. On one hand, often encouraged by nurses, children adopted ballads such as the 'Tale of Cock Robin' or political rhymes such as 'Mary, Mary Quite Contrary'. On the other they took up such out-of-fashion romance tales as 'Guy of Warwick' or 'Bevis of Southampton' or 'Valentine and Orson' and appropriated them as childhood reading.

In *The Governess: or, Little Female Academy* (1749), a work of fiction by Fielding's sister, Sarah, the delightfully bad girls in the school of Mistress Teachum spend their mornings and evenings telling one another just such stories. Miss Jenny Peace begins with the sort of tale which John Locke sought to expel from the classroom: 'The Story of the cruel Giant *Barbarico*, the good Giant *Beneficio*, and the pretty Dwarf *Mignon*.' She is then succeeded by Miss Dolly Friendly, who tells 'The Story of Celia and Chloe', a romance of the sort with which Fielding himself played (in the story of Leonora) in *Joseph Andrews* (1742). Dolly is in turn followed by Miss Jenny Peace, who first reads a fairytale, 'The Princess Hebe', and then concludes the series with a fable, 'The Assembly of the Birds'.

The Governess is a book for children, but its analogies with the comic-epic structure of *Tom Jones* and *Joseph Andrews* suggest the interesting interchange between the imaginative worlds of adult and juvenile fiction. Sarah Fielding shows children taking traditional popular fictions and

weaving them into their lives, without reproof and even with encouragement. But they are doing no more than what such writers as Swift and
Henry Fielding themselves had done. Swift appropriated the tales of the
Arabian Nights and the *Contes des Fees* in *Gulliver's Travels*;[11] Fielding
appropriated French romance and the popular literature of 'true histories' in
Joseph Andrews. Moreover, children soon learned how to dispense with
literature that was merely improving and instructive.

Children also managed to read fictions as imaginative even where the
work's intention was otherwise. Bunyan's pilgrim may have set his face
against 'dismal stories' and resolved that 'Hobgoblin nor foul fiend | Can
daunt his spirit',[12] but it was the giant Apollyon and the terrors of the
dungeon that drew children to *Pilgrim's Progress* (1678). Bunyan's work
seeks to transmute romance into instructive allegory, but the romance gets
out and the adventure is as irrepressible as it is in the 11-year-old Francis
Godolphin's account of a visit to Cornwall 12 years later. For him, St
Michael's Mount was exciting because there were 'two Dungeons in this
house, and very deep ones too'. And the wild and rugged coastline of Land's
End, though as forbidding as much of Bunyan's landscape, was a place for
adventures. ''Tis a long range of Rocks steep and craggie,' he writes, 'but
with help I got down pretty near the sea.'[13]

That letter was written to John Evelyn, Francis Godolphin's honorary
'grand-papa', who responded to it enthusiastically: 'Methinks, whiles I was
Reading it, I was *Travelling* with you, and saw the *Cities, Palaces, Bridges,
Rivers, Seas*, Harbors, *Mounts* and *Rocks* and horrid *precipices*, thro which
you have gon, and other remarkable Adventures.'

Although Evelyn was a sort of guardian to Francis and already 70 years
old, his reply to the boy was in language entirely subversive of the solemnity
of high literature and authority. This account, he says, is better than that of
Ulysses 'that all the World for above *3000* yeares cryed up for so renoun'd
a *Leg-strecher*'. For the stories of that other *Odyssey*, he writes,

> are all *damn'd Lyes*; Sung about by one *Homer*, an old Blind, squalid
> *Ballad-singer*: who with a *Bagpiper* and his Trull roam'd about to the
> *Wakes* and *Faires* of *Greece*, and where the Country-*Bumkins* met at
> *Foote-ball* Matches, *Pitching* the Bar, Cricket and *Ninepins* for *Cakes*
> and *Ale*: And this was that they cal'd th'*Olympic* Games forsooth, and
> make such a noise with in storie.[14]

Evelyn there places Francis's account of a 'hurling' competition inside the
popular culture of a West-Country world still recognizable even as late as
Thomas Hardy's time. But he also turns *The Odyssey* from a schoolroom
text into a lived adventure, and rescues it from what he calls the 'Tyrannical
Grammaticasters [who] *scourge* and *torment* poore Boys posteriors' and
turn epic adventures into grammar texts. Evelyn was no less pious than
Lady Anne Halket who published her *Instruction for Youth* only a decade
later, but in Evelyn's letter there is no sense of her belief that 'the

Imagination of mans Heart is evil, from his Youth.'[15] On the contrary, Evelyn rescues the fantastical creatures of the imagination as legitimate subjects for the boy's interests. Tell me, he writes in a letter to Francis before the boy went on his trip, 'of the most remarkable *Places* and *Curiosities*: The *Lakes*, *Rivers*, and *Mountaines*, *Wildernesses*, *Dens*, *Wild-Beasts* and *Monsters*, and what manner of *Creatures*, the *Miners* and *Tin-men* are; and what *Spirits* (besides *Brandie*) they meete with underground.'[16]

Such accounts, like the ballads and romances, generally appeared in 'chapbooks': cheap paper copies that were hawked about from village to village, sometimes by the very men (called 'running patterers' or 'running stationers') who were later to be the first publishers of literature specifically directed at children. One of these publishers was Mary Cooper, who also published such adult poets as Richard Savage. Her *Tommy Thumb's Pretty Songbook* (1744) has good claim to be the first book in English for children that was not overtly didactic or moralizing. A collection of classic nursery rhymes, many of them are here between covers in this book for the first time. Some of them are still familiar to children today: 'Hickery, dickery dock', 'Ride a Cock Horse', 'Oranges and Lemons', 'London Bridge', 'Ladybird, Ladybird'. But often these rhymes appear in forms quite different from the ones we know now. Several of the poems included, indeed, would now be thought as inappropriate for children by many twentieth-century publishers as they would have been by Bunyan and Watts:

> Piss a Bed,
> Piss a Bed,
> Barley Butt,
> Your Bum is so heavy
> You cant get up.[17]

This is a long way from the sententious preaching of Watts's *Divine and Moral Songs* – such poems as 'The Sluggard', subtitled 'Against Idleness and Mischief':

> How doth the little busy Bee
> Improve each shining Hour,
> And gather Honey all the day
> From every opening Flower!

Blake's much later *Songs of Innocence* (1789) were written in reaction against that sort of moralizing children's poetry. But his poems may also be read in the context of the different attitude to childhood that Mary Cooper represents: one in which freedom and gaiety is not overshadowed by caution and admonition. In this Cooper was one of Blake's predecessors and represents a sort of underground stream which resurfaces only fitfully until the nineteenth century:

> Girls and Boys,
> Come out to play,
> The Moon does shine,
> As bright as Day,
> Come with a Hoop,
> Come with a Call,
> Come with a good will,
> Or not at all.

If the subversion of adult authority is a common feature of children's literature in English, moreover, this tiny illustrated book is certainly a foundation stone of that process. Long before the nonsense verse of the early nineteenth century, Cooper included as rhymes for children the poetry of an upside-down world that had only previously appeared in anti-authoritarian political satires:

> When I was a little boy,
> I wash'd my
> Mothers Dishes,
>
> I put my finger in my
> Ear, and pull'd out
> Little fishes.
>
> My Mother call'd me
> Good boy,
> And bid me pull out more,
>
> I put my finger
> In my Ear,
> And pull'd out fourscore.

Cooper also preserved material that was anathema to Locke in these rhymes. In them the old world of fantasy and the supernatural, of giants and hobgoblins, that was potent for Swift and remained so for Dr Johnson, is alive and well. A little girl speaks to her doll:

> This Pig went to Market
> Then creep Mouse,
> Mouse, Mouse, Mousey
> Then Shoe, Shoe, Shoe,
> The Wild Colt,
> And here to your own
> Dol —— Dousy.
> Get you gone Raw Head
> And Bloody bones,

> Here's a child don't fear ye.
> Come kissy and pissy
> My Jewel and then a, a, a,
> My Deary.

Cooper's work is addressed to children just beyond infancy proper, that is children who have learned to speak but are only beginning to read. In her advertisement to the book she coaxes adults to purchase:

> The Childs Plaything
> I recommend for Cheating
> Children into Learning
> Without any Beating.

The distinction between infancy and childhood was a commonplace in the seventeenth century; indeed, it was the second stage which most pre-occupied many Puritan writers of the mid-century and after. Concerned as they were with educating children out of a state of damnation, the vast majority of their books for little children in this period have a pedagogical agenda; they address such subjects as obedience to parents, the saintly lives of other children, and the need to be on continual guard against evil.[18]

But it is worth considering how much the popular literature of childhood – the ballads, fairytales, and folk-tales which it appropriated – was as much a strategy of resistance to this sort of 'improvement' for children as it was for adults against the values of mercantile capitalism. In 1647 Richard Corbet's ballad, 'The Fairies' Farewell', was published as a rebuke to the suppression of traditional tales and ballads which Puritan writers sought to carry out. Invoking the opening words of 'The Wife of Bath's Tale', Corbet's poem is a lament for the loss of the supernatural world of fairies and changelings incorporated even by Milton in his poem 'L'Allegro'.

> Farewell, rewards and fairies
>   Good housewives now may say;
> For now foul sluts in dairies
>   Do fare as well as they,
> And though they sweep their hearths no less
>   Than maids were wont to do,
> Yet who of late for cleanliness
>   Finds sixpence in her shoe?
>
> Lament, lament old abbeys,
>   The fairies lost command;
> They did but change priests's babies,
>   But some have changed your land;

> And all your children sprung from thence
> Are now grown Puritans,
> Who live as changelings ever since,
> For love of your demesnes.[19]

William Herbert's *Careful Father and Pious Child* (1648) rebukes this world of fairytale and folk-tale, establishing the relation between old religion and the fanciful folk customs which it also seeks to abolish. The book is, says the author, 'a Work, in which the Catholick Truth is Asserted, and above 600 Errors, Heresies, and points of Poperie are briefly confuted'. Among the last are included a whole series of popular customs such as bonfires and bob-apples:

> Watching in the Church-yard, to know who shall dye that yeare: fasting a day, then at night watching with meate and drinke, to see the shape of their future husbands; or for the same end hanging a smock (a neere, though dumb witness of lust) upon a hedge, and sitting by it at night; or looking in one of their shoes, the first time they heare the Cuckoe, to find a haire of the colour of the mans, they must have.[20]

There are only a handful of exceptions to such books in the late seventeenth century, but they are significant. The anonymous J. G.'s *A Play-Book for Children* (1694) has several features that were not to be common until the end of the eighteenth century: small pages with wide margins and large type, lists of words by syllables (up to six), and groups of such increasingly difficult sentences as 'A Pan - ther is a spot - ed wild beast ve - ry like a Leo - pard if it be not the same crea - ture.'

At this time it was still rare to recognize such pedagogical problems; the rod was the answer for the slow learner. It was rarer still for a family to address what we call 'learning disabilities', and probably only the well-off could afford to do so. Sir William Trumbull's concern to cure his 4-year-old son of stammering by soliciting the advice of a specialist in 1712 is remarkable enough. That this 'specialist', a Mr Foord, recommended curing the child by getting him to spell and pronounce the syllables on which he stammered is even more remarkable.[21]

In 1712, William Ronksley published *The Child's Weeks-work: Or, A Little Book, So nicely Suited to the Genius and Capacity of a* LITTLE CHILD, *Both for* MATTER *and* METHOD, *That it will infallibly Allure and Lead him into a Way of* READING. This too suggests an increasing sense of the child as a different creature from the adult and extends J. G.'s method in an engaging and attractive way. 'Children,' Ronksley writes, 'can't so well relish grave and serious Discourses, nor are capable of observing Elegancy of Speech, and quick turns of Wit,' but they do love rhymes and verses. 'And because generally *Verse* is more taking than *Prose*' it is 'within the reach of Little Ones, and now and then gratifying their gay and airy Temper; with this peculiar Advantage, that no word in it exceeds *One Syllable*.'[22]

The 'Invitation' to this little book is worlds away from the schoolroom tyranny of *Tom Jones*, where the Reverend Mr Thwackum's name speaks for itself and for his belief 'that the human Mind, since the Fall, was nothing but a Sink of Iniquity'.[23] Indeed, without Thwackum, Mr Allworthy could not be what his name suggests: a man who sees the worthiness of human nature in the teeth of Thwackum's 'damn 'em and flog 'em' principles. Like Mary Cooper and a group of educational reformers whose principles can be traced to social reform during the Commonwealth, Ronksley takes the opposite course:

> Sweet Lines as these
> Are Learnd with Ease;
>   No long Words you meet
> With here; for those
> Stand nigh the Close:
>   All here is short and sweet.

This 'Invitation' is followed by four weeks' worth of lessons arranged according to the difficulty of words; and here again, even in a schoolbook, one hears the sound of Blake's *Songs*:

> The Sun doth rise,
> And climb the Skies
> To give us Light by Day:
> The Moon at Night
> Sends forth her Light,
> To guide us in our Way.
>
> The Horse doth Prance
> (Nay, some can Dance,)
> Leap, Jump, Pace, Trot, and Run,
> He Kicks and Rears,
> The Earth he Tears,
> He Fears nor Sword or Gun.[24]

The poems for Saturday afternoon, moreover, suggest that the schoolmaster as much as the schoolboys is eager to:

> lay our Books
> In some off Nooks,
> Till the next Day but one.

And the proverbs from Week Two again sound like Blake, in this case his 'Proverbs of Hell'. They are a mixture of the Biblical and traditional popular wisdom: 'Give a man luck, and throw him into the *Sea*.'[25]

There is little enough of this admiration for fancy and play in most of the books for and about children in this period. Mark Lewis, who had no more room for the imagination than Locke, none the less recognized, like Ronksley, that Jack would be a dull boy without break-time and play, and that memorizing grammar rules was not true education.

Children shall never be at their Book above an hour and a half at a time, but have frequent Intermissions of an hour and a half, or two hours; For instance, they may be at School an hour and a half before Break-fast, half an hour may be allowed for Break-fast, then one hour may be spent in these delightful Exercises, the Children shall be at School again one hour and a half before Dinner, then one hour may be allowed for Dinner and Play, and then one hour may be ordered for delightful Learning, etc. I suppose all Men can remember how tedious it was to them when they were Boys, to sit four or five hours at one time, in a bit-ter cold School in the *Winter*, or a sultery [*sic*] hot School in the *Summer*, under a Tyrannical Master, and an unintelligible Grammar.[26]

Thomas Tryon, another educator of this period, had no more patience than Blake for the intellectual dead wood that oppressed the imagination. Like Swift's King of Brobdingnag, he also insisted on an education that made the lot of man better, though he also had some of Swift's savage indignation about the daily business of the world. Like the innocent folly of children, the innocent self-revelations of the mad, he believed, were preferable to the cunning hypocrisies of the ostensibly righteous. Raised as a wool-spinner and shepherd, Tryon early learned 'the vast usefulness of Reading' and came to write a pioneering treatise on the subject of madness.[27] In the dedication to his *A New Method of Educating Children* (1695), he explains that the healer Aesculapius is conventionally depicted as an older man than Apollo, the supposed god of wisdom, because Aesculapius's practical wisdom is the wisdom of maturity.

This position is absolutely that of the practical reformers of the Hartlib circle two generations earlier: men as concerned with education as they were with agriculture. John Dury's *The Reformed School* (c. 1650) made it the first rule that 'nothing is to be taught but that which is useful in itself to the society of mankind'. Although Dury was hostile to such pastimes as dancing that 'foment pride and satisfy curiosity and imaginary delights', the second of his rules of education none the less recognized that imagination took its place with sensation and memory in the educational process.[28] It was in this tradition that Tryon argued that 'the managing of Gardens, and Art of Husbandry, with a thousand other Employments [are] more honourable and more diverting than their idle Sports and Games'.[29]

Here Tryon speaks with the voice of Hartlib's circle and against what he calls 'the ill Custom of sending Children to be instructed at publick *Dancing-Schools*' instead of teaching them 'Musick, Painting, Housewifery, etc.'[30] But Tryon is different from that generation in three important ways: his belief in the importance of the imagination, his aversion to corporal punishment, and his insistence on the place of women in the instruction of children.

Like Traherne and Vaughan, he believed that children's imaginations were free from the curse of believing merely in reason. As Traherne put it:

> In unexperienc'd Infancy
> Many a sweet Mistake doth ly:
> Mistake tho false, intending tru:
> A *Seeming* somwhat more than *View*;
> That doth instruct the Mind
> In Things that ly behind,
> And many Secrets to us show
> Which afterwards we com to know.
> ('Shadows in the Water')

Children 'are, as it were, like Incorporeal Beings', Tryon wrote; 'their Imaginations and Fancies are not bounded or mis-led by that we call Reason.'

> For this Reason [cause] it was, that our Saviour commanded *little Children* to be brought unto him. Which had not relation to their Innocency, but to their Capacity; their minds being, as it were, Free and Empty, not yet bound Apprentice unto the Vanity of Custom and Prejudice.[31]

In his treatise on madness Tryon goes even further in defence of the imagination, seeming almost to foreshadow Blake:

> the Imagination and the Desire have a most wonderfull deep and hidden Original; and if its mighty property were not captivated, darkned, and as it were chained in the Clouds of gross flesh, and dark Powers of the outward and corporeal Nature, it would do wonders.[32]

Tryon also disapproved of corporal punishment at a time when the maxim 'spare the rod and spoil the child' was generally subscribed to. 'It is the Craft of your common *School Masters*,' he wrote, 'to keep Children (like Spirits in a Circle) a long time under the Terror of their Jurisdiction and Discipline, in order to promote their own Profit and Interest.' By contrast, the school that he was proposing was one in which:

> the *Master* and *Tutors* shall neither Whip, Beat nor shew Anger or Passion toward any Child, be he never so dull: But instead of such Correction, shall take the dull Child aside, and Commend and Praise him for his Endeavours.[33]

Believing that languages were best learned by speaking, Tryon recommended they be taught early, not by '*half-speaking* and Lisping' but by 'plain Discourses, and Words properly, fully and distinctly pronounced.' For this, he asserted, no tutors are as good as mothers, and that is why women's education in all branches of learning is important:

It is a great Truth, though very little believed, That the Females are naturally as fit for, and capable of all excellent Learning, as Men, even the Mathematicks it self; and if there be any difference, the Advantage is on the Womens side. They are of curious and apt Capacities, to apprehend all things, that depend upon the Power of the Fancy and Imagination, being of a more delicate Contexture and wrought with a finer Thread than Man.[34]

Tryon was not the first to argue for women's education, though few had made the case that women had a greater intellectual capacity, and could bring fancy and imagination to the process of education. His predecessor in this feminist argument was (not suprisingly) a woman: the poet and educationist Bathshua Makin. In *An Essay to Revive the Antient Education of Gentlewomen* (1673), Makin had to pretend to be a male writer who wished no harm to the privileges of his own sex in order to be in a position to argue against a system where women were 'outwardly dressed like Puppets, rather than inwardly adorned with Knowledge'. The force of her irony is evident when she continues: 'They are the weaker Sex, yet capable of impressions of great things, something like to the best of men.'[35]

The book is dedicated to the 11-year-old Princess Mary, who was to become queen 15 years later: a testimony to Makin's belief in the tradition of intelligent women from antiquity to the present day. Among her contemporaries she was able to cite such learned women as Margaret Cavendish Duchess of Newcastle, Mary Sidney Countess of Pembroke, the Duchess of Huntingdon (whom she herself had taught), the continental educational reformer Anna Schurmann, the poets Anne Bradstreet, Katherine Philips, and Anne Killigrew, Ladies Russell and Bacon, and the three daughters of Lord Burleigh: not an inconsiderable list in a time when women were regarded increasingly as ineducable.

Her enemies, she believed, were not other thinkers but courtiers and wastrels: the Barbarous custom to breed Women low, is grown general amongst us, and hath prevailed so far, that it is verily believed (especially amongst a sort of debauched Sots) that Women are not endued with such Reason, as men; not capable of improvment by Education, as they are.[36]

Makin's educational arguments, however, were far more based on reason than Tryon's. Like Lewis (and in advance of Locke) she believed in the reasonable and practical as the chief grounds for education. 'Had God intended Women onely as a finer sort of Cattle,' she wrote, 'he would not have made them reasonable.'[37] Like her colleague, Mark Lewis, she picked up the practical discourse of the Hartlib reformers but took it further and applied it to the education of girls. Her curriculum is what Defoe's Moll Flanders had to pick up by her own wits in the streets.

To buy Wooll and Flax, to die Scarlet and Purple, requires skill in

Natural Philosophy. To consider a Field, the quality and quantity, requires knowledge in Geometry. To plant a Vineyard, requires understanding in Husbandry: She could not Merchandize without knowing her Arithmetick: She could not govern so great a Family well without knowledge in Politicks and Oeconomicks: She could not look well into the ways of her Houshold, except she understood Physick and Chirurgery: She could not open her Mouth with Wisdom, and have in her Tongue the Law of kindness, unless she understood Grammar, Rhetorick and Logick.[38]

Moll Flanders's education is in fact little different from that of many of the boys of the underclass in Defoe: Captain Singleton and Colonel Jack, for example. Gay describes such a child in *Trivia*, an orphan long before Captain Coram's foundation for orphans and foundlings had been established (1742):

> At length he sighing cried; That boy was blest,
> Whose infant lips have drain'd a mother's breast;
> But happier far are those (if such be known)
> Whom both a father and a mother own:
> But I, alas! hard fortune's utmost scorn,
> Who ne'er knew parent, was an orphan born! . . .
> Had I the precepts of a father learn'd,
> Perhaps I then the coachman's fare had earn'd,
> For lesser boys can drive.
>   (II. 177–82, 187–9)

But Moll is also a mother, and her attitude towards her children, especially the girls, is problematic to the modern reader. Is she an 'unnatural mother', as her husband-brother accuses her of being, or is that accusation a piece of male manipulation? Is her return to Newgate a punishment for her attitude towards her children?[39]

Neither of these seem questions that can easily be answered. Moll has, after all, been left at birth in Newgate by her own mother. On the first page of the novel, Moll states (what Defoe knew to be the case) that many foreign nations make charitable provision for the care and education of the children of criminals:

Had this been the Custom in our Country, I had not been left a poor desolate Girl without Friends, without Cloaths, without Help or Helper in the World, as was my Fate; and by which, I was not only expos'd to very great Distresses, even before I was capable, either of Understanding my Case, or how to Amend it, nor brought into a Course of Life, which was not only not scandalous in itself, but which in its ordinary Course, tended to the swift Destruction both of Soul and Body.[40]

In what sense, in her subsequent life in a world run by what Makin calls 'debauched Sots', is it possible for her to act freely? And does the opening not suggest that our response to her is as culturally constructed as her actions? What she does has at least to be seen within the context of the argument about female education and women's freedom: an argument about *episteme* vs. *techne* (education *vs.* mere skills). How is moral choice possible in a world of apparent economic determinisms? Does not Pamela's subsequent ability to parley her virginity for respectable marriage in Richardson's novel confirm Moll's dilemma? How are these questions related to the debate about knowledge and education which Milton canvasses in *Areopagitica* and *Of Education* and explores imaginatively in the context of women in the middle books of *Paradise Lost*?

These questions touch schooling at large. Like Milton, both Lewis and Makin believed that the curriculum, and especially the teaching of languages, was in need of reform. In *Of Education* (1644) Milton condemns the practice of spending 'seven or eight years meerly in scraping together so much miserable Latin, and Greek, as might be learnt otherwise easily and delightfully in one yeer' if pupils were not forced to 'compose Theams, verses, and Orations'. He also sets out an elaborate curriculum which excludes logic and rhetoric but includes (beyond languages) the sciences of agriculture, geography, geology, biology, and mathematics: all of them to be taught in conjunction with the experience of men who use these sciences. This, he says, 'will give them such a reall tincture of natural knowledge, as they shall never forget'.[41]

Milton's concern with an easy and pleasant access to knowledge is one that Makin and Lewis also shared with Tryon. But although Milton declines 'to search what many modern *Janua's* and *Didactics*' have to say on the subject before beginning to write his essay, the most famous of these *Januas* or introductions was to have a profound effect on attitudes to childhood learning in the last half of the seventeenth century. It was the work of John Amos Comenius (or Komensky), a Polish educational reformer who came to England at the invitation of Hartlib in 1641 and had already published, at that time, his *Janua Linguarum Reserata* (*The Gateway of Languages Unlocked*, 1631).

This book was republished in 1658 along with the first appearance of his more famous work, the *Orbis Sensualium Pictus* (*A Picture of the World of the Senses*). As the first instructional book primarily to use pictures as a means of teaching, the *Orbis* had a great impact on educators, not least on Makin and Lewis. As educational reformers in the Bacon-Hartlib mould, both writers affirmed the relation between words and things that Comenius's work illustrated. 'Words are but the marks of things,'[42] Makin wrote, anticipating Locke. Lewis sets this empirical argument out even more elaborately:

Whilst we instruct Children, according to the Law of Nature, we must proceed by Sense: By Sense, I mean, the Sense of Seeing; Words are not the Objects of Feeling, Tasting, or Smelling; words spoken are but transient marks of things, and so the Objects of Hearing; Words written or printed, are permanent marks, and so are objects of Seeing. The use of the outward Senses is, to be *mediums*, to let in Notions to the inward. When the understanding is enlightned through the Senses, the memory freely keeps any thing for use laid up in it. Children are very inquisitive, and desirous of Knowledge, whilst the progress is natural from the Senses to the Understanding; and from thence to the Memory.

This is Locke more than 20 years before Locke, and it comes with the same suspicion of the imaginative and fanciful. At the same time, Milton had just written the most famous epic in the language about an unfallen world which (by definition) the senses of fallen man could not know; Dryden was writing that a rhyme had often helped him to a thought; and Robert Boyle was imagining the chemical elements to be inhabited by angels. Even John Locke, however, could not have been more scathing about the dangers of childish imaginations than Lewis:

> if you pervert the order of Nature, and represent things otherwise, as the Limmer [painter] did, who painted the Running Horse with his Heels upward; your Notions, like Monsters, affright Children, and are burthensom to the Memory, as nauseous things are to the Stomach. This is the reason, that going to School is so burthensom. Things not brought down to Childrens capacities by Sense, are like confused Objects, they see at a great distance, which the Eye is weary in beholding. Instruction of Children ought to be *zoographicon logon*, made so plain that they may look upon Words as Pictures.[43]

If this was a recipe for dullness in illustration, however, Lewis's complaint against dessicated vocabulary-crunching and grammar rules was better taken, but ultimately just as limiting of the child's imagination. This complaint had a long ancestry, but it acquired an especial force in the wake of Bacon's stress on practical knowledge and induction. 'Things may be learnt with Words by shewing the things themselves from Repositories, by using *Maps* and *Globes*, and *Pictures*, where the things themselves cannot be had; ... This will make Learning pleasant.'[44]

This model of language was, of course, just the one that that champion of fairytales and giants, Jonathan Swift, was to make fun of. In Book III of *Gulliver's Travels*, the scholars of Lagado carry about with them sacks of things as a substitute for words. Swift, as a believer in a concept of faith 'as the evidence of things unseen', would have agreed with the twentieth-century American writer, Flannery O'Connor, who claimed that a child's drawing only appears distorted to an adult who no longer understands that the concept of motion is part of 'seeing'.

Admirable as Lewis and Makin's concern was for an easier mode of reading and learning, of proceeding from the known to the unknown, as Lewis put it, their reforms came at the expense of eliminating the playful world of sound-making and storytelling which constitutes so much of the world of childhood. In *A Model for a School for the better Education of YOUTH* (1675), Lewis argued that it was as foolish 'to hurry Children with so much pains through an abundance of Authors meerly for the words' as it would be to go all over the world to see all the animals in creation. All of these, he pointed out, could be found in Comenius's *Janua*.[45] We are perilously close here to the famous call for 'facts' at the beginning of Dickens's *Hard Times*, and to Bitzer's definition of a horse there as 'a gramnivorous quadruped'. For Sissy Jupe, the circus showman's daughter in that novel, such a rationalized horse was as much an abomination as it is for Swift in Book IV of *Gulliver's Travels*.

Lewis's proposals look initially as attractive as many such platforms of educational reform, and his Baconian sense that words without things are empty wind ('Copia of words') seems common sense:

> Look upon one bred in the way commonly practised in the best publick Schools in *England*, that in seven years (the usual time from *In Speech* allowed even to the best parts) hath got a good Copia of words in *Latin, Greek,* and *Hebrew*, is a competent Orator, Historian, Rhetorician, and Poet, but understands little of things, or other Arts, mainly necessary in the Life of Man, or of other Languages.

His alternative to this seems altogether admirable on first reading, containing as it does the spectrum of modern knowledge:

> On the other side, look upon one bred in this Method here proposed, that besides all these things before mentioned, understands *French*, *Italian*, and *Spanish*: hath a Foundation laid to attain several other Languages, when he pleases, in a short time, with little trouble: and further hath made a good progress into Natural Philosophy, and the History of things; into Logick, the Mathematicks; as Arithmetick, Geometry, Astronomy, Geography, things mainly useful almost in any station: Moreover hath digested some System of Divinity, is well read in the Scriptures; all which may be done in the same time by all Lads of ordinary parts, were things constituted as hath been proposed.[46]

Only when we look again does a nagging doubt emerge about what is missing here: the faculty that allows a Galileo to imagine a heliocentric universe when his senses tell him that it is geocentric – the imagination. On second reading, the text that comes to mind is Wordsworth's description of the so-called 'ideal child' of modern educational systems, the child produced by the very sort of systems put in place by Locke:

> 'tis a Child, no Child,
> But a dwarf Man; in knowledge, virtue, skill; . . .
> The Ensigns of the Empire which he holds,
> The globe and sceptre of his royalties,

> Are telescopes, and crucibles, and maps. . . .
> He knows the policies of foreign Lands;
> Can string you names of districts, cities, towns,
> The whole world over, tight as beads of dew
> Upon a gossamer thread.[47]

Wordsworth compares this educational programme to Satan's work in *Paradise Lost*, and contrasts it both to the neglected playthings that nature has designed for the child and the very world of folk-tale and fairytale that such reformers as Locke sought to exclude: 'The child, whose love is here, at least, doth reap | One precious gain, that he forgets himself.'[48]

John Evelyn's notion of an ideal education included many of the elements that Lewis and Makin proposed. In pedagogy he was both an ancient and a modern. But as I have suggested, his concept of a child's education included more than the schoolroom, and embraced the imaginative and the fantastic. None the less, when he wrote to his father-in-law in the autumn of 1656, like Lewis he commended not rules but exercises for his four-year-old son's education:

> My boy Dick dos reade English, Latine, and French in all characters that are printed without the least hesitation, and failes very little in the prosodia, he has wonderfully many latine words, which he daily increases, and takes that strange delight in reading, that by his good will he would be continualy at his booke.

Evelyn then goes on to explain that the method of education he proposes for his son is in opposition to the dry-as-dust prescriptions of the famous text by William Lilly that had been used in grammar schools since Tudor times:

> I shall at Christmas put him to his nownes and verbs (for the business of reading is overcome perfectly) after a particular method which my Cousin Wase (now scholemaster of a famous Freeschoole in Essex or Suffolk neere Colchester) is now printing for his school; I will bring him up to few Lillian rules, but to exercise.[49]

Christopher Wase was a cousin of Evelyn's wife who came early in the 1670s to be a beadle at Oxford. His *An Essay of A Practical Grammar*, was first designed to be 'an easie Method' of learning Latin. 'Practical' also in the sense of 'practice', it was primarily dependent on the use of proverbial phrases in English and Latin as a means of introducing students to the rules through exercise. And in this, like Makin and Lewis, he looked to 'that great Regulator of *School-Policy*, who hath much matured the Learning of *Tongues*, the Reverend and Singularly Ingenious *Comenius*'.[50]

Wase precedes Makin, Lewis, and Tryon in using the modern discourse of business and trade which the Royal Society was to make popular. 'It would turn to better account,' he writes, 'if, as the children are intrusted with any stock, they were required to trade with it,' and for that they need '*Technical*

Books'.[51] Wase did not share Milton's hostility to making 'theams', but both men shared the hope that 'the *understanding* would run parallel with the *memory'*, and Wase's comparison of learning to the ascent of a hill is also Milton's. For these introductory compositions, Wase recommends not passages out of the classics – 'nothing sublime or profound, nothing anomalous, nothing preposterous'[52] – but the stuff of common knowledge.

Unfortunately, however, Evelyn's little son Richard was not to live to benefit from his or Wase's method. Having been rescued at the age of 2 from a bone stuck in his throat, he was to die of an inflamed liver at the age of 6 in 1658, a prodigy of piety and learning who could 'turne English into Lat: and *vice versa*, construe and prove what he read and did, the government and use of Relatives, Verbs *Transitive, Substantives* etc: Elipses and many figures and tropes, and made a considerable progresse in *Commenius's Janua.'*[53]

Evelyn's third son, John, was longer-lived, however; and it concerned Evelyn's friend John Beale that at the age of 11 'he may be entred into Mathematics', thereby confounding the Aristotelian enemies of modern learning.[54] One of the consolations of Evelyn's old age, however, was the education of his grandson, John's son, Jack (later Sir John) Evelyn. Four years younger than Evelyn's other 'grandson', Francis Godolphin, Jack had been sent to the French school at Greenwich (near Evelyn's estate at Deptford) in 1689; a bill for his school expenses there from the school-master, M. Severin, still survives. But it was at Eton that he shone. Writing to his first son's tutor, Dr Bohun, in 1697, Evelyn complained of his son's health and his own financial difficulties, but his grandson (by then at Eton) was plainly his consolation:

> Little *Jack* (my *Grand-son*) is in truth, a very good Child, of an honest, steady, and sweete nature; of a good Understanding and I believe will be a solid man, having already an extraordinary sense of things beyond my imagination: and as to Book-learning now in the fift forme at Eaton; so as there is no dealing with him in *Homer, Vergil, Horace,* etc. In summ: Mr *Newbery* (the chiefe Mr of that Schoole) told me that this 20 years he never had any so forward and good a proficient as *Jack.*[55]

During Jack's time at Eton, the most influential work on pedagogy in the early eighteenth century was published: Locke's *Some Thoughts Concerning Education.* Written originally as advice to his friend Edward Clarke on the education of his son (a contemporary of Jack Evelyn's), *Some Thoughts* was grounded in the same empiricist model of knowledge as *An Essay on Human Understanding,* published the previous year. Central to its pedagogy was the concept of the child's mind as a *tabula rasa,* a concept that appears in Evelyn's translation of of St John Chrysostom's *Golden Book* nearly 40 years earlier: the book he published as a memorial to his dead son Richard. Commenting on a Greek passage, Evelyn writes:

Tis reported that when pearls are first taken up, they are only little drops of water, etc. And it was only a report, taken up by S. Chrysostom to metaphorize his discourse: but it is apparently true of glasses, which from a fluid metal receive their figure from the will of the blower of them, which is afterwards firm, and not to be new moulded. The French have an expression, *Il a prins son pli,* A tender twig soon yeelds. Hence that of Persius,

> *Udum, et molle lutum es, nunc properandus et acri*
> *Fingendus sine fine rotâ*
>
> (Sat.3.)

[You are soft wet clay; now be off at once and have yourself shaped (into a pot) on the ceaslessly whirling wheel.]

Children are *rasae Tabulae,* or rather *cereae,* apt for every inscription and impression.[56]

Evelyn's correction to what was to become Locke's famous phrase, *tabula rasa,* is instructive. '*Cereae*' means 'of wax' and suggests a continuous process of erasure and change (or even moulding and shaping) that is not in the word '*rasae*', which means only 'blank' and has the connotation of inert passivity. Locke has generally been credited with the origin of the notion of the *tabula rasa,* but he largely consolidated and popularized an idea that can be found in previous thinkers: Ascham, Montaigne, Richard Hooker, Erasmus, St Thomas Aquinas, Cicero, and Aristotle.[57]

After Bacon's *Advancement of Learning* (1605), moreover, versions of the concept of *tabula rasa* were a commonplace among educational and social reformers in England, though Locke himself seems to have been ignorant of many of these writers. Locke, however, published his work in a society eager for consensus and for ensuring the consolidation of the values of the Revolution of 1688. The gradualism implicit in his educational theories struck a wide popular chord in a society keen on gradual change through education as an alternative to violent revolution.[58]

Some Thoughts Concerning Education, moreover, proposed a system of education more suitable for the middle-class values of an empire of trade and commerce than such previous courtesy books for gentlemen as Henry Peacham's *The Compleat Gentleman* (1622). Although Locke's book was addressed to a country squire (Edward Clarke) and meant for the education of Clarke's son as a gentleman, it includes an emphasis on practical skills, accounting, and foreign languages.[59] And the book has little time for many of the traditional gentleman's pastimes – music or fencing or riding – which would have been found in *The Compleat Gentleman.* As for poetry, Locke says dismissively, 'It is very seldom seen that any one discovers Mines of Gold or Silver in *Parnassus.*'[60]

Locke's influence on childhood education in the eighteenth century was primarily through his linking of instruction with delight. He recognized that children 'must play, and have Play-things',[61] and he gave the lead to later publishers by suggesting how educational toys and games might be made. But some of his recommendations had an effect disproportionate to their place in his book. His advice that children be taught kindness to animals, for instance, appealed to a society that was keen to assert its oneness with the natural world,[62] and was much reiterated. And his recommendation that (male) children be hardened to physical discomfort was certainly welcome to an expanding military and imperial power.

Like many of the reforming writers to whom I have referred, Locke believed that examples were better than rules. 'Children are *not* to be *taught by Rules*,' he wrote, 'which will be always slipping out of their Memories.'[63] And his celebration of curiosity as 'the great Instrument Nature has provided to remove . . . Ignorance' was revolutionary in its time, though he was careful to restrict that curiosity from being 'too Curious' about the nature of God. But what must have been most appealing to the adult purchasers of the book was Locke's insistence on a combination of obedience and reasonableness in a child: an obedience achieved by discipline and stifling the imagination.

Locke's major legacy to eighteenth-century children was his hostility to what he called the 'bugbear' stories nurses tell which stamp frightening ideas in the child's imagination. This served as a text to attack the whole panoply of popular literature which children had inherited and adopted: folk-tales, fairytales, and ballads. In retrospect, Locke's dislike of stories about '*Goblins, Spectres*, and *Apparitions*'[64] seems almost pathological, but it is indicative of something more ominous in his work: his suspicion of the imagination generally. Coleridge was to say that fairytales had accommodated his imagination to the idea of the vast; but Locke would have no more of that than did the whole host of repressive writers for children who used Locke at the end of the eighteenth century as the ground for teaching 'rational morality'.

Locke knew virtually nothing about the speculative aspect of science. In praising 'such Writers, as have imploy'd themselves in making rational Experiments and Observations' he denigrates what he calls 'barely speculative Systems'.[65] He has room in his account of knowledge for a Newton observing the law of gravity in the fall of an apple, but not for the mind of Newton which Wordsworth described 'voyaging through strange seas of thought alone'. In fact, for all his supposed rationality, Locke thought the universe incomprehensible and even the law of gravity 'impossible to be explained by any natural Operation of Matter, or any other Law of Motion, but the positive Will of a Superiour Being [i.e. God], so ordering it'.[66] His friend Edward Molyneux believed that 'Experiment is matter of Fact, and strikes the senses so forcibly, that there is no opposing it,'[67] but Locke none the less did not understand the 'facts' (the mathematical principles) on which Newton erected his theories. In that instance he was content to be reassured that they were true, and to examine only the reasonings and corollaries that followed from them.[68]

At first glance it would seem that Locke stands with Pope and Swift in their suspicion of 'mad mathesis' and arrogant speculation. But in fact it was Locke's desire for scientific certainties which Pope deplored in *The Essay on Man*, and the absurdities of experimentation which Swift mocked in Book III of *Gulliver's Travels*. Locke's doubt was that any scientific system had yet been found in which a student might 'be sure to find Truth and Certainty, which is, what all Sciences give an expectation of'.[69] But he was not in doubt, as Pope and Swift were, about science's claim for certainty. And because his system of education depended so much upon factual evidence and experimentation, it opened the door to the sort of fact-mongering that Mr M'Choakumchild employs in Gradgrind's academy in *Hard Times* and which Wordsworth was to deplore in *The Prelude*.

Like Peter Ramus, the so-called reformer of logic at the end of the sixteenth century, Locke consolidated a ratiocinative and practical trend in education into what amounted to a system. Like many of the members of the Royal Society, he was, in fact, a child of Ramus in the sense that Ramus had divided knowing from its expression (or logic from rhetoric). Dryden said that a rhyme often helped him to a thought, and no one who has read Pope's couplets with attention is unaware how often a rhyme is a revelation of such thoughts. Locke's belief in 'facts' was at the expense of the language which shapes those facts and the imagination that constructs their arrangement. What he elides is the way in which a society constructs the world in its own image, as France and England were (at this very time) constructing the botanical taxonomy of the rest of the world in the image of their own philosophical and epistemological preoccupations.

In *Some Thoughts Concerning Education*, Locke had nothing to say about the education of the vast majority of his society. What he thought the poor should have, however, was set out in a document he wrote in 1697: a proposal for working schools that was to be very useful to the government commissioners who set up the workhouses in 1834. These schools were designed to ensure that such children between the ages of 3 and 14 'from infancy be inured to work' for 'the making of them sober and industrious all their lives'.[70] And they were not intended to educate in anything but trades, so that the boys (at least) might be apprenticed afterwards. Any such children 'found begging out of the parish where they dwell' were to be 'sent to the next working school, there to be soundly whipped and kept working till evening'.[71] Enter Oliver Twist!

Locke's *Thoughts*, then, were never intended as a thorough system of education for the whole population; but they were widely taken up by the middle classes. In the second part of Richardson's enormously popular novel, *Pamela* (1740), much of the space is devoted to Pamela's mastery of Locke's theories so that she may set up an educational system for her son.[72]

Even earlier in the century his theories were widely disseminated by the prolific Nonconformist minister, Isaac Watts. Probably the most popular children's book ever published, Watts's *Moral Songs*, had reached 8 million copies by the early twentieth century.

Though Watts has been described as a 'kindly Puritan' (a misnomer on both counts), many of his popular *Divine and Moral Songs* for children (first published in 1715 and later expanded) contain the stuff of childhood nightmares. Watts's God is one of punishments. Children who scoff at the Lord will have their lips cut off, and even his famous 'Cradle Hymn' contains the lines: ''Twas to save thee, Child, from dying, | Save my Dear from burning flame.' His *Preservative from the Sins and Follies of Childhood and Youth Written by Way of Question and Answer* (1730) tells all in its title. Like Locke, moreover, Watts did not believe that the lower classes should be educated above their station. The charity school he envisages for them 'might have partly the character of a *Work-House*', he says, 'as well as of a *School*'.[73] Watts also makes the imperial agenda of this new system of education overt. In the sixth of his *Divine Songs* he addresses his thanks to God:

> 'Tis to thy sovreign Grace I owe,
> That I was born on *British* Ground,
> Where Streams of Heavenly Mercy flow,
> And words of sweet Salvation sound.
>
> Lord I ascribe it to Thy Grace,
> And not to chance, as others do,
> That I was born of Christian Race,
> And not a Heathen or a Jew.

Knowledge is, for Watts, a matter of conforming the mind to authority, a process in which memory is central. (Small wonder that Blake, who hated memory, parodied Watts in his *Songs of Innocence and Experience*!) For Watts, the mind is not an instrument of discovery but a repository, its operation not unlike the primitive calculator that we find in the third book of *Gulliver's Travels*. In his *Logick* (1725) Watts describes the imagination as that which has no place in the mind's growth; and in *The Improvement of the Mind* (1741) he is as dismissive of fairytales as Locke. In his mechanistic view of a universe of clear ideas, nothing could be further from Coleridge's connection of fairytales with the child's conception of the infinite. In *The Improvement of the Mind* Watts wrote:

Fancy with all her Images is fatigued and overwhelmed in following the planetary Worlds through such immense stages, such astonishing journies as these are, and resigns its place to the pure intellect, which learns by degrees to take in such ideas as these, and to adore its Creator with new and sublime devotion.[74]

Perhaps Watts's greatest gift to children's literature, though, was an unconscious one. In his definition of man in his *Logic* (1724)[75] he objected to the standard formulation that man is 'a rational animal' because the animal in man is not rational but rather united to reason. 'If a spirit should be united to a horse, and make it a rational being, surely this would not be a man,' he argues, taking up a familiar argument in logic. Only two years later, Swift's Gulliver encounters just such creatures, the Houyhnhnms, dispassionately propounding a rational dystopia in which genocide seems perfectly rational.[76] That way, as Gulliver demonstrates, lies madness.

Fortunately neither Locke nor Watts seems to have been very successful in expelling popular literature from children's reading in this period. Five years after Locke's death, Sir Richard Steele wrote (in *Tatler* 95) of a little girl whose chief reading was 'in Fairies and Sprights',[77] . . . indeed, much the same reading that Swift was amusing himself with at the time, that is Mme. d'Aulnoy's *Contes des Fées*.

Fairytales, like most folk-tales, are about prevailing against the odds, chiefly against the odds of a superior and tyrannical authority. Even literary authorities like Dr Johnson thought them preferable for children to the books of improvement and instruction that came in the wake of Watts. Johnson reproved Coleridge's friend, Mrs Barbauld, for her rationalist condescension in her children's books:

> She tells the children, 'This is a cat, and that is a dog, with four legs and a tail; see there! you are much better than a cat or a dog, for you can speak.' If I had bestowed such an education on a daughter . . . I would have sent her to the *Congress*.[7]

He means the American Congress: Johnson's idea of a madhouse.

Like Wordsworth, Johnson had similar views about folk-tales. '*Jack the Giant-Killer, Parismus and Parismenus*, and *The Seven Champions of Christendom*' were fitter for children, he believed, than the works of Mrs Barbauld.[79]

It is often claimed that children had to wait for the famous bookseller John Newbery to liberate them from the shackles of improving rationalist books. But in fact most of Newbery's works have an instructional sting in the tail. His *Little Pretty Pocket-Book* (1744) is a pleasant exception. It begins with a justification for the book in a 'Method of Reasoning', but once the parents are safely out of the way its alphabet trails off into a farrago of nonsense:

> Here's great K, and L,
> Pray Dame can you tell,
> Who put the Pig-Hog
> Down into the Well.

Children, in any case, seem to have been perfectly able to subvert the instructional agendas of their elders. In 1672 John Prideaux attacked 'superstitious *Romances*' and 'the Bastard sort of Histories' for 'stuffing the Fancy and Memory with ridiculous *Chimerah's*, and wandering Imaginations, to the excluding and stifling of more serious and profitable meditations'.[80] Swift, who was no friend of fancies posing as truth, was equally opposed to this sort of learned pedagogical dullness. In his time he had seen Aesop's *Fables* change from Ogilby's version in which diverting narratives were accompanied by brief 'morals', to L'Estrange's version in which the moral outweighs the narrative.

At the begining of the most famous passage in *The Battle of the Books* – the very Aesopic story of the spider and the bee – Aesop himself, with his title-page missing and his leaves half-torn, escapes from this mistreatment by the Moderns back to his proper home with the Ancients. And in *A Tale of a Tub*, Swift manages to reduce Dryden's *The Hind and the Panther* to a child's beast-fable while poking satiric fun at dull modern scholars who have found arcane meanings in such children's classics as 'Reynard the Fox', 'Tom Thumb', and 'Whittington and His Cat'.

But even John Bunyan, who attacked romances as 'fingle-fangle', was indebted to one of them, *Valentine and Orson*, for the encounter with the giant Apollyon. When Sir Richard Steele asked his 8-year-old godson in 1709 whether he liked romances more than Aesop's *Fables*, the boy replied that he preferred 'the Lives and Adventures of Don *Bellianis* of *Greece*, *Guy* of *Warwick*, the *Seven Champions*, and other Historians of that age.'[81] It was a candid answer, but cunning too. One of the educational claims for the *Fables*, certainly by the early eighteenth century, was that they taught natural history at the same time as inculcating morals, and so had a double advantage over such merely entertaining literature as romances. By identifying the authors of folk romances as historians, Steele's godson made them a respectable part of the structure of scientific knowledge and gave what he knew to be an adult's reason for preferring imaginative adventure stories to moral tales.

Notes

1 'Children in Early Modern England', in *Children and their Books*, ed. Gillian Avery and Julia Briggs (Oxford: Clarendon, 1989), p. 50.
2 See Linda Pollock, *A Lasting Relationship: Parents and Children Over Three Centuries* (London: Fourth Estate, 1987), pp. 11–12.
3 See Linda Pollock, *Forgotten Children: Parent-Child Relations from 1500 to 1900* (Cambridge: Cambridge University Press, 1983); Lawrence Stone, *The Family, Sex and Marriage in England 1500–1800* (London: Weidenfeld & Nicolson, 1977); Philip Aries, *Centuries of Childhood* (London: Jonathan Cape, 1960); and *The Essayes of Montaigne*, trans. John Florio (New York: Modern Library, 1933), pp. 107–40.
4 British Library, Ms. Harl. 382, Jone Elyott to her sister-in-law, Elizabeth D'Ewes, 18 December [1643?], fo. 40.

5 *The Diary of John Evelyn*, ed. E. S. de Beer (Oxford: Clarendon, 1955), iii. p. 220. For an extensive survey of the subject of childhood death and parental grief, see Rayomnd A. Anselment, '"The Teares of Nature": Seventeenth-Century Parental Bereavement', *Modern Philology*, 91 (1993), pp. 26–53.

6 British Library, Evelyn Papers, Family Bound Letters 1449, 5 July 1658.

7 Letter to her father, Sir Richard Browne, 1 April, 1659. Evelyn Papers, Mary Evelyn Box 2: Bundle ME to various.

8 *The Diary of the Rev. Ralph Josselin 1616–1683*, ed. E. Hockliffe (Camden, 3rd ser., xv. 1908), p. 74.

9 'Against Disobedience'.

10 'This is the reason why I think it is not possible for anyone to imagine any other quantities in bodies, howsoever constituted, whereby they can be taken notice of, besides, sounds, tastes, smells, visible and tangible qualities', *An Essay Concerning Human Understanding* (1690), ii. Ch. 2. This passage contains the only use of the word 'imagination' in Locke's work.

11 In a letter (possibly to Lady Rich), in 1717, Pope's one-time friend, Lady Mary Wortley Montagu, indignantly asserted her accounts of Turkey to be true: 'Would you have me write novels like the Countess of D'Aulnoy?' [i.e. the *Contes des Fées*] *The Turkish Embassy Letters*, ed. Malcolm Jack (London: Virago, 1994), p. 41. In a letter to John Evelyn on 5 July 1669 John Beale refers to himself as 'plung'd in the Region of darknesse; And like the Spirit enclos'd in the Magicians bottle, I must cry out to you that are in the light, to unseale the Bottle, that I may see what you are doing.' British Library, Evelyn Papers, Incoming Letterbook. This suggests that stories from *The Arabian Nights* were common currency in England at least by then.

12 'Whoso would Valiant Be.'

13 British Library, Evelyn Papers, Incoming Letters G–J, No. 848, Letter of 5 July 1690.

14 Ibid., Letterbook II, Ep. 624, Letter of 9 August 1690.

15 Edinburgh, 1701, p. 4. Halket's book was addressed to 'young Noblemen and Gentlemen', that is, of the same class as Francis Godolphin.

16 British Library, Evelyn Papers, Letterbook II, Ep. 624, Letter of 4 April 1690.

17 *Pretty Songbook*, p. 34. This is from vol. ii of a work for which vol. i. is no longer extant. Even vol. ii. exists in only one copy in the British Library.

18 There is also a category of books of advice from fathers to sons, but many of these, such as the Marquis of Argyll's *Instructions to a Son* (1661), are in fact addressed to adults.

19 *The New Oxford Book of Seventeenth-Century Verse*, ed. Alastair Fowler (Oxford: Oxford University Press, 1991), p. 176.

20 sig. [Q3v]. In *Trivia* (1716) Gay gives an account of the strength of these customary beliefs in London 70 years later.

21 British Library, Trumbull Papers: Stubbes File IV, Letter from the Rev. Richard Stubbe, 1712.

22 *The Child's Week's-Work*, sig. A2.

23 *Tom Jones*, i. ch. 3.

24 *The Child's Week's-Work*, pp. 8, 14

25 Ibid., p. 30.

26 *Vestibulum Technicum: Or, An Artificial Vestibulum* (London, 1675), p. [5].

27 *Some Memoirs of the Life of Tho. Tryon* (London, 1705), p. 14. *A Discourse of the Causes, Natures and Cure of Phrensie, Madness or Distraction*, appendixed to *A Treatise of Dreams and Visions* (London, 1689).

28 *The Reformed School*, ed. H. M. Knox, (Liverpool: Liverpool University Press, 1958), pp. 25–6, 41.

29 Ibid., p. 50.

30 Tryon, *A New Method of Education Children* (1695), p. 46.

31 Ibid., pp. 28, 27.

32 *A Discourse of . . . Madness*, pp. 260–1.

33 sig. A3, p. 71. John Evelyn dreaded going to Eton as a little boy just for this reason: see *Diary*, ed. de Beer, ii. p. 11. Tryon also differed from his contemporaries in thinking that humane treatment of the mad was preferable to beatings and quack cures. *A Discourse of . . . Madness*, pp. 288–90.

34 *New Method*, pp.15–16. Twenty years earlier Bathshua Makin made the same argument for mothers as tutors in languages, in *An Essay to Revive the Antient Education of Gentlewomen* (London, 1673), p. 17.

35 Ibid., p. 31.

36 Ibid., p. 3.

37 Ibid., p. 23.

38 Ibid., p. 35.

39 David Blewett, *Defoe's Art of Fiction: Robinson Crusoe, Moll Flanders, Colonel Jack and Roxana* (Toronto: University of Toronto Press, 1979), p. 65.

40 *Moll Flanders*, ed. G. A. Starr (Oxford: Oxford University Press – World's Classics, 1971), p. 8.

41 *The Prose of John Milton*, ed. J. Max Patrick (New York: New York University, 1968), pp. 231, 235.

42 *An Essay to Revive the Antient Education of Gentlewomen*, p. 36.

43 *An Essay to Facilitate the Education of YOUTH, by bringing down the Rudiments of Grammar to the Sense of SEEING* (London, [1670]), pp. 1–2.

44 Ibid., p. 7.

45 Echoing Bacon's famous title, Lewis wrote in Comenius's praise: 'Doubtless *Comenius* hath done more for the advancement of Learning than any other man of his age, let prejudiced persons say what they will', sig. [A7]. Thomas Lye's *The Childs Delight* (1671) also uses pictures, but in a more primitive way. His practice of teaching language by syllables and by similar sounds, however, is considerably in advance of its time and reflects the influence of educational reform that he himself acknowledges in the work of John Wilkins.

46 *A Model for a School*, p. 15.

47 *The Prelude* (1850) v. ll. 294–5, 328–30, 334–7.

48 Ibid., V. 368–69.

49 Evelyn Papers, Family Bound Letters, 1439. Evelyn to Sir Richard Browne, 29 Nov. 1656. Wase was a cousin of Evelyn's wife, Mary Browne. He was a classicist whose school was, in fact, at Dedham in Essex, and he subsequently became Headmaster of Tonbridge School before being employed in state service. He also wrote the epitaph for Evelyn's son, Richard. Lewis also attacked Lilly as a 'huge Fardle of useless Rules' in *Plain, and short Rules For Pointing Periods* (London, [1675?]), p. 7, as does Makin.

50 *Methodi Practicae Specimen. An Essay of a Practical Grammar* (London, 1660), sig. A2. Wase also refers to 'divers happy pieces' on this subject that have been printed in England, among which he includes Charles Hoole's *A New Discovery of the Old Art of Teaching School*. Doubtless it was Wase's identification with the modern methods of Comenius that led John Beale to suggest to Evelyn that Wase be conscripted into an early stage of the ancients-vs.-moderns controversy in which the Royal Society got embroiled in the early 1670s. See British Library Evelyn Papers, Incoming Letterbook, Letter from Beale of 25 Sept. 1671.

51 Ibid., A2–A2v.

52 Ibid., [A5v].

53 *The Diary of John Evelyn*, iii. p. 207.

54 British Library, Evelyn Papers, Incoming Letterbook, 16 Feb. 1666.

55 Letter of 18 Jan., 1697, *Seven Letters of John Evelyn*, ed. F. E. R. Heygate (Oxford: Horace Hart, 1914), p. 12.

56 *Miscellanea*, ed. William Upcott (London: Henry Colburn, 1825), p. 139.

57 See Neal Wood, '*Tabula Rasa*, Social Environmentalism, and the "English Paradigm"', *Journal of the History of Ideas*, 53 (1992), p. 651.

58 Although not published until 1693, the work was begun in the 1680s and reflects the constitutional struggle of the period that led to the deposition of James II and the emplacement of a modern constitutional monarchy.

59 Locke's proposals were addressed to the middle classes. His proposals for the poor are contained in H. R. Fox Bourne, *The Life of John Locke* (New York: Harper & Brothers, 1876), ii. 377–90. The passage concerning the education of the poor is on pp. 383–6.

60 *The Educational Writings of John Locke*, ed. James L. Axtell (Cambridge: Cambridge University Press, 1968), p. 285. All subsequent citations from *Some Thoughts Concerning Education* are from Axtell's edition and are referred to only by page number.

61 Axtell, p. 143.

62 See Keith Thomas, *Man and the Natural World* (New York: Pantheon, 1983), pp. 92–142.

63 Axtell, p. 158.

64 Ibid., p. 303.

65 Ibid., pp. 305–6.

66 Ibid., p. 303.

67 Ibid., p. 306, n. 1.

68 Ibid., p. 307, n. 1.

69 Ibid., p. 304.

70 *The Life of John Locke*, ii. 384.

71 Ibid., ii. 381.

72 Richardson had written two educational works himself in the 1730s, *The Apprentice's Vade Mecum* (1733) and a depoliticized edition of *Aesop's Fables* (1739).

73 *An Essay Towards the Encouragement of Charity Schools* (London, 1728), p. 15.

74 Berwick, 1806, pp. 138–9. This comes, paradoxically, after a passage in which Watts explains the usefulness of such a poem as *Paradise Lost* in enlarging the mind by use of tropes and figures. Plainly his concept of 'mind' here, however, does not include fancy.

75 *Logic: Or the Right Use of Reason* (Edinburgh, 1807), p. 100.

76 It seems likely that Swift would first have encountered this debate in the *Institutiones Logicae* (1681) of Narcissus Marsh, the Provost of Trinity College, Dublin. Swift, however, was an undergraduate at Trinity in the late 1680s; *Gulliver* was not written until more than 30 years later. See also R. S. Crane, 'The Houyhnhnms, the Yahoos and the History of Ideas', in *Reason and the Imagination: Studies in the History of Ideas*, ed. J. A. Mazzeo (New York: Columbia University Press, 1962), pp. 231–53.

77 No. 95, 17 Nov. 1709 (London, 1743), ii. p. 242.

78 *Boswell's Life of Johnson*, ed. G. B. Hill (Oxford: Clarendon Press, 1934), iv. p. 8, n. 3.

79 *Life of Johnson*, ii. pp. 408–9.

80 *An Easy and Compendious Introduction for Histories* (Oxford, 1661).

81 No. 95, Nov. 17 1709 (London, 1743), ii. p. 242.

|7|

Conclusion: The Discourse of Resistance

One of the most powerful passages in Romantic literature is in Thomas De Quincey's description of a dream in his *Confessions of an English Opium-Eater*. In it De Quincey remembers 'seeing' in his mind a reconstruction of an engraving by the eighteenth-century Italian artist, Piranesi. Taken from Piranesi's series of imaginary prison drawings, the *Carceri*, this print shows a figure endlessly toiling up flights of a broken circular staircase: a subject that overwhelms de Quincey in its scale and hopelessness. It was, says De Quincey, an allegory of power and the resistance to it.[1]

In fact, De Quincey had never seen this print and had been told about it (inaccurately, it seems) by Coleridge. Piranesi, moreover, had never seen prisons of this kind. None such existed in Rome. The whole of this series was an exercise of his imagination at play with the scale of Roman ruins from antiquity. We have here, then, a recollection of a dream based on a narrative about an engraving of a non-existent subject. The whole process of subject-object possession recounted here (from De Quincey through Coleridge and Piranesi) is an analogue of how art, like mapping, subjects experience in order to possess it.

Piranesi's print (published in 1750) is of a subject that is part of the discourse of sublimity that Burke in his *Philosophical Enquiry into the Origin of Our Ideas of the Sublime and Beautiful* defined, in English at any rate, in 1757. Arising from the ancient work *On the Sublime* by Longinus, it reified a whole area of knowledge that challenged the mechanical model of the world at the very moment when Sir John Hill published his canonization of Linnaeus's classificatory work in English. 'Perhaps it is not too much to hope,' Sir John wrote to his dedicatee Lord Bute,

> that under such Auspices the subject will be pursued successfully, till not a Flower of the East or Western World shall be wanting in our Gardens; till the Science, traced in Nature only, *Paulatim vitia atque Errores exuit omnes* [and little by little all the mistakes and errors will vanish].[2]

The onward course of botany's empire which Hill traces there was in fact already being enacted by the Earl of Bute, who was beginning to make the Royal Botanic Garden at Kew. But just as the empirical stemmas of Linnaean taxonomy began to take hold of English consciousness, Laurence Sterne began to publish *Tristram Shandy* (1759–67), a sustained comic attack on the very correspondence between language and things which Sir John celebrated, and on his certainty that everything would now be known by its proper name.

It is not my business to trace the continued and increasing resistance to the mechanical model of knowledge in the later eighteenth century; but Sterne's Dr Slop – the 'man-midwife' in *Tristram Shandy* – might stand as exemplary of this distrust. Based on the York anatomist and gynaecologist Dr John Burton, Slop's mechanical view of nature very nearly destroys Tristram at birth. And Sterne's subsequent comic play with the gap between words and the things they signify is a virtuoso examination of the follies of empiricism. Where Richardson, in *Pamela* part II (1741), shows us his heroine engaged in Lockean schemes of paediatric and educational reform, Sterne's novel manifests the disastrous absurdity of any such schemes.

Not for Sterne Francis Lodowyck's confidence that the numerical sign '5' would signify the same thing in every culture. Uncle Toby proposes to show the Widow Wadman where he was wounded at the Siege of Namur. He means on the model of the siege that he has built in the garden; she hopes to see his exposed body. Clear and perspicuous prose may be what Bernard Mandeville espouses in his preface to *The Fable of the Bees* (1714), but what he disparagingly calls the terms of 'Art and Education'[3] are none the less very evident in his work. Like Bacon, Mandeville was scarcely artless in the style of his writing; his colourful narrative digressions are a chief feature of the supposedly transparent realism of his prose.

Sterne's Dr Slop is a parody of Dr Burton's belief (in his *Essay on Midwifery*, 1751) that women's bodies could be unfolded as texts and read unambiguously.[4] Slop has no masculine qualms about his ability to read this feminine text. In this Slop and Burton are at the opposite pole from Barbara Duden's scrupulous German physician, Johann Storch, keeping (like Sir Thomas Browne and Milton) the possibility of more than one model in mind.[5] Storch (whether consciously or not) and Sterne stand against the inscription of the world in merely masculine terms: against the phallocentrism that defines children in relation only to their fathers, for example.

Sterne's novel makes a mockery of the privileged phallus not only in the scene where Tristram almost loses his in the sash window, but in the very act of Tristram's conception, when his mother is reminded of clock-winding by the action of her husband. Anything but passive in the conception of her child, Mrs Shandy enacts what one critic has called 'double invagination'[6]: a place of self-articulation where women can belong without definition by men, indeed where men's definitions have nothing to do with what women are. Over against the expected patrilineal discourse and structure of the novel, a whole range of other meanings suggest the inadequacy of that dominating model.

But Dr Burton's somatic appropriation has a cultural history in writing about the body. In *A Tale of a Tub* (1704), Swift's hack writer views a flayed human body or a corpse with the detached equanimity of a Nazi doctor in a death camp:

> Last Week I saw a Woman *flay'd*, and you will hardly believe, how much it altered her Person for the worse. Yesterday I ordered the Carcass of a *Beau* to be stript in my Presence; when we were all amazed to find so many unsuspected Faults under one Suit of Cloaths: Then I laid open his *Brain*, his *Heart*, and his *Spleen*; But I plainly perceived at every Operation, that the farther we proceeded, we found the Defects increase upon us in Number and Bulk.[7]

Swift's discourse there is of the anatomy theatre. By the early eighteenth century such theatres began to be established in London hospitals, but Swift's work (written in the 1690s) antedates them and the great popular hostility to them later in the eighteenth century.[8] Anatomy had, however, been an interest of the sort of *virtuosi* that were associated with the Royal Society. Not only were such anatomical demonstrations a popular feature of the Grand Tour, they had been part of the curriculum at Oxford since 1624 when the Tomlins Lectureship in anatomy there was established. The Statute establishing this lectureship links it directly to the law: 'the procuring of a Sounde body of one of the Executed persons' at the Lent Assizes. With an attendant surgeon 'for the severing lyfting up and shewing of the parts', the Reader of this lectureship is to 'shew the Scituation, nature and office of the partes commonly called Natural vidilicet [that is] Liver Spleene Stomake Guttes etc.' This process is to be continued for 3 days, on the third of which the Reader is to deal with the brain.[9]

Thomas Willis, an early exponent of the functions of the brain, lectured on the subject in Oxford in the 1650s. There he was the assistant to William Petty, who was acting Tomlins Reader in Anatomy, a medical career obscured by his later fame for surveying and statistics. In 1650 Willis and Petty were responsible for one of the great cases of the century, the strange 'resurrection' of Ann Green. Green was accused of infanticide, condemned, and hanged at the judicial assizes. After the execution, her corpse would thus have been available for dissection. But it was discovered that she was still alive and so she was resuscitated by Petty, and was subsequently pardoned, and married and had three children. This case, not surprisingly, had wide publicity and was still remembered by John Evelyn in a letter to William Wotton in 1703.[10] Indeed, it is hard to imagine a better example of the subjection of a body to scrutiny as a text.

Willis was an exact contemporary of Evelyn and, like him, both a Royalist and an early participant in one of the learned groups that led to the foundation of the Royal Society. One of Willis's pupils at Oxford in the 1650s was John Locke, whose lecture notes provide us with evidence of Willis's early views on the structure of the brain. As an iatrochemist (a scientist interested in the interrelation of chemistry and medicine) Willis also combined Baconian empiricism with William Harvey's mechanical model of the body's circulatory system.

It is scarcely surprising that such a combination appealed to the young Locke, nor is it surprising that Willis's analogy for the operation of the brain is distillation in a laboratory. For him, too, the imagination is a matter of blood flow:

> Through these interconnections the imaginations and the passions, conceived in the cerebrum, may be communicated through the cerebellum to the praecordia, and similarly the passions from the praecordia may reach the imagination and the cerebrum. Hence, love, anger, etc. cause various praecordial motions accompanied by divers modulations and fluxes of the blood.[11]

It is no great step from Willis to the mad modern 'projectors' of Swift's *A Tale of a Tub*. In 'Sect. IX A Digression Concerning The Original, The Use And Improvment of Madness In A Commonwealth', madness, whether in the state or in the academy, is attributed by the hack writer to a '*Phoenomenon of Vapours*, ascending from the lower Faculties to overshadow the Brain, and thence distilling into Conceptions, for which the Narrowness of our Mother-Tongue has not yet assigned any other Name, besides *Madness* or *Phrenzy*'. Louis XIV's desire to conquer Europe, he explains, is directly connected with a disorder in the rectum: 'The same Spirits which in their superior Progress would conquer a Kingdom, descending upon the *Anus*, conclude in a *Fistula*.'[12]

It would be unfair to Willis, however, to identify him with the hack's mere belief in outward appearances. Unlike the hack, Willis was one of those 'who held *Anatomy* to be the ultimate End of *Physick*' (medicine), and not a mere curiosity.[13] 'The *Academy of Modern Bedlam*' for which the hack speaks, on the other hand, is a place where reason means preferring speculation to anything but the most superficial observation. In what David Nokes has called this 'physico-logical' system, large ears in a man may be marks of inward grace, and experiments are only for the purpose of satisfying curiosity. The flaying of a woman or the anatomy of a beau have no more to do with real knowledge than the infamous experiment recorded by John Evelyn at the Royal Society in 1667, when a vivisection was performed on a dog that had air pumped into its lungs to keep it alive.[14]

In 1667 *Paradise Lost* also first appeared: a work in which, in Book XI, Michael displays to Adam the history of the world in a series of tableaux. Most of these revelations to the disconsolate Adam are of scenes from the Old Testament: historical narratives of Cain and Abel, or Enoch, or Noah. The second, however, is very different in kind. It shows the consequences of death's entry into the world, a spectacle of mortality: 'A Lazar house, it seemd, wherein were laid/Numbers of all diseas'd.'

What the poem then offers is a gruesome catalogue of ailments – 'Convulsions, Epilepsies, fierce Catarrhs' – that might have been gleaned from the Great Plague of London only 2 years earlier. This scene presents the body in a new light: not in action, but passive to the spectacle of suffering. In describing this scene to Adam, Michael blames these illnesses on the victims' ungoverned appetite 'Inductive mainly to the sin of *Eve*./Therefore so abject is their punishment.'

'Inductive' and 'abject' are potent words, especially in conjunction. The abjection of the body is linked to the induction of Eve: her willingness to believe Satan's claim that knowledge comes only from inductive experience.[15] In this passage the world of inductive sensation is linked to the sort of physical abjection suffered by Ann Green: a story still widely talked about well after the publication of *Paradise Lost*. Here, startlingly, is the world of medical demonstration in which objective display and fact seem to prevail over subjective understanding. Like the corpse in Rembrandt's 'The Anatomy Lesson of Dr. Tulp', these bodies are pathic: subject to the horrified gaze of Adam as similar medical displays were subject to the gaze of young Englishmen on the Grand Tour of the continent at the time.

That this show of horrors does not prevail over Adam is one of the dramatic ironies of the discursive tutorial which Michael is having with him. First of all, this 'scene' is within a stream of larger and more conventional narratives of (ultimately) providential history. Though it follows the murder of Cain, it precedes stories of the righteous. Those histories, moreover, are not merely what Ben Jonson called 'mighty shows' but part of a process of gradual illumination in Adam: illumination in which Michael's 'intermixture' of consolation is a chief part. The sequence as a whole leads to the spoken revelations of Book XII and reveals the greater potency of discourse then mere 'scientific' demonstration. It also critiques the incongruity of this heterogenous scene: its macabre claims to domination and possession; its prefiguration of the world of modern medicine and mechanical systems of the body.

In the year of the publication of *Paradise Lost*, one of the Fellows of the Royal Society, Nathaniel Fairfax, wrote to its Secretary, Henry Oldenburg, about the case of a 'monstrous birth' to a woman called Burroughs in Woodbridge, Suffolk. Like many of his contemporaries, Fairfax was fascinated by what action on her part might have led to what we would now call Siamese twins, and whether these two bodies had only one soul. Fairfax's manner of explaining himself is anything but straightforward, but his rambling conclusions display a scepticism about human ability to understand the relation between body and soul that is a long way from Descartes' conviction that the latter lay in the pineal gland. Reflecting on how 'the head powers' of one body might be common to what appear to be two persons, he observes that it would be as difficult to imagine 'how one whole soul may snugg to, or ly hid in another'. In spite of his admiration for the Royal Society's advancement of knowledge, however, Fairfax stops there with what amounts to a rebuke to Descartes and the claims of the mechanical model of the body. Fairfax's comments reflect sceptically on the inadequacy of the discourse of one subject to another in a manner that rebukes Descartes:

> but I doubt this question will nere be rightly handled, till we leave speaking of these things asunder which should here be taken together . . . and till we forbear to imploy those words about the soul which are framed to and bounded by the kind [nature] and working of a body.[16]

For Swift's hack, Descartes' system is a romance, but Descartes' *cogito ergo sum* is his nemesis in *The Battle of the Books*, where a blow to the head does him in. Associated there with such other Moderns as John Wilkins and William Harvey, in *A Tale of Tub* Descartes is among the 'Grand Innovators' whom the world has deemed crazy. What is demonstrably mad in all of this, for Swift, is a man's belief in a system that could 'reduce the Notions of all Mankind, exactly to the same Length and Breadth, and Heighth of his own'.[17]

A. Rupert Hall has charted three stages in the emplacement of the mechanistic model of the universe. The first he attributes to Descartes' *Principles of Philosophy* (1644); the second to the biological theory of the organism as a machine; and the third is the adoption of mechanical models in physics and chemistry.[18] The first stage of this process, however, seems to have been more complex. Willis's mechanical model of the body is derived from William Harvey's *Circulation of the Blood* (1628), but it is also contemporary with the early work of Descartes. Descartes had been in Holland at the time when Rembrandt was painting 'The Anatomy Lesson of Dr. Tulp', a work that drew popular attention to the anatomy of the brain and nerves. His analogy for their operation is as mechanical as Harvey's, but it is drawn from the artificial machines or *automata* that were commonplace in the great gardens of Europe at this time:

> And indeed one might truly compare the nerves to a machine like the machines of fountains . . . even breathing . . . is like the movement of a watch or of a mill where the flow of water renders it continuous . . . Exterior objects that come up against the organs of sense are simply like strangers who, coming into a grotto with statues that move by water, activate them. The reasonable mind is that machine and has its chief seat in the brain.[19]

For Descartes, as Marie Boas Hall has pointed out, the mechanical view of the world seemed an effective way of ridding that world of magical occultism: 'Laws of nature could now be apprehended as expressions of the way in which God had built the machine, and the way in which he intended it to run.'[20] In fact its impact in England was no more sweeping in this regard than Bacon's reforms had been. Not everyone accepted this mechanical explanation of the body. As a Royalist exile in Paris, Margaret Cavendish would have encountered Descartes' 'mechanical philosophy'; but she no more accepted it than she would have accepted the work of her Royalist contemporary, Willis. At virtually the same time as Willis she was writing that 'the Rational Animate matter is as much in the Heart, as in the Head,' and that it is passions that 'Raise Imaginations, Corrupt Judgement, Disorder Reason, and Blind-fold Understanding; And Imaginations will raise Passions, as Fear, Love, Hate, Doubt, Hope, and the like'.[21]

Only a year later (in 1656), the Cambridge Platonist, Henry More, was to write that if a man's imagination when he is awake

> were so strong as to bear it self against all the occursions and impulses of outward Objects, so as not to be broken, but to keep it self entire and in *equall* splendour and vigour with what is represented from *without*, and . . . the Party thus affected would not fail to take his own Imagination for a reall Object of Sense.[22]

In their respective treatises, More and Cavendish represent resistance to empirical induction as the sole means of knowledge. Their insistence on another kind of knowing, whether from the passions or the imagination, offers a challenge *avant la lettre* to the model of the mind that Locke was to put in place in 1690. Nor did Locke pass unchallenged at the time. The educationist, Thomas Tryon, as I have noted, believed equally strongly in the strength of the imagination. He also drew upon an extensive classical and Biblical tradition when he affirmed that dreams were significant portents of future events. And he joined the eminent physician and scholar, Robert Burton, in believing that astrology was 'the Method of God's Government in Nature, and Administration of the World'.[23]

But Milton deployed both dreams and astrology in *Paradise Lost*. Eve's portentous dream in Book V is Milton's invention, and in Book IV Milton's God hangs out an astrological sign (Libra) to signify the conclusion to the War in Heaven. Indeed, Adam's dream, described in Book VIII, is one from which (as Keats says) 'he waked to find it truth'. Overcome by his 'celestial Colloquie sublime' with God, Adam sees in a dream-vison what he could not otherwise apprehend: the creation of Eve from his own side. It is with what he calls 'the Cell of Fancie my internal sight' that he understands what his sensations cannot tell. This is also a discursive moment in the poem; Adam is relating his dream to Raphael in another kind of educative colloquy. Both the dream and the familiar conversation about it rebuke Adam's desire for absolute knowledge that characterizes the opening third of the book. Milton not only privileges words over things here, but imagination ('Fancie') over induction.

How far this is from Thomas Willis, Milton's contemporary, is signalled by Willis's thinking of himself as engaging in the Baconian enterprise of 'a thorough instauration of Physick'.[24] 'In a Brain rightly disposed,' says Willis, 'the motion of the animal Spirits is perform'd in certain Numbers and Measure.' This is a model of the mind that Mandeville, another physician, repudiated in the second part of The Fable of the Bees (1729). While he guardedly accepted that 'the Structure and Motions of the Body, may, perhaps, be mechanically accounted for', he also asserted that, 'We can have no Help from any Part of the Mechanicks, in the Discovery of Things infinitely remote from Sight.'[25]

Willis's model of the brain, however, was mechanical. In fact it was little different than that of George Dalgarno, the author of Ars Signorum (The Art of Signs), who in the late 1650s observed in a 'Grammatical Observation':

> The soules of men, though of a spirituall and heavenly substance; yet in respect of that neare and strict union betwixt them and their bodies while they are in this state of mortality, are not able to act and exert their intellectuall faculties, without the ministration of the corporeall organs of the Inferior faculties of the senses.[26]

Small wonder that Blake celebrated Milton as the champion of liberated imagination and the opponent of this sort of mechanism of the sensations! What Adam is describing in Book VIII of Paradise Lost is what Willis would have called 'Delirium', that is, a short-lived aberration in which the imagination presents 'erroneous appearances by a variegated, and distorted Glass [mirror]'. The result is that

> the animal Spirits either being too much irritated or put in confusion, are carried hither and thither within the globous Frame of the Brain (where the Fansy and Memory have their Seats) in a disorderly and tumultuous manner, for so while the various Species of the Imagination and Memory being rais'd together, are confounded with each other, only obsurd [absurd] and incongruous Phantasms are presented to the Rational Soul, and therefore the Acts of the Understanding and Will are wrought only irregularly.[27]

Half a century before Tristram Shandy, Swift published the work that included A Tale of a Tub, The Battle of the Books, and The Mechanical Operation of the Spirit. In the last, in a characteristic way, Swift managed both to pillory the absurdities of radical enthusiasm in religion and to do so by describing it in the terms of modern mechanical physiology. As if defining religious enthusiasm as some mad modern doctor would, he explained that 'Practitioners of this famous Art' believe:

> That, the Corruption of the Senses is the Generation of the Spirit: Because the Senses in Men are so many Avenues to the Fort of Reason, which in the Operation is wholly block'd up. All Endeavours must be therefore used, either to divert, bind up, stupify, fluster, and amuse the

Senses, or else to justle them out of their Stations; and while they are either absent, or otherwise employ'd or engaged in Civil War against each other, the *Spirit* enters and performs its Part.[28]

Alan Bennett's 1992 play, *The Madness of George III* (1993), depicts the king himself as the imprisoned victim of a combination of just such pseudo-science and power. But the king's own Declaration, prefaced to the 'Thirty-Nine Articles' in a joint edition of Prayer Book and Bible of 1763, bespeaks the very culture of 'discipline and punish' to which he himself was later subjected. Lamenting that the Church has too long been exercised by disputes, the Declaration commands that 'all further curious Search be laid aside', and that 'No Man hereafter shall either print or preach to draw the Article aside any way, but shall submit to it in the plain and full Meaning thereof.'[29]

The concept of transparent meaning implicit in this declaration is quite breathtaking, especially in relation to a document famous for its openness to different meanings. This Declaration represents the consolidation of unitary meaning with unitary power: the very consolidation that the aptly named Dr Willis in Bennett's play puts to use. 'I have you in my eye,' he says to the refractory king, in just the way that Jeremy Bentham's panopticon prison was to propose: universal surveillance.

Whatever Swift's attachment to the established church or his espousal of reason, neither was so denotative or mechanical as the unitary concept of George III's Declaration implies. Indeed, it was the very unity of signifying in philosophical systems that Swift distrusted. In *A Tale of a Tub* he makes fun of the ancient doctrine of the dramatic unities as applied to Modern wit precisely because of its absurd notion of conformity. Wit is to be as straitened as a walk in a formal garden.

It is a sign of Swift's indignation that his hack writer first compares this aspect of the Modern learning to commerce and then goes on to 'bewail, that no famous *Modern* hath ever yet attempted an universal System in a small portable Volume, of all Things that are to be Known, or Believed, or Imagined, or Practised in Life'. What Swift recognizes, however, is that such systems are no more than a revival of mediaeval encyclopedias: 'Abstracts, Summaries, Compendiums, Extracts, Collections, Medulla's, Excerpta quaedam's, Florilegia's *and the like, all disposed into great Order, and reducible upon Paper.*'[30]

In the name of Modernity and system, the hack proposes to include in his work 'all that Human Imagination can *Rise* or *Fall* to', not least 'An *Universal Rule of Reason, or Every Man his own Carver*'. Although he credits Homer with having discovered the compass, gunpowder, and the circulation of the blood (all of them modern inventions), he regrets that Homer has written nothing about such important subjects as the spleen, tea, political wagering, or salivation without mercury. Here then is knowledge reduced to factoids (what he calls an 'Infinity of Matter') and thrown into a meaningless information system of indexes, compendiums, quotations, commentators and lexicons. 'By these Methods,' he claims, anyone can be an expert on anything:

> in a few Weeks, there starts up many a Writer, capable of managing the profoundest, and most universal Subjects. For, what tho' his *Head* be empty, provided his *Common-place-Book* be full; And if you will bate [supply] him but the Circumstances of *Method* and *Style*, and *Grammar* and *Invention*; allow him but the common Priviledges of transcribing from others, and digressing from himself, as often as he shall see Occasion; He will desire no more Ingredients towards fitting up a Treatise.[31]

All criticism runs the risk of falling into the hack's systematizing, and a study of this kind is equally in danger of slipping into the facile dualism of mechanism *vs.* 'rival knowledge'. There is no Alexandrian sword to separate the mechanists from the rest, any more than there is for dividing ancients from moderns. Sir William Temple was a defender of the ancients, but his famous garden at Moor Park introduced elements unknown to the Romans. His champion, the Earl of Orrery, moreover, gave his name to a modern model of the universe. John Evelyn's career is also a useful corrective to easy categorization. A classicist by training and inclination, he was none the less engaged in reforming modern knowledge in at least twenty different fields. His largest work, 'Elysium Britannicum', was part of this modern 'great instauration', and yet it was more on the side of description than definition, more like Sir Thomas Browne than Newton. As a translator of Lucretius, Evelyn looked to ancient texts even for scientific authority; but the two Modern critics, Wotton and Bentley, who were involved in the ancients and moderns controversy were his protégés.

Pope proved Dryden wrong. His 'Epistle to Arbuthnot' refuted Dryden's observation that a poem cannot be made from closing a door. Pope's gesture seems to me more than a simple joke at Dryden's expense; it takes on the challenge of regulation and rule and undermines it in just the way that subcultures of the period learned to do. In an age of mapping, prescribing, and bounding, the discourse of resistance is a potent imaginative force, keeping even its adversary alert to the many voices that might be heard and the variety of human experience available to literature.

Notes

1 *The Opium Eater and Other Writings* (London: Cassell & Co., 1908), p. 215.
2 Sir John Hill, Dedication to the Earl of Bute, *Eden* (London, 1757).
3 This is from the later Preface added to the 1705 edition of Mandeville's poem *The Grumbling Hive*. The edition cited is *The Fable of the Bees*, ed. F. B. Kaye

(Oxford: Clarendon Press, 1924), p. 4. Mandeville's 'realist' view of human nature was indebted to Hobbes and in reaction to the benevolence of Lord Shaftesbury, a benevolence that Sterne also shared.

4 Burton's more famous contemporary in this was Dr William Hunter (1718–83), whose elaborately illustrated work *On the Human Gravid Uterus* was first published in Latin in 1774 and in English in 1794.

5 See especially 'Johann Storch and Women's Complaints', in *The Woman Beneath the Skin* (Cambridge, Mass.: Harvard University Press, 1991).

6 See Gayatri Chakravorty Spivak, 'Displacement and the Discourse of Woman', in *Displacement: Derrida and After*, ed. Mark Krupnick (Bloomington, Ind.: Indiana University Press, 1983), pp. 169–91. Spivak scrupulously establishes that she is not simply setting up a feminine alternative to phallocentrism but exposing the impossibility of a phallocentric language's constructing anything other than a model of language in its own image.

7 *Gulliver's Travels and Other Writings*, ed. Ricardo Quintana (New York: Modern Library, 1958), p. 343.

8 See Peter Linebaugh, 'The Tyburn Riot Against the Surgeons', in *Albion's Fatal Tree: Crime and Society in Eighteenth-Century England* (London: Penguin, 1977), pp. 65–117.

9 D. W. Sylvester, *Educational Documents 800–1816* (London: Methuen, 1970), p. 154.

10 Letter of 12 Sept. 1703. A version of this letter is published in *Diary and Correspondence of John Evelyn*, ed. William Bray (London: Henry G. Bohn, 1859), iii. pp. 390–8. The original is in British Library Add. MS 4229, fo. 56-[57v] of which Add. MS 28104, fo. 21 is a copy.

11 *Thomas Willis's Oxford Lectures*, ed. Kenneth Dewhurst (Oxford: Sandford Publications, 1980), p. 144.

12 *Gulliver's Travels And Other Writings*, pp. 339, 338.

13 Ibid., p. 343.

14 'To *Lond*: dined with the *Swedish Resident*: where was a disection of a dog, the poore curr, kept long alive after the Thorax was open, by blowing with bellows into its lungs, and that long after his heart was out, and the lungs both gashed and pierced, his eyes quick all the while: This was an experiment of more cruelty than pleased me.' *Diary*, ed. de Beer, ii. 497–8.

15 Alastair Fowler notes that 'inductive' means 'resulting from', *The Poems of John Milton*, ed. John Carey and Alastair Fowler (London: Longman Green & Co., 1968), p. 1009. But the word is too potent in the Royal Society's post-Baconian discourse to be innocent of its other more 'scientific' meaning, especially in this context.

16 *The Correspondence of Henry Oldenburg*, ed. A. R. and M. B. Hall (Madison: University of Wisconsin Press, 1966), iii. 197. I have expanded the contractions in this quotation.

17 *Gulliver's Travels and Other Writings*, p. 339.

18 *The Scientific Revolution 1500–1800* (London: Longman, 1954), p. 205.

19 *Treatise on Man, Le Monde* (1662), *Oeuvres*, ed. Charles Adam and Paul Tannery (Paris: Leopold, 1909), xi. p. 131. Descartes would have seen the fountains at Fontainebleau, but there were many other contemporary accounts of similar mechanisms at Pratolino, Lubeck, and Amsterdam.

20 'The Machinery of Nature', *The Making of Modern Science*, ed. A. R. Hall (Leicester: Leicester University Press, 1960), pp. 32–3.

21 *Philosophical and Physical Opinions* (London, 1663), pp. 265, 262. The first edition was in 1655. The British Library 1663 edition is inscribed '*Ex dono nobilissimae Heroinae, Authoris*' and seems to have been corrected by her hand or at least a contemporary.

22 *Enthusiasmus Triumphatus* (2nd edn, London, 1662), p. 4.

23 *Some Memoirs of the Life of Mr Thomas Tryon* (London, 1705), pp. 22–3.

24 Cited from Samuel Pordage's 1684 translation of Willis's *Diatribae dua Medicao-Philosophicae* (1659), p. 53.

25 Oxford: Clarendon, 1924, ii. p. 161.

26 British Library, Sloane MS 4377, published with Francis Lodowyck's *A Common Writing* (London, 1647) in the Scolar Press series 'English Linguistics' (Menston, England: 1969), No. 147.

27 *The London Practise of Physick, Being the Practical Part of Physick* (London, 1692), pp. 458–9. This work is derived from Willis's *Pharmaceutice Rationalis*, first published in 1674, itself a digest of Willis's work on the brain dating from the 1650s. Although Milton certainly recognized that the senses could dictate falsely and misinform the will, this did not mean that the imagination was dispensable.

28 *Gulliver's Travels And Other Writings*, ed. Ricardo Quintana (New York: Modern Library, 1958) p. 397.

29 (London, 1763), sig. [G6v].

30 *Gulliver's Travels and Other Writings*, pp. 316, 317.

31 Ibid., p. 329.

8

Postscript: What We Have Forgotten

What this book is about is also a question of how it came to be written. Several years ago I had to have a colonoscopy: a medical examination of the bowel and colon for cancer. This is done with a tube to which a light and a camera are attached. Because the process can be painful, the patient is given a relaxant drug (usually valium); even so, it is also possible to watch the whole business on a TV monitor. What I saw, in a slightly hallucinatory fashion, was what looked like a space odyssey inside my body: an intimate text of myself that I had never known. What it revealed was that here was another sense of myself, a self seen from inner space. The experience radically altered the image that I had of who I was, as radically as our first pictures from space changed our notion of the planet we inhabit. The addition to knowledge was not simply incremental – a few more facts about myself – it was a revelation of how what we know comes to be constructed in the first place and how that is related to what is deemed to be knowledge.

Just before the outbreak of World War II, as the most technologically advanced nation on the planet was preparing for mass destruction, W. B. Yeats's 'Under Ben Bulben' affirmed that 'measurement began our might'. And another of his poems from the same year (1938) asserted that it was 'calculation, number, [and] measurement' that (as he said) put down 'Asiatic vague immensities' and what the poem called 'this filthy modern tide'.[1] Recent studies of the brain, however, have questioned whether there can be any confidence in the objectivity of this sort of measurement or indeed of any field of knowledge, given the obviously subjective nature of the brain's functioning.[2]

There has also been considerable disquiet about the supposedly objective instruments with which we measure intelligence. Stephen Jay Gould's *The Mismeasure of Man* (1981) and Howard Gardner's *Frames of Mind: The Theory of Multiple Intelligences* (1983) both question in their different ways the notion of absolute intelligence free from the prejudices of the cultural constructs that have been erected to measure it. Even in popular culture there has been an increasing disquiet with the quantification of experience. A song such as Laurie Anderson's 'Big Science' is a critique of a world of mere mensuration and utility: a world in which 'economy' has ceased to mean 'stewardship' and means instead 'speculation' and the Gatsby-ish mythologies that accompany it.

As Barbara Duden's *The Woman Beneath the Skin* points out, women have had good reason to be particularly suspicious of medicine on this score. While I was writing this book, it was revealed that the commonly cited statistic that women have fewer heart attacks than men was based on a model of human physiology which excluded women. But a similar discovery about the absolutism of medicine's models was made years ago by many people with AIDS. An early case of infection who did not die of the virus's complications was simply deemed not to have had it in the first place.

'It is the scientific establishment that makes itself esoteric and is the scourge of heresy,' James Lovelock has observed.[3] Lovelock was writing in the wake of the Mariner probe to Mars which had been programmed to ask questions that make no sense outside our own planet. Like the Voyager mission that carried stylized images of earthly Caucasians into the universe, the scientists had assumed that any form of intelligence would recognize the symbols we have made up for ourselves. The 'heresy' that opposes this absurdity is what Oliver Sacks has called being 'an anthropologist on Mars': aware that the universe we observe is one that we construct. Or as the daughter of friends of mine observed about kindergarten: 'Who thought this thing up anyway?'

One of the consequences of the orthodoxies of what has been called 'scientism' is that western culture has lost many kinds of liminal knowledge: knowledge that is somewhere between intuition and sensation. Part of this knowledge is what Wendell Berry means when he writes of 'a kind of knowledge inestimably valuable and probably indispensable, that comes out of a common culture and cannot be taught as part of a formal curriculum of a school'.[4] One aspect of this is simply attention at a higher level: the countryman's attention to his environment, Berry would claim, which is eroded by a world of switches and dials.

'O! the one Life within us and abroad,' Coleridge wrote in 1795 of this kind of knowledge, a knowledge which he elsewhere called the 'esemplastic imagination' that makes the imaginer one with the initial and ongoing act of creation.[5] In his work *Desert Solitaire* (1968) the American writer about nature, Edward Abbey, describes having watched two gopher snakes mating in an elaborate ritual dance: a performance that he crawled under his cabin in Arizona to observe, only to find the snakes coming suddenly towards him. Like D. H. Lawrence in his famous poem 'The Snake', Abbey backed out in fear and so lost a chance to remember a kind of knowledge that his ratiocinative culture had excluded. His regret for what Lawrence called 'pettiness' is for lost knowledge: 'if I had been as capable of trust as I am susceptible to fear I might have learned something new, or some truth so very old we have forgotten it.'[6]

Many of the writers dealt with in this book not only recognized this 'forgotten' knowledge, but kept it alive at a time when quantification and mere ratiocination were in the ascendent. Not only Milton, Defoe, Pope, Swift, and Fielding, but a whole range of lesser-known figures espoused the unity of all knowledge during a period when it was becoming (in Collinson's memorable phrase) fragmented into branches of study that 'none but real professors can pretend to attain'. Writing about Aby Warburg, the founder of the Warburg Institute, Simon Schama defines the turning-point in Warburg's career as the moment when, in an asylum for the mentally ill, Warburg affirmed the cultural inseparability of reason and unreason in a learned paper and so won his release.[7] It is a moment that the writers I have dealt with here would have understood: the alliance of 'great wits' and 'madness' that Dryden affirmed.

In his *Apology for Poetry* (1579–80), Sir Philip Sidney said that poetry dealt with 'notable images of virtues, vices, or what else'.[8] 'What else' is a useful phrase: a 'liminal' reminder that most interesting literature is not easily categorizable. Even the well-planned schemes of librarians are open to debate. In the Library of Congress system, Canadian literature may be either 'PR' or 'PS' depending on whether you regard the subject as a subset of English literature or as a part of American. Canadians long ago got used to the imperialism of other people's definitions.

The works that have most influenced my thinking about this book are not easily catalogued either: Bruce Chatwin's *The Songlines* (1987), Clifford Geertz's *Local Knowledge* (1983), Charles Bazerman's *Shaping Written Knowledge* (1988), Robert Logan's *The Alphabet Effect* (1986), Mary Douglas's *Purity and Danger* (1966), Mary Louise Pratt's *Imperial Eyes* (1992), Stephen Jay Gould's *Bully for Brontosaurus* (1991), Marguerite Yourcenar's *The Dark Brain of Piranesi* (1985), and Jacob Bronowski's *The Ascent of Man* (1973).

In his long poem, 'A Ordinary Evening in New Haven' (1950), Wallace Stevens writes of 'coming back and coming back/To the real', but to a reality that is 'Naked Alpha, not the hierophant Omega.' The poet's approach to this problem involves 'A few words, an and yet, and yet, and yet.' That is also the critic's problem, and one that I hope I have addressed here.

Notes

1 The second poem is 'The Statues'. Both were collected in *Last Poems and Plays* (London: Macmillan & Co., 1940).

2 See e.g. Paul D. MacLean's *The Triune Brain in Evolution* (New York: Plenum Press, 1990) in which the author argues that the human brain is composed of three intermeshing brains: one common to late mammals, one to early mammals, and one to reptiles.

3 *The Ages of Gaia* (Oxford: Oxford University Press, 1988), p. xv.
4 Wendell Berry, *What Are People For?* (San Francisco : North Point Press, 1990).
5 'The Eolian Harp', l. 26.
6 'The Serpents of Paradise', in *Desert Solitaire* (New York: McGraw-Hill, 1968), p. 21.
7 *Landscape and Memory* (Toronto: Random House, 1995), p. 212.
8 ed. Geoffrey Shepherd (London: Nelson, 1965), p. 103.

Appendix of Original Documents

Introduction

The following excerpts indicate the range of 'non-literary' work upon which the argument of the book depends. The four plans suggest not only the importance of mapping to imaginative literature in this period but to the control of landscape and the environment. Knyff and Kip's plan of Badminton is as much about the power of survey as about topography, and is a good example of the appropriation of surrounding countryside by radial avenues in the French style of the Brompton Nursery firm (London & Wise). And John Evelyn's plans for a restored London after the Great Fire show the desire to rectify and correct society which is present in his earlier urban studies, *A Character of England* (1659) and *Fumifugium* (1661). Wenceslas Hollar's map of London after the Great Fire is the earliest example of an exact survey of the City. The two details from William Morgan's *London &c. Actually Survey'd* show the topography of the world of Moll Flanders and the young Col. Jack.

The desire for a general and thorough reform of society and knowledge is usually thought of as a product of the Royal Society. But long before its foundation, writers often associated with the circle of Samuel Hartlib were proposing visionary schemes. The proposal for a 'universal character' or language is often attributed to John Wilkins, but George Dalgarno's suggested reforms precede him and set the tone of the kind of new science which Swift was to parody.

Both Herman Moll's *A View of the Coasts* and George Warren's *An Impartial Account of Surinam* are more than introductions to *Oroonoko* and *Robinson Crusoe*. They suggest the powerful mythology of untold riches and recaptured Eden which also animates much of the literature of the heyday of the South Sea Company before its collapse in 1721, a mythology reflected in *Captain Singleton* and *Moll Flanders* as well as in James Thomson's *The Seasons*. It is also a mythology to which Pope responds from his early work,

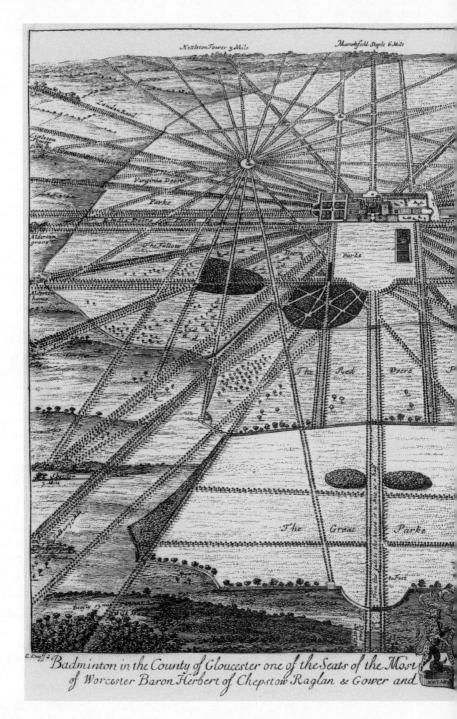

Within the image:
Nettleton Tower 3 Mile
Marshfield Steple 6 Mile

Badminton in the County of Gloucester one of the Seats of the Most
of Worcester Baron Herbert of Chepstow Raglan & Gower and

Fig. 1 Leonard Knyff & James Kip, 'Badminton, Glos.', *Britannia Illustrata* (London, 1707).

Tormarton Warren   Tormarton Mill   Lugrove House

A Colchetts Coach

The Fallow   Deere Parks

the Red Lane

Parks

Warren

The Hare Warren

London Road to Bath   Kilcott Wood

I Kip S

Noble & Potent Prince Henry Duke of Beaufort Marquesse & Earle
Knight of the Most Noble order of the Garter.

11

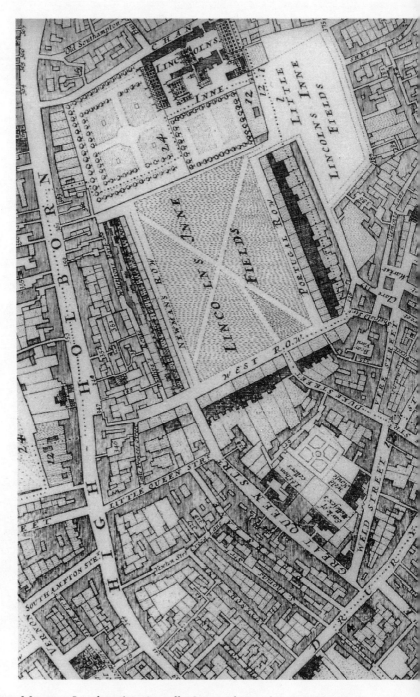

Fig. 2 William Morgan, *London &c. Actually Survey'd* (London, 1682). Covent Garden, Drury Lane, and the area around the Strand.

Fig. 3 William Morgan, *London &c. Actually Survey'd*, (London, 1682). Fenchurch Street and the eastern edge of the City.

Fig. 4 Wenceslas Hollar, Fenchurch Street and the eastern edge of the City after the Great Fire, *An Exact Survey of the Streetes Lanes and Churches Contained Within the Ruines of the City of London* (London, 1667).

102

Duke's Place

C

New Prison for Rebells &c.

Aldgate

Leadenhall Street

D

Fanchurch street

H

Red lane

Mincion lane

A

Tower hill

Tower Street

S. Mary hill

Mill lane

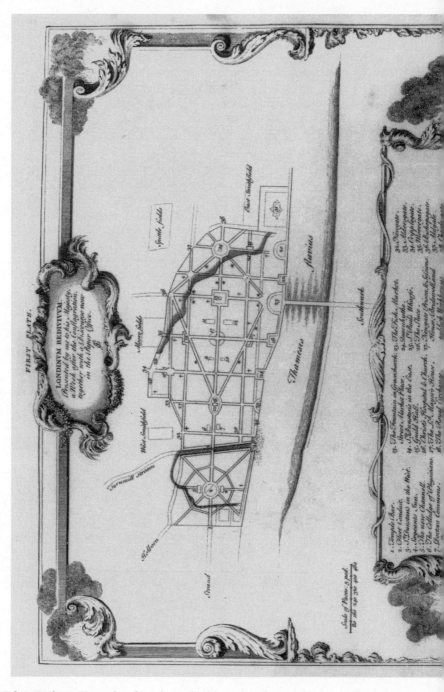

Fig. 5 John Evelyn, *Two sketches for rebuilding London* (1666), engraved by George Vertue.

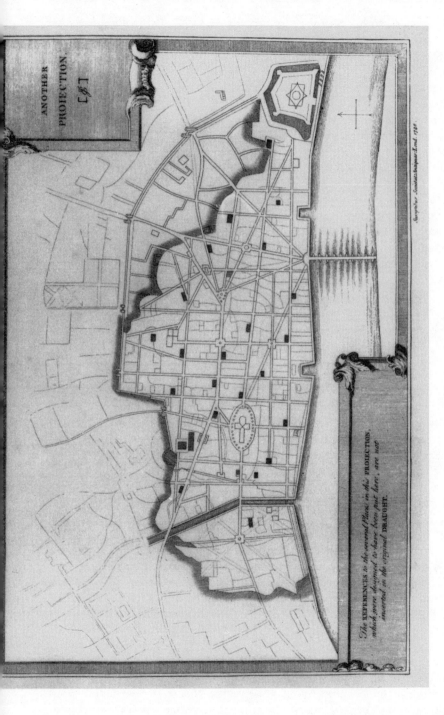

Windsor Forest, to his *Moral Epistles* of the early 1730s. In *Paradise Lost* Milton was early to detect its Satanic economic consequences, consquences which Swift was to spell out in many of his pamphlets on agriculture.

The longest extract here is from John Harris's *Navigantium*, a collection of voyages and travels including the story of Captain Knox and his son that William the Quaker tells in *Captain Singleton*. Defoe's version is very little different from *Navigantium*: a work (to my knowledge) never republished. Its geographical accuracy is not easy to authenticate, though the modern cities of Columbo, Kandy, and Jaffna are mentioned; and Anarogdburro is probably modern Anuradhapura, as the Malwateyan River is probably the Malwatu Oya.

I include virtually all of this tale because it contains so many of the tropes of this kind of writing which are also the hallmarks of early fiction, Defoe's in particular: the deviousness of foreigners, the terrors of wild beasts, the pathlessness of the wilderness, the rewards of industry and a trust in providence, the frustration of expectations, the meticulousness of detail, and the narrative jumps. But it is also a telling example of the thin line between 'literary' and 'non-literary' works in the period.

The mythology of riches, but of a different (agricultural) kind, enters the discourse of the work of agricultural apologists and reformers. The great distance that separates Ralph Austen from John Cowper on the subject of enclosure bespeaks what had happened to this mythology in less than a century, as what had been a scheme for agricultural utopianism became co-opted for the private gain of the powerful. Austen speaks with the idealism of the Hartlib circle; indeed, his proposals for fruit trees were to be promoted by another Hartlibean, John Beale, in his *Pomona* more than than 20 years later. What Worlidge shares with Richard Bradley, the Professor of Botany at Cambridge, is what both might have found in John Evelyn's works: the sense of the classical heritage and dignity of agriculture and its revival as part of what is often called 'Augustanism'.

The idealism of agricultural reform was of a piece with educational reform. Hartlib's circle had included writers on both subjects. Most of the excerpts from works for and about children are largely concerned with language instruction at an early age. Comenius's influential *Orbis Sensualium Pictus* is here introduced by the influential seventeenth-century schoolmaster and educational reformer, Charles Hoole. Christopher Wase, Mark Lewis, and Thomas Tryon all wrote (in Thomas Tryon's phrase on the title-page of his *A New Method*) 'to dis-engage the World from those ill Customs in Education, it has been so long used to'. They represent the ongoing attempt to wrench early childhood education out of the hands of what John Evelyn called 'Tyrannical Grammaticasters' while at the same time making it more useful to a new culture based on trade. The stress in all of them is on luring children to learning by easy steps: the theme of instruction with delight that was to be a hallmark of eighteenth-century writers about childhood and education.

But this liberation was to have little to do with girls and women. In Part II of Samuel Richardson's novel, Pamela writes about the education of her son. Girls like herself, however, would continue to get short shrift educationally. John Locke's neglect of girls and women in *Some Thoughts Concerning Education*, as in his proposals for the children of the poor, are the more telling in the wake of Bathshua Makin's trenchant defence of women's education in her *Essay to Revive the Antient Education of Gentlewomen*. Its powerful defence of women's learning is representative of the resistance throughout this period (though seldom in written form) to an increasingly mechanical society which retained power at the expense of its underclass.

Many of these passages are prefaces and were originally set entirely in italics. In transcribing them I have reversed the use of type. What was in italic is now in Roman and vice versa.

GEORGE DALGARNO. *NEWS TO THE WHOLE WORLD OF AN UNIVERSAL CHARACTER, AND A NEW RATIONAL LANGUAGE* (LONDON, C. 1652)

This Design has been numbered as one of the chief *Desiderata* of Learning, and much longed for by the Learned, both of the present and former Ages, witness hereunto the renowned Lord *Verulam*, the learned Doctor *Ward*, D. *Pettie*, Mr. *Comenius*, Mr. *Lodovicke*, with many others. High thoughts of advantage towards the advancement of all the parts of Humane Literature, and a more universal encrease of Knowledge, have been conceived from the discovery hereof; several attempts have been to this effect, but as yet without success or issue. I hope it shall appear from the following general Assertions, the truth whereof shall hereafter be demonstrated in particulars, that this present Undertaking shall be able to reach the production of all those desireable Fruits and Advantages to the World, which ever by any have been apprehended of it: Provided that, it being now ripe, and come to the birth, the cherishing care of the Supreme Authorities, and Universities of this Commonwealth (whom chiefly it doth concern) do tender its safe delivery, with suitable Encouragements to the exigency of the Affair; For if it be preserved from Injuries in its Birth, it will immediately thereafter be able both to nurse and arme it self against all prejudices, and will, as its nature requires, not onely spread it self, but carry along with it the fame and names of its first Patrons, over the whole World, to remain in an honorable remembrance to Posterity.

1. This Character shall immediately represent things, and not the sounds of Words, and therefore universal, and equally applicable to all Languages. 2. The Art hereof, shall not rest onely in a dumb Character, but by the same Rules it shall be made effable [pronounceable], in distinct and dearticulate sounds. 3. Which does chiefly commend the Art (though I know it will exceed the beleif of many) both the Character and Language shall be

perfectly attainable by any of ordinary capacity and diligence, in less then a months time, so that two of quite different Languages may be made to understand one another, either in Writing or Speaking within the said space. 4. This Character shall go far beyond all received Brachigraphy [shorthand], for contraction and speed in Writing. 5. Whereas it is scarce known that Brachygraphy hath been improved in any Langyage but the English, this shall be equally practicable and useful in all Languages. 6. This Character shall be more accommodated for an emphatick delivery of real Truths, and the grounds and precepts of Arts and Sciences, then any other language; this will be easily apprehended by those, who are versed in late [recent] Mathematical Writers, who have begun to follow this way, by expressing words of frequent use with real Characters; and that partly because it works a more real and lively apprehension of the thing treated of, and partly for compendiousness of delivery. 7. The Grammatical Rules of this Art, shall be few, plain, and easie, obvious to every capacity, because they shall be altogether grounded upon Nature and Reason, without any irregularities or exceptions (which Nature and Reason abhors) without any superfluity of univocations [words meaning the same thing], or ambiguity of equivocations [seeming to say one thing while saying another]. 8. The construction and Phrasiology of this Character and Language, shall be such as Nature and Reason requires, and not to follow the impertinency, and non-sence of phrase of Languages; but to deliver Truth in plain and down-right terms. 9. The true pronounciation and accent of this Language shall be easily attainable by the people of all nations. 10. There shall be no occa-sion of error, or mistake in the Orthography [spelling] of this Language; for the Writing shall be perfectly conformable to the speaking, and e contra [vice versa]. 11. This Character shall be a ready way, and a singular mean, to convey Knowledge to deaf and dumb people (which is a secret of Learning heretofore not discovered) and it is conceived upon good ground that a deaf man might be taught to communicate in this Character, in the sixth part of the time that any other man could learn a foreign Language. 12. From the method and contrivance of this Design can be discovered, a more easie way of the Art of memory then any commonly known. 13. From it may be drawn an exceeding useful *Janus* [introduction], whereby to enter the study of any Language. 14. It shall be a singular help to Discourse, affording variety of apposite words and epithets, and shall make a man understand his own Language, or any other he is Master of, more fully then he did, and shall teach him to distinguish betwixt Phrase and Sence. 15. All these things being made out, it cannot be denied, but that it will prove the most comprehensive, and advantagious peece of Knowledge that ever was received in Schools, for the education of Youth; for they shall be so far from losing of precious time in acquiring this Art, that by following the method and practice thereof, they shall redeem the half of that time, which others lose either in the study of Languages, or Philosophy, and besides have the practice of this Art, *gratis*, and by way of *over-plus*. If those whom it concerns, will mind the education of Youth, and Publick good so far as to make it practical this way; undoubtedly, the world will in a short time reap more plentiful fruits of it, then can now be apprehended. For 16. It may by Gods blessing be a great help for propagating the Gospel; and if neglected by reformed States and Churches, will certainly be improved by the Jesuites to that end. 17. It may be of singular use to civilize barbarous Nations, destitute even of the first elements of Literature. 18. It may unite the Nations of the World, by a more familiar and frequent intercourse and commerce, the cheif hinderance whereof is the diversity and difficulty of Languages. 19. Arts and Sciences may flourish more everywhere, not onely because of the easiness of this key of Language, whereby to enter them; but also because the method of this invention, discovers a way of abreviating and facilitating all other parts of Learning. From these brief Assertions, I leave it to every intelligent Reader to answer that great question to himself proposed to new Designs, *viz. Cui bono?* [who will it profit?] Here I do profess that my main intent in publishing this Paper was to try if any would appear to own publick good, and the advancement of Learning so far, as to bring this design upon the Stage of a publick trial: For besides the testimony of several of the most eminent Doctors of the both the Universities ready to be produced; I hope to rational men the thing shall be a sufficient testimony to itself. Any who desires the knowledge of this Art, or further satisfaction in those Proposals, may learn where to finde the Author, at the center of all usefull and solid Learning, Mr. *Samuel Hartlibs* house, near Charing-Cross over against Angel Court.

HERMAN MOLL. *A VIEW OF THE COASTS, COUNTRYS, & ISLANDS WITHIN THE LIMITS OF THE SOUTH-SEA COMPANY* (SECOND EDITION. LONDON, 1720?)

The Preface
When the Publick Welfare of these Kingdoms depend so much on the Success of the *Company* newly Establish'd to carry on a Trade to the South Seas, it cou'd not but excite the Curiosity of all who wish well to it, to know what are the *Countries, Commerce* and *Riches* which are the Subject of our present *Views* and *Expectations*.

All the *Voyages* that have been hitherto Publish'd are imperfect to this End: None of 'em treat of the greatest part of the *Eastern* Coasts of the Continent within the Limits of the *Act*, from the River *Aranoca* to *Port Desire*: And Sir *John Narborough*, who begins there, goes no farther than *Baldivia* in the *South Sea*, where the Gold and Silver Mines scarce begin. *Wafer* enlarges most on that Part of the Isthmus of *Darien* which is not in the *Company*'s Charter. *Wood* keeps to *Narborough*'s Voyage. *Dampier* treats of *Mexico, Campeachy*, and other Places of the *North Sea* [Gulf of Mexico], not within their Limits; and is large on those in the *South Sea*

[Caribbean] to the North of the Isles of *Lobos* only. *Sharp, Cowly,* and other Voyagers, say little of either side of the Continent, and what they do say is without Order. *Funnel* is the most particular, but then he follow'd an old *Spanish* Draught, which though it appears to be very regular in naming *Ports, Harbours, Rivers* and *Creeks,* yet is it not very certain. The greater *Voyagers* are full of *Historical* and *Romantick* Accounts of these Countries, and enter very little into what we want to know most of, the *Trade, Product,* etc. Now taking from all these such Observations as are most to the purpose; as also from the *History* of the *Bucaniers* in *English* and *French,* from *De Lussan*'s Adventures of the *Free-Booters*; from *F. Gemelli, Techo, Seppe,* and other Voyagers of the *Missionaries*; and from a *Spanish Manuscript* lately translated into *French*; what relates to the *New Design,* we have in *One View* presented to the Reader, with whatever concerns the *Coasts, Countries* and *Islands;* the *Product, Trade* and *Present State* of all the *Places* within the Limits of the *New Act of Parliament,* to which we have entirely confin'd our selves; and by comparing all our own Authors one with another, and with Foreign Writers, 'tis hop'd we may reasonably affirm there is nothing extant in any Language so exact and so proper to inform the Concern'd in this Company, as this Treatise, which is design'd for their Service. All the Voyages that have been formerly or lately Publish'd, are crouded with Accounts of *Countries* that have little or no Relation to those included in the *Act*; for where there is most of that Relation, there is not a fourth Part but treats of other *Places* and *Trades,* most of them so uncertain or obsolete, that without the same Trouble, we have been at, and which will save the Reader, 'tis impossible for any to have a just *Idea* of the *Settlements* that may be made, the *Trade* that may be carry'd on, and the *Advantages* that may arise from this *South-Sea Company.*

GEORGE WARREN. *AN IMPARTIAL DESCRIPTION OF SURINAM*
(LONDON, 1667)

To the Reader
This is a present of three years Collection, not without many hazards to my self: for the delights of Warm Countries are mingled with sharp Sawces, and indeed from the Constant breathings through the Pores, more there than in Colder Regions, 'tis rationally believed, our Spirits must make hast out of Bodies exhaust by heat; but I have often seen many both Natives, and others at *Surinam,* very vigorous in extreme Old Age. In this Continent, the *Indians* will tell you of Mighty Princes upwards, and Golden Cities how true I know not. But a brave Country it is, and it may be truly said, to a Mind untaint with Ambition (and that can live according to Nature) no place is more accommodate; whether we regard health, a luxuriant Soyle, or kind Women. I have made it no design of mine either to hide the inconveniences of the Country, or to extol the happiness there beyond truth: Such as it is, is

here expos'd. Some there are, who confidently believe, these warm Climates were the Dwellings of the Antient Learned Heathens: to which opinion, for the pleasure of the same places, I could assent, but that the most Acute Philosophers held a gross Doctrine, that under, or neer the Line [Equator], 'twas not habitable, whereof dayly Experience affords a Confutation: And it's great ignorance to think any considerable Improvements can be made far distant from the Sun. What advantage hath Accrewed to the *English* Scepter, How Navigation hath been increased by the only Trade of *Tobacco* and *Sugar* in our New Plantations, Who hath not heard? As for my self, I held it more Ingenuous to venture thy Censure for appearing in Print, than that you should lose the light of these Observations.

Chap. V. Of the Fruits

Which are *Oranges, Limmons, Limes, Pomcitrons* [Citron], both Water, and Musk *Melons*, with some *Grapes*; all which are forc'd, not natural to the Country, though as good, and thrive as well there as in any other place. Those originally found there, are *Plantons*, [Plantains], *Bonanoes*, [Bananas], *Semerrimars* [Mangoes?], *Guavers, Pines* [Pineapples], and abundance of Wilde Trash, which perhaps if Transplanted, might prove not so Contemptible as they now are. The *Planton* I have already spoken of, from which the *Bonano* is little different, but rather the better of the two, though neither of them, in my opinion, very pleasing. The *Semmerimarre* grows upon a pretty tall Tree, 'tis almost like a *Peach*, wooly on the outside, and is not to be eaten till rotten, when, the taste is not unlike to that of *Marmalade* of *Quince*. The *Guaver* is about the bigness of a *Medlar*, yellow, and full of Seeds, 'tis truly a most delicious fruit, and when quite ripe, tastes very like a *Strawberry*: it grows upon small Trees, commonly in Savanna's, or Pastures. The *Pine*, or rather the Prince of Fruits, is ordinarily eight or nine inches about, and a foot in length, the outside is green and chequer'd; and within yellow, juicy, and full of holes, like a Hony-Combe; on the Top it has a fair coronet of Leaves, as 'twere denoting its Supremacy; nor do I think it a usurper, being incomparably the best, and most beautiful that I ever saw or tasted: it grows upon a small Bush, about four foot high, the stalk coming from the root like an *Artichoke*: the crown being cut off and planted, bears again in ten months.

JOHN HARRIS. *NAVIGANTIUM ATQUE ITINERARIUM BIBLIOTHECA: OR, A COMPLEAT COLLECTION OF VOYAGES AND TRAVELS* (LONDON, 1705), VOL. II, BOOK II, PP. 450–2

An Historical Account of the Island of Ceilon in the East-Indies: Written by Robert Knox, a Captive there near Twenty Years
In the year 1657, the *Ann* Frigat of *London*, Capt. *Robert Knox* Commander, on the 21st Day of *January* set Sail out of the *Downs*, in the

Service of the Honourable *East India* Company of *England*, bound for Fort St. *George*, on the Coast of *Coramandel*, to trade for one Year from Port to Port in *India*, which having performed, as he was lading his Goods to return for *England*, being in the Road of *Matlipatan*, on the 19th of *November*, 1659, there happn'd such a mighty Storm that in it several Ships were cast-away, and he was forced to cut his Main-Mast by the Board, which so disabled the Ship, that he could not proceed in his Voyage; whereupon *Cotiar*, in the Island of Ceilon being a very commodious Bay, fit for her present Distress, *Thomas Chambers*, Esq; (since Sir *Thomas*) the Agent at Fort St. *George*, order'd, that the Ship should take in some Cloth and *Indian* Merchants belonging to *Porta Nova*, who might trade there, till she lay to set her Mast, and repair the other Damages sustain'd by the Storm. At her first coming thither, after the *Indian* Merchants were set on Shore, the Captain and his Men were very jealous of the People of the Place, by reason the *English* never had any Commerce or Dealing with them, but after they had been there 20 Days, and going ashore, and returning again at Pleasure, without any Molestation, they began to lay aside all suspicious Thoughts of the People that dwelt thereabouts, who had kindly entertain'd them for their Monies.

By this time the King of the Country had Notice of their Arrival, and not being acquainted with their Intents, he sent down a *Dissuava*, or General, with an Army to them, who immediately sent a Messenger on purpose to the Captain on Board to desire him to come ashore to him, pretending a Letter from the King. The Captain saluted the Message with Firing of Guns, and ordering his son *Robert Knox* and Mr. *John Loveland*, Merchant of the Ship, to go ashore and wait on him. When they were come before him, he demanded, *Who they were, and how long they should stay?* They told him, *They were* English *Men, and not to stay above 20 or 30 Days, and desired Permission to trade in his Majesty's Port.* His Answer was, *That the King was glad to hear that the English were come into his Country, and had commanded him to assist them, as they should desire, and had sent a Letter to be delivered to the Captain himself.* They were then 12 Miles from the Sea-side, and therefore reply'd, *That the Captain could not leave his Ship to come so far, but if he pleased to go down to the Sea-side, the Captain would wait on him to receive the Letter*: Whereupon the *Dessuava* desired them to stay that Day, and on the Morrow he would go down with them, which rather than displease him in so small a matter, they consented to. In the Evening the *Dissuava* sent a Present to the Captain of Cattle, Fruits, etc. which being carried all Night long by the Messengers, was delivered to him in the Morning, who told him withal, That his Men were coming down with the *Dissuava*, and desired his Company on Shore against his coming, having a Letter from the King to deliver into his own Hand. The Captain mistrusting nothing came ashore with his Boat, and sitting down under a Tamarind-Tree, waited for the *Dissuava*. In the meantime the Native Soldiers privately surrounded him, and the 7 Men he had with him, and seizing them carried them to meet the *Dissuava*, bearing the Captain in a Hammock on their Shoulders.

The next Day the Long-Boats Crew, not knowing what had happn'd, came ashore to cut down a Tree to make Checks for the Main-Mast, and were made Prisoners after the same Manner, tho' with more Violence, because they were more rough with them, and made Resistance; yet they were not brought to the Captain and his Company, but quarter'd in another House in the same Town.

The *Dissuava* having thus gotten 2 Boats and 18 Men, his next Care was to gain the Ship; and to that End, telling the Captain, That he and his Men were only detain'd because the King inteded to send Letters with a Present to the *English* Nation by him, desired him to send some Men on Board his Ship to order her Stay, and because the Ship was in danger of being fired by the *Dutch*, if she stay'd long in the Bay, to bring her up the River. The Captain did not approve of the Advice, but dare not own his Dislike, and so sent his Son with the Order, but with a solemn Conjuration [order] to return again, which he accordingly did, bringing a Letter from the Company in the Ship, *That they would not obey the Captain, nor any other, in this Matter, but were resolv'd to stand on their own Defence*. This Letter satisfied the *Dissuava*, who thereupon gave the Captain Leave to write for what he would have brought him from the Ship, pretending that he had not the King's Order to release them, tho' it would suddenly come.

The Captain seeing he was held in Suspence, and the Season of the Year spending for the Ship to proceed on her Voyage to some Place, sent Order to Mr *John Burford*, the chief Mate, to take Charge of the Ship, and set Sail to *Porta Nova*, from whence they came, and there to follow the Agent's Order.

And now began that long and sad Captivity they all along fear'd. The Ship being gone, the *Dissuava* was called up to the King, and they were kept under Guards a while, till a special Order came down from the King to part them, and put them in one Town for the Conveniency of their Maintenance, which the King ordered to be at the Charge of the Country. On *Sept.* 16. 1660. the Captain and his Son were placed in a Town, called *Bonder coeswat*, in the Country of *Hotcurly*, distant from the City of *Candi* Northward 30 Miles, and from the rest of the *English* a full Day's Journey. Here they had their Provisions brought them twice a Day without Money, so much as they could eat, and as good as the Country yielded. The Situation of the Place was very pleasant and commodious; but that Year that Part of the Land was very sickly by Agues and Fevers, of which many died. The Captain and his Son after some time were visited with the common Distemper, and the Captain being also loaded with Grief for his deplorable Condition, languish'd more than 3 Months, and then died, *Feb.* 9. 1660 [1661].

Robert Knox, his Son, being now left desolate, sick and in Captivity, having none to comfort him but God, who is the Father of the Fatherless, and hears the Groans of such as are in Captivity, began alone to enter upon a long Scene of Misery and Calamity, oppressed with Weakness of Body and Grief of Soul for the Loss of his Father, and the remediless Trouble that he was like to endure. And the first Instance of it was in the Burial of his Father; for he sent his black Boy to the People of the Town to desire their Assistance, because he understood not their Language; but they sent him only a Rope to drag him by the Neck into the Woods, and told him, *That they would afford him no other Help, unless he would pay for it.* This barbarous Answer encreas'd his Trouble for his father's Death, that now he was likely to lie unburied, and be made a Prey to the wild Beasts in the Woods, for the Ground was very hard, and they had not Tools to dig with, and so 'twas impossible for them to bury him; but having a small Matter of Money left him, *viz.* a Pagoda and a Gold Ring, he hired a Man, and so buried him in as decent a Manner as his Condition would permit.

His dead Father being thus removed out of his Sight, but his Ague continuing, he was reduced very low, partly by Sorrow, and partly by his Disease. All the Comfort he had was to go into the Woods and Fields with a Book (*viz*, either *The Practice of Piety*, or Mr. *Roger's Seven Treatises*, which were the only 2 Books he had) and meditate and read, and sometimes pray, in which his Anguish made him often insert *Elijah's* Petition, *That he might die*, because his Life was a Burthen to him. God, tho' he was pleased to prolong his Life, yet he found a Way to lighten his Grief by removing his Ague, and granting him a Desire, which above all things were acceptable to him. He had read his 2 Books over so often that he had them both almost by Heart, and tho' they were both pious and good Writings, yet he long'd for the Truth from the Original Fountain, and thought it his greatest Unhappiness that he had not a Bible, and did believe he should never see one again: But, contrary to his Expectation, God brought him one after this Manner. As he was fishing one Day with his black Boy to catch some Fish to relieve his Hunger, an old Man passed by them, and asked his Boy, whether his Master could read, and when the Boy had answer'd *Yes*, he told him, *That he had gotten a Book from the Portuguese when these left* Columbo, *and if his Master pleased he would sell it him.* The Boy told his Master, who bid him go and see what Book it was. The Boy having served the *English* some time, knew the Book, and as soon as he had got it into his Hand, came running to him, calling out before he came to him, *'Tis the Bible.* The Words startled him, and he flang down his Angle [fishing rod] to meet him, and finding it true, was mighty rejoyced to see it, but yet was afraid he should not have enough to purchase it, tho' he was resolv'd to part with all the Money he had (which was but one *Pagoda*) to buy it, but his black Boy perswading him to slight it, and leave it to him to buy it, he at length obtain'd it for a knit Cap.

This Accident he could not but look upon as a great Miracle, that God should bestow upon him such an extrardinary Blessing, and bring him a Bible in his own Native Language in such a remote Part of the World, where his Name was not known, and where it was never heard of that an *English*

Man had ever been before. The Enjoyment of this Mercy was a great Comfort to him in his Captivity, and though he wanted no bodily Convenience that the Country did afford (for the King immediately after his Father's Death had sent an express Order to the People of the Town that they should be kind to him, and give him good Victuals [provisions]); and after he had been some time in the Country, and understood the Language, he got him good Conveniences, as an House and Garden, and falling to Husbandry, God so prosper'd him, that he had Plenty not only for himself, but to lend others, which being according to the Custom of the Country, at *50 per Cent.* a Year, much enrich'd him; He had also Goats, which serv'd him for Mutton, and Hogs and Hens. Notwithstanding this Plenty, I say (for he lived as finely as any of their Noblemen) he could not so far forget his Native Country, as to be contented to dwell in a strange Land, where there was to him a Famine of God's Word and Sacraments, the Want of which made other Things to be of little Value to him; and therefore as he made it his daily and fervent Prayer to God in his good time to restore him to both, so at length he, with one *Stephen Rutland*, who had liv'd with him 2 Years before, resolv'd to make their Escape, and about the Year 1673, meditated all secret Ways to compass it. They had before taken up a Way of Peddling about the Country, and buying Tobacco, Pepper, Garlick, Combs, and all sorts of Iron-Ware, where they wanted them: And now to promote their Design, as they went with their Commodities from Place to Place, they discoursed with the Country-People (for they could now speak their Language well) concerning the Ways and Inhabitants; where the Isle was thinnest and fullest Inhabited; where and how the Watches [guards] lay from one Country to another; and what Commodities were proper for them to carry into all Parts, pretending that they would furnish themselves with such Wares as the respective Places wanted. None doubted but that they did upon the Account of Trade, because Mr. *Knox* was so well seated, could not be suppos'd to leave such an Estate, and run away. By Enquiry they found, that the easiest and most probable Way to make an Escape was by travelling Northward, because that Part of the Land was least inhabited, and so furnishing themselves with such Wares as were vendible in those Parts, they set forth, and steer'd their Course towards the N. Parts of the Isle, knowing very little of the Ways, which were generally intricate and perplex'd, because they have no publick Roads, but a Multitude of little Paths from one Town to another, and those so often changing; and for white Men to enquire about the Ways was very dangerous, because the People would presently suspect their Design.

At this time they travell'd from *Candi Uda* as far as the County of *Nearecalava*, which is in the furthest Parts of the King's Dominions, and about 3 Days Journey from their Dwelling. They were very thankful to Providence that they had got passed all their Difficulties so far, but yet durst not go any further, because they had no Wares left to traffick with, and it being the first time they had been absent so long from Home, they fear'd the

Townsmen would come after them to seek for them, and so they return'd Home, and went 8 or 10 times with their Wares into those Parts, till they became well acquainted both with the People and the Paths.

In these Parts Mr. *Knox* met his black Boy, whom he had turn'd away divers Years before. He had now got a Wife and Children, and was very poor, but being acquainted with those Quarters he not only took Directions of him, but agreed with him for a good Reward to conduct him and his Companion to the *Dutch*. He gladly undertook it, and a Time was appointed between them; but Mr. *Knox* being disabled by a grievous Pain, which seiz'd him on his Right side and held him 5 Days, that he could not travel, this Appointment was in vain; for tho' he went as soon as he was well, his Guide was gone into another Country about his Business, and they durst not at that time venture to run away without him.

These Attempts took up 5 or 9 [6?] Years, various Accidents hindring their Designs, but most commonly the dry Weather, because they fear'd in the Woods they should be starv'd with Thirst, all the Country being in such a Condition almost 4 or 5 Years together for lack of Rain.

On *Sept.* 22. 1679 they set forth again, furnish'd with Knives and small Axes for their Defence (because they could carry them privately) and several sorts of Wares to sell, as formerly, and as necessary Provisions, the Moon being 27 Days old, that they might have Light to run away by, to try what Success God Almighty would now give them in seeking their Liberty. Their first stage was to *Anarodgburro*, in the Way to which lay a Wilderness, called *Parroah Mocclane*, full of wild Elephants, Tigers and Bears; and because 'tis the utmost Confines of the King's Dominions, there is always a Watch kept.

In the midst of their Way they heard, that the Governour's Officers of these Parts were out to gather up the King's Revenues and Duties, to send them up to the City; which put them into no small Fear, lest finding them, they should send them back again; whereupon they withdrew to the Western Parts of *Kepoulpot*, and sat down to Knitting till they heard that the Officers were gone. As soon as they were departed they went onwards of their Journey, having gotten a good parcel of Cotton-Yarn to knit Caps with, and having kept their Wares, as they pretended, to exchange for dried Flesh, which was sold only in those lower Parts. Their Way lay necessarily thro' the Governor's Yard at *Collinilla*, who dwells there on purpose to examine all that go and come. This greatly distressed them, because he would easily suspect they were out of their Bounds, being Captives; however, they went resolutely to his House, and meeting him, presented him with a small Parcel of Tobacco and Betel, and shewing him their Wares, told him, That they came there to get dry'd Flesh to carry back with them. The Governour did not suspect them, but told them, He was sorry they came in so dry a Time, when no Deer could be catched; but if some Rain fell he would soon supply them. This Answer pleased them, and they seem'd contented to stay, and accordingly abiding with him 2 or 3 Days, and no Rain falling, they presented the Governour with 5 or 6 Charges of Gun-powder, which is a Rarity among them, and leaving a Bundle at his House, they desired him to shoot them some Deer, while they made a Step to *Anarodgburro*. Here also they were put into a great Fright, by the coming of certain Soldiers from the King to the Governour to give him Orders to set a secure Guard at the Watches, that no suspicious Persons might pass, which tho' it was intended only to prevent the Flight of the Relations of certain Nobles whom the king had clapp'd up [imprisoned], yet they fear'd they might wonder to see white Men here, and so send them back again: But God so order'd it, that they were very kind to them, and left them to their Business, and so they got safe to *Anarodgburro*. Their Pretence was for dry'd Flesh, tho' they knew there was none to be had; but their real Business was to search the Way down to the *Dutch*, which they staid 3 Days to do: But finding that in the Road to *Jafnapatan*, which is one of the *Dutch* Ports, there was a Watch which could hardly be passed, and other Inconveniences not surmountable, they resolved to go back, and take the River *Malwateyan*, which they had before judged would be a probable Guide to lead them to the Sea; and that they might not be pursued, left *Anarodgburro* just at Night (when the People never travelled for fear of wild Beasts) on *Sunday, Octob.* 12. being stored with all Things needful for their Journey, *viz.* Ten Days Provision, a Basin to boil their Provisions in, 2 Calabashes to fetch Water in, and 2 great Tallipat-Leaves for Tents, with Jaggory, Sweet-meets, Tobacco, Betel, Tinder-Boxes, and a Deer-Skin for Shooes, to keep their Feet from Thorns, because to them they chiefly trusted. Being come to the River, they struck into the Woods, and kept by the side of it, yet not going on the Sand, lest their Footsteps should be discern'd, unless forced, and then going backwards.

Being gotten a good Way into the Woods, it began to rain, wherefore they erected their Tents, made a Fire, and refresh'd themselves against the Rising of the Moon, which was then 18 Days old, and having tied Deers Skin about their Feet, and eased themselves of their Wares, they proceeded in their Journey. When they had travell'd 3 or 4 Hours with Difficulty, because the Moon gave but little Light among the thick Trees, they found an Elephant in their Way before them, and because they could not scare him away, they were forced to stay till Morning, and so they kindled a Fire, and took a Pipe of Tobacco. By the Light they could not discern that ever any Body had been there, nothing being to be seen but Woods, and so they were in great Hopes, that they were past all Danger, being beyond all Inhabitants; but they were mistaken, for the River winding Northward, brought them into the midst of a Parcel of Towns, called *Tissea Wava*, where being in danger of being seen, they were under a mighty Terrour (for had the People found them, they would have beat them, and sent them up to the King) and to avoid it, they crept into an hollow Tree, and sat there in Mud and Wet until it began to grow dark, and then betaking themselves to their Legs, travell'd till the darkness of the Night stopt them. They heard Voices behind them, and fear'd that 'twas some Body in Pursuit of them; but at length discerning 'twas only an Hollowing [hallooing] to keep the wild Beasts out of the Corn, they pitched their Tents by the River, and having boiled Rice and roasted Meat for their Suppers, and satisfied their Hunger, they commended themselves to God's Keeping, and laid them down to sleep.

The next Morning, to prevent the worst, they got up early, and hastn'd on their Journey, and tho' they were now got out of all Danger of the tame *Chingulays*, they were in great Danger of the wild ones, of whom these Woods were full; and though they saw their Tents, yet they were all gone since the Rains had fallen from the River into the Wood, and so God kept them from that Danger; for had they med the Wild Men they had been shot.

Thus they travell'd from Morning to Night several Days thro' Bushes and Thorns, which made their Arms and Shoulders, which were naked, all of a Gore-Blood. They often met with Bears, Hogs, Deer, and wild Buffaloes; but they all run away as soon as they saw them. The River was exceeding full of Alligators. In the Evening they used to pitch their Tents and make great Fires both before and behind them, to affright the wild Beasts, and tho' they heard the Voices of all sorts, they saw none.

On *Thursday* at Noon they cross'd the River *Coronda Oyah*, which parts the country of the *Malabars* from the King's and on *Friday* about 9 or 10 in the Morning came among the Inhabitants of whom they were as much afraid as of the *Chingulays* before; for tho' the *Wanniounay*, or Prince of this People, payeth Tribute to the *Dutch* out of Fear, yet he is better affected to the King of *Candi*, and if he had took them would have sent them up to their old Master; but not knowing any Way to escape, they kept on their Journey by the River side by Day, because the Woods were not to be travell'd by Night for Thorns and Wild Beasts, who came down to the River to drink. In all the *Malabars* Country they met with only 2 *Bramins*, who treated them civilly, and for their Money one of them conducted them until they came into the Territories of the *Dutch*, and out of all Danger of the King of *Candi*, which did not a little rejoyce them; but yet they were in no small Trouble how to find the Way out of the Woods, till a *Malabar* for the Lucre [reward] of a Knife conducted them to a *Dutch* Town, where they found Guides to direct them from Town to Town, till they came to the Fort, called *Arrepa*, where they arriv'd *Saturday, Octob.* 18. 1679 and there thankfully ador'd God's wonderful Providence in thus compleating their Deliverance from a long Captivity of 19 Years and 6 Months.

RALPH AUSTEN. *A TREATISE OF FRUIT TREES* (OXFORD, 1653)

The Epistle Dedicatory

If men would *Plant Fruit-trees*, not only in *Gardens*, but also in many of their *Fields and Hedges*; This course (after some years) might save the experice of *many Thousand Quarters of Mault*, yearely, in the Nation. And many Thousand *Loades of Wood*, and other *Fuell*, in making Mault, and as much (it may be) in Brewing *Beere*. And many thousand Acres sowed yearely with *Barly*, might be sowed with *Bread-corne*, or turned into *Pasture-grounds*, by reason of the abundance of those most healthful Liquors, *Cyder* and *Perry* that might be yearely made, Besides great store of *Wood*, would be got for Fuell, by the *Prunings of the Fruit-trees*, and Old Trees past bearing, with spetiall *Wood for Joyners*, and many other purposes.

This likewise might be one chiefe way (among others) for imploying and setting on worke, very many *Poore People*, (in Inclosing, and preparing Grounds for Planting, and many other Workes) (according to the late consultations of the Parliament) whereby they might maintaine themselves, and profit others, in stead of burthening of them.

Yea: hereby would accrue to the *Poore* (and the *whole Nation*) many great advantages, in severall respects: First, a Freedome, and deliverance of multitudes from *Idleness, Beggery, Shame*, and consequently, *Theft, Murther*, and (at last) *the Gallowes*.

Secondly, *Positive advantages; Meate, Drinke, Clothing, Riches, and Profits*, to themselves and others.

If the higher powers (whom God hath set up to designe, and labour for the welfare, and prosperity of his People) would please to make a *Law*, (there being *Lawes* of a thousand times less consequence) for the *Inclosure and Plantation*, of some of the *Wast, and Common Grounds*, Whereof there are many Thousand Acres in this Nation, (such as are most fit for *Improvement*, according as is largely, and with wisdome and judgement, set forth in the late *Treatise* entituled *Bread for the Poore*; And in another *Treatise*, entituled *A Design for Plenty*:) there would (by the blessing of God on our Labours) be *Bread* indeed for the *Poore*, and *Wine* too; Yea, *Riches, and Lands of Inheritance*, to those who are not now worth a *Groat*.

For in divisions, and inclosures of *Wast*, and *Common Grounds*, (by Persons appoynted for that purpose,) why should not the *Poore* have their share, and proportion, as well as their rich Neighbours, and that to them, and their heires for ever; yea, let the *Poore* be first provided for.

JOHN WORLIDGE. *SYSTEMA AGRICULTURAE, THE MYSTERY OF HUSBANDRY DISCOVERED* (LONDON, 1668)

Prooemium *In Laudem Agriculturae*, Being The Preface or Introduction to the Work
It is most evident that this Art of *Agriculture* doth not require so great charge and expence as it doth Judgement, Labour, and Industry, which to possess men withal, and encourage them unto, is the intent and scope of the Learned, both Ancient and Modern Authors, that we may not spend

the best of our times in the most vain, costly, unnecessary and trifling studies and affaires; For in former times (*Cato* testifies) he was highly commended and praised that was esteemed a good Husband; It cannot be thought that so learned and wise Men could set so high a value and esteem upon this Art of *Agriculture*, but upon very solid and weighty grounds and reasons: Not to speak of the various delights, pleasures, and contents, that these *Rusticities* plentifully heap upon us, they supply us for our necessities, and advantages, for without this Art none in *City* or *Countrey* could subsist, as the Mother suckles the Infant with her Milk, so doth the Earth the Mother of us all universally feed and nourish us at an easie, liberal, and profitable rate, whereof we have daily experience, that our Industry, Labour, and Costs are returned upon us, with a manifold increase and advantage, unless the *celestial* influences impede; *Chrysostom* also shews how necessary the Art of *Agriculture* is (when enumerating the several advantages of *Mechanick* Arts) at length concludes that this Art is by far more worthy, excellent, and necessary than all the other: we all know how ill we can subsist without Garments and other necessaries of that nature; But without the Fruits and other increase of the Earth we cannot live. The *Scythians, Hamaxobians*, and *Gymnosophists*, esteemed all other Arts as vain and unprofitable, but this Art of *Agriculture* they accounted the onely necessary for human life, they exercised and applied all their Industry, Ingenuity, Practises, and studies, principally onely to this Art.

RICHARD BRADLEY. *A SURVEY OF THE ANCIENT HUSBANDRY AND GARDENING* (LONDON, 1725)

The Preface
The following Work, as it contains the Sum of what the ancient Writers of Husbandry have written concerning the Improvement of Land, so it likewise brings to our View the Esteem and Respect with which the ancient *Greeks* and *Romans* were honour'd, who had any way signaliz'd themselves in that Study: We find that Husbandry was accounted a Study so extremely beneficial to the Commonwealth, that Persons of the highest Rank and Figure did not only promote the Practice and Improvement of it among the Common People, but took a Pride to distinguish themselves by such new Inventions and Contrivances as might add any thing to an Art of so general Advantage. I remember to have read somewhere, in an Author of good Reasoning, that a Country well managed in point of Husbandry, might bring as much Profit to the People as their foreign Trade, although the latter was upon the best footing; and especially I think *Britain* might yet be brought to a much greater Perfection in Agriculture than it is at present, if our Farmers had Opportunities and Judgment to try Experiments, or had some fix'd Place, where they might see Examples of all Kinds of Husbandry, as a School, for

their Information; which I hope to compass, as soon as a Physick Garden is compleated at *Cambridge*; where besides collecting such Plants as are used in Physick [medicine], and choice Vegetables from foreign Countries, a little Room may be spared for Experiments tending to the Improvement of Land, which may be a Means of encreasing the Estate of every Man in *England*; for in such an Undertaking every Kind of Soil must be used and every Situation imitated.

JOHN AMOS COMENIUS. *ORBIS SENSUALIUM PICTUS*, TRANS. CHARLES HOOLE (LONDON, 1705)

The Preface
I. *To entice witty Children to it* [instruction], that they may not conceit a torment to be in the School, but dainty-fare. For it is apparent, that Children (even from their Infancy almost) are delighted with Pictures, and willingly please their eyes with these sights: And it will be very well worth the Pains to have once brought to pass, that scare-crows may be taken away from Wisdoms Gardens.

II. This same little Book will serve *to stir up the Attention, which is to be fastned upon things, and ever to be sharpned more and more*; which is also a great matter. For the senses (being the main guides of Childhood, because therein the mind doth not as yet raise up itself to an abstracted contemplation of things) evermore seek their own objects, and if they be away, they grow dull, and wry themselves hither and thither out of a weariness of themselves: but when their Objects are present, they grow merry, wax lively, and willingly suffer themselves to be fastned upon them, till the thing be sufficiently discerned. This Book then will do a good piece of service in taking (especially flickering) Wits, and preparing them for deeper Studies.

III. Whence a third good will follow; that *Children being won hereunto, and drawn over with this way of breeding, may be furnished with the knowledge of the prime things that are in the world, by sport and merry pastime*. In a word, this Book will serve for the more pleasing using of *the Vestibulum and Janua Linguarum*, for which end it was even at the first intended.

CHRISTOPHER WASE. *METHODI PRACTICAE SPECIMEN. AN ESSAY OF A PRACTICAL GRAMMAR* (LONDON, 1667, 5TH EDITION)

To the Reader
We bring them [children] to pearse [parse] *Latin*, by leading them through *senentiae Pureiles*, and *Pueriles Confabulatiunculae*, and *Corderius*

Colloquies, and so to *Aesop's Fables, Cato's Distichs, Terence*, and the easier pieces of *Ovid* and *Tully* [Cicero]. Ought not the same condescension to be used in requiring the *Work* from them? should they be at once, at the very first engaged upon the whole *work* of *Grammar* promiscuously? Allowing that they have the whole *body* of *Grammar* in their *memories*; yet if they have it not in their *understandings*, it is but like Cash committed to their keeping locked up; they should be accountable onely for so much as is intrusted to them under their own Key. Now a single *example* does very difficultly open to *young Beginners* a *general rule*; but manifold practice sliding from the *Vulgar* to the *Latin* Tongue, is a more certain and ready Key ... as a *Seaman* attains by custom to run up and down the *Ladder* of a *Mast*, which would be difficult to one not practised to it ... It hinders not, that a child may grow up to travel in rugged ways, who hath learned to set his steps upon the smoothest *pavement*, and from before whom, at first, all causes of stumbling have been studiously removed.

MARK LEWIS. *VESTIBULUM TECHNICUM: OR, AN ARTIFICIAL VESTIBULUM* (LONDON, 1675)

To the Reader
This Generation seems more inquisitive after the Education of Youth, than former Ages have been; as it doth appear by those multitude of Grammars lately Printed, and those various Methods and Models of Education every where talked of. We all conclude our method is not right here in *England*; because our Neighbours raise their youth to greater perfection in shorter time, and with less toyl than we do. It's true, some few amongst us prove very famous, which is to be ascribed to the Genius of our Climate; but for one of those, that at the end of seven or eight years bondage spent at Schools as bad as *Bridewell* [a prison of correction], who do make any competent progress in the Tongues (which is all we aim at) five drudge out that time to little purpose; as appears, if we look amongst our Gentry, and the best of our Tradesmen.

In other places, most Children (that are not natural fools) in this time, are bred with a great deal of freedom to some competent understanding in four or five Languages, and to some general knowledge of things, that they are capable of benefitting themselves, and serving their Country.

The defect is not in our natural parts, it's evident we are not inferior to the best in *Europe*: but our minds are not polished as they ought and might be, were Schools ordered as they are elsewhere. Our misery is, there is a sort of Road-witted persons (like the Irish that dragged their Ploughs by their Horses tails) will by no means have it otherwise; but rail, like bawling Curs [dogs], at all men that would make a plainer road, and go faster than the common pace.

There are divers reasons for this Epidemical miscarriage.

The first and great remora [obstacle] is a tedious impracticable Grammar [probably William Lily's *Grammar* of 1527], I shall pass by all the Sphalmata [errors in copying] that the *Oxford* Annotator finds in it, and that large comment, more difficult to be learn'd than the Grammar it self, which he puts upon it. It is crime enough that it is in *Latin*, and a great part of it in Verses. The Accidence [basic rules of grammar] in the *Etymologia* consists of Logical definitions, and the Syntax of second notions, neither of which I am sure the Child can understand.

A Second inconvenience is, we take a tedious course, and run a mad Wildgoose chase in getting words, reading Classick Authors proper to get the idiom by, and when we have done all, we have not above two parts of three of words useful in common conversation.

A third mischief in our Education is, we do not so much as endeavour to teach our Children any thing but words that are empty sounds, and a little History; but wholly neglect things obvious to sense, which Children can understand, and would delight in.

THOMAS TRYON. *A NEW METHOD OF EDUCATING CHILDREN*
(LONDON, 1695)

To *Parents, Tutors, Nurses*, and all others, concern'd in the Education of Children
I have seen in *Holland*, and other parts of the World, Children entred upon Business, and very capable of managing it, at those Years, it may be, ours here in *England* are learning to *Spell* and *Pronounce*.

Is it not a scandalous thing, to see a great Boy, of Fifteen or Sixteen Years old, trudging to School, with a great Bundle of Books under his Arm, to learn to decline a *Noun* and *Conjugate Verb*, and yet after all, remains uncertain, whether the *Genders* of *Nouns* be *Three* or *Seven*? But by this time he is it seems a hopeful Youth, and his Master thinks fit that he be sent to the *University*. Now there's no help for it, he must be a Schollar: And yet perhaps, when he comes to commence *Batchelour of Arts*, shall hardly be capable of determining whether the *Conclusion* be part of a *Syllogism*.

This indeed is the Craft of your common *School Masters*, to keep Children (like Spirits in a Circle) a long time under the Terror of their Jurisdiction and Discipline, in order only to promote their own Profit and Interest. A mischievous way this, and ought to be taken notice of by the Government: Why shou'd the Publick for so many Years be deprived of the Service of so many hopeful Boys, who are ter [desirous?] to enter upon Action, and intrusted with the management of Business, than to be compelled to sit in Torment eight Hours in a day under the *grum* [sic] and unpleasing Aspect of an harsh and ill-natured *Pedagogue*.

[BATHSHUA MAKIN]. *AN ESSAY TO REVIVE THE ANTIENT EDUCATION
OF GENTLEWOMEN* (LONDON, 1673)

These for my much Honoured and Worthy Friend, &c
Sir

Your great Question is, Whether to breed up Women in Arts and
Tongues, is not a mere new Device, never before practised in the World. This
you doubt the more Because Women are of low Parts, and not capable of
Improvement by this Education. If they could be improved, you doubt,
whether it would benefit them? If it would benefit them, you enquire where
such education may be had? or, whether they must go to School with Boys?
to be made twice more impudent than learned. At last you muster up a
Legion of Objections.

I shall speak distinctly to your Questions, and then answer your
Objections . . .

Women Educated in Arts and Tongues, have been eminent in them
I should be too tedious, if I should commemorate all upon Record, that have
been Smatterers in Learning. I shall mention some few Ladies that have been
equal to most Men . . .

The present Dutchess of *New-Castle*, by her own Genius, rather than any
timely Instruction, over-tops many grave Gown-Men.

I am forbidden to mention the Countess *Dowager* of *Huntington*
(instructed sometimes by Mrs. *Makin*) how well she understands *Latin,
Greek, Hebrew, French* and *Spanish*; or what a proficient she is in Arts, sub-
servient to Divinity, in which (if I durst would tell you) she excels.

The Princess *Elizabeth*, daugher to King *Charles* the first, to whom Mrs.
Makin was Tutress, at nine Years old could write, read, and in some measure understand, *Latin, Greek, Hebrew, French* and *Italian*. Had she lived,
what a Miracle would She have been of her Sex!

The Princess *Elizabeth*, eldest Daughter to the Queen of *Bohemia*, yet living, is versed in all sorts of choice Literature.

Mrs. *Thorold*, Daughter of the Lady *Car* in Lincolnshire, was excellent in
Philosophy, and all sorts of Learning.

I cannot without Injury forget the Lady *Mildmay*, and Dr *Loves*
Daughters; Their Worth and Excellency in Learning is yet fresh in the
Memory of many Men. . . .

Women have been good Poets
How excellent a Poet Mrs. *Bradstreet* is, (now in *America*) her Works do
testifie.

We need no other Encomium of Mrs. *Philips*, than what Mr. *Cowley*
gives, he plucks the Lawrel from his own Brow, to crown hers, as best
deserving it. Besides, her Works in print speak for her.

Sir *John Harington* in his Allegory upon the 37 Books of *Ariosto*, commends unto us the four Daughters of Sir *Anthony Cook*; also the Lady *Russel*, the Lady *Bacon*, the Lady *Killegrew*, giving to each of them, for Poetry, a worthy Character; whither I refer the Reader.

In the same place the Author commends to us, a great *Italian* Lady, *Vittoria*, who write largely and learnedly of her dead Husband. With whom I may rank (if the comparison I do not underprize) the beautiful and learned Lady *Mary*, Countess of *Pembrook*, the worthy Sister to that incomparable Person Sir *Philip Sidney*.

H. R. FOX BOURNE. *THE LIFE OF JOHN LOCKE* (NEW YORK, 1876),
2 VOLS

John Locke: Proposed Poor Law Reform, 17 Nov., 1697

2. Besides the grown people above mentioned, the children of labouring people are an ordinary burden to the parish, and are usually maintained in idleness, so that their labour also is generally lost to the public till they are twelve or fourteen years old.

The most effectual remedy for this that we are able to conceive, and which we therefore humbly propose, is, that, in the fore-mentioned new law to be enacted, it be further provided that working schools be set up in every parish, to which the children of all such as demand relief of the parish, above three and under fourteen years of age, whilst they live at home with their parents, and are not otherwise employed for their livelihood by the allowance of the overseers of the poor, shall be obliged to come.

By this means the mother will be eased of a great part of her trouble in looking after and providing for them at home, and so be at the more liberty to work; the children will be kept in much better order, be better provided for, and from infancy be inured to work, which is of no small consequence to the making of them sober and industrious all their lives after; and the parish will be either eased of this burden or at least of the misuse in the present management of it. For, a great number of children giving a poor man a title to an allowance from the parish, this allowance is given once a week or once a month to the father in money, which he not seldom spends on himself at the alehouse, whilst his children, for whose sake he had it, are left to suffer, or perish under the want of necessaries, unless the charity of neighbours relieve them.

We humbly conceive that a man and his wife in health may be able by their ordinary labour to maintain themselves and two children. More than two children at one time under the age of three years will seldom happen in one family. If therefore all the children above three years old be taken off from their hands those who have never so many, whilst they remain themselves in health, will not need any allowance for them.

We do not suppose that children of three years old will be able at that age to get their livelihoods at the working school, but we are sure that what is

necessary for their relief will more effectually have that use if it be distributed to them in bread at that school than if it be given to their fathers in
money. What they have at home from their parents is seldom more than
bread and water, and that, many of them, very scantily too. If therfore care
be taken that they have each of them their belly-full of bread daily at school,
they will be in no danger of famishing, but on the contrary, they will be
healthier and stronger than those who are bred otherwise. Nor will this
practice cost the overseers any trouble; for a baker may be agreed with to
furnish and bring ito the school-house every day the allowance of bread
necessary for all the scholars that are there. And to this may be also added,
without any trouble, in cold weather, if it be thought needful, a little warm
water-gruel; for the same fire that warms the room may be made use of to
boil a pot of it.

From this method the children will not only reap the fore-mentioned
advantages with far less charge to the parish than what is now done for
them, but they will be also thereby the more obliged to come to school and
apply themselves to work, because otherwise they will have no victuals, and
also for the benefit thereby both to themselves and the parish will daily
increase; for, the earnings of their labour at school every day increasing, it
may reasonably be concluded that, computing all the earnings of a child
from three to fourteen years of age, the nourishment and teaching of such a
child during that whole time will cost the parish nothing; whereas there is
now child now which from its birth is maintained by the parish but, before
the age of fourteen, costs the parish 50 *l.* or 60 *l.* Vol. ii, 383–5.

Index